SCIENCE EDUCATION

SCIENCE EDUCATION

Editor
Prof. Ramesh Chandra

Publications
KALPAZ PUBLICATIONS
DELHI-110052

Science Education

ISBN: 81-7835-232-X

This book is Vol. No. 4 of Universal Education and Technology in 21st Century (Set)

Published in 2005 in India by
Kalpaz Publications,
C-30, Satyawati Nagar, Delhi-110052
E-mail : Kalpaz@hotmail.com

Laser Typesetting at : Master Computers, Delhi
Printed at : Rajdhani Printers, Delhi

Contents

Preface

The general aim of science education is to help develop science education is to help develop well-defined abilities in cognitive and affective domains, besides enhancing psychomotor skills. It helps to foster an uninhibited spirit of inquiry, characterized by creative, innovative and objective approaches. Educational programmes are designed to help unravel the mysteries of the interrelationship between science and day-to-day life, health, agriculture, industry, and indeed, the individual and the universe. Scientific wisdom, knowledge and skills are ammunitions that instil confidence and inspire the individuals to challenge existing beliefs, prejudices and practices. They work as a liberating force and serve as a reliable tool in one's search for truth, harmony and order in different aspects of life.

Over the last two decades many developing countries have invested heavily in improving access to, and enhancing the quality of science education. Human resource development has become a central feature of most national development strategies and within this the emphasis has more often than not been on the acquisition of scientific and technological skills and capabilities. In many developing countries there is now more than two decades of experience with system reforms, curriculum development, and teacher training for science education at secondary and higher levels.

Science education, as one of the most expensive areas of the curriculum, has become vulnerable to the effects of parsimonious resourcing. Radically new technologies of production and access to information are beginning to permeate the developing world. Greater and greater proportions of the labour force are being employed in occupations where scientific literacy is an advantage. Scientific competence and understanding is required for growing numbers of professionals.

This book takes a hard look at science education reform efforts and the issues it raises for learners who differ along gender, socioeconomic, ethnic, cultural, linguistic lines, or disability status. It is designed to be used in preservice science teacher education classes in tandem with the regular text or course readings.

Editor

1

Scope of Science Education

The scope of science education varied greatly from one country to another, with more or less emphasis placed on scientific content, methods (inquiry, problem-solving, cooperative learning, etc.), tools or values. China, for instance, distinguished among six different domains in science teaching, i.e.: the knowledge domain (ability to master important facts, major concepts and principles of science); the operational skills domain (ability to use apparatus and instruments); the scientific process skills domain (ability to observe, measure, group, question, formulate hypotheses and experiment); the application domain (ability to apply concepts and skills in new situations); the creative domain (ability to formulate questions, to give explanations and new ideas); and the attitude domain (ability to develop a positive feeling towards science and studying science).

The United Kingdom put a stronger emphasis on the social value of science, by referring not only to the knowledge and understanding of the scientific content as well as the scientific approach to inquiry, but also to science as a 'social enterprise' - that is, the social practices of the community. Japan and Israel included technology in the scope of science education. Japan talked about the capacity of making use of computers and Israel spoke of problem-solving within a 'technological and scientific environment', putting stress on the significant impact of technological process on the individual and society. New Zealand called for a new definition of literacy and numeracy that would see science education as 'a tool to understand the world in which we live'. Israel insisted on the necessity for primary school curriculum to enhance scientific and technological literacy for all, and Japan described the difficulty of promoting national scientific literacy, given that after graduation, students seem to forget the scientific concepts that they are supposed to have acquired. From this reflection on the importance of scientific literary emerged the necessity to modify the scope of science education according to the level of education concerned.

While the need for scientific literacy at primary level was recognized, the need for progressively specialized science education beginning at the secondary level was also underlined. This would imply that the aims, methods and approaches of science teaching should be adapted to primary, secondary and higher education, which is not always the case in countries whose school system is highly selective as early as primary level and that choose to base their selection process on scientific subjects.

Useful Concepts

Two opposing concepts-knowledge and competencies-were raised several times by participants. China, for instance, declared that in the Chinese school system, undue stress was put on knowledge, neglecting the development of the students' ability to apply science knowledge and skills in problem-solving; as a consequence, teachers were failing to develop students' scientific attitudes, values, process skills and high-order thinking skills. This emphasis on knowledge was associated by Indonesia with the importance given to content rather than to process in syllabus design. The rigidity of the syllabus coupled with no (or insufficient) curriculum guidelines) was described as limiting teachers' creativity in teaching science.

The concepts of integrated subjects and of interdisciplinarity were frequently used for qualifying different matters. Japan gave examples of integrated subjects to be taught at various school level; at upper secondary level for instance, 'Integrated science A' will be added to traditional subjects as from 2002: it will consist in inquiring into 'the natural events with relation to our daily life like matters and energy; centering the relation between scientific technology and human beings; and fostering the integrated view of nature, and the ability and attitude to inquire nature'. It is planned that the organization of these integrated subjects will be a function of the ability and intention of teachers 'in each school.

China also called for a change in its own system from subject division towards subject integration. It intends to offer comprehensive courses (such as humanities, comprehensive science, sports and health, etc.), in addition to traditional disciplines (such as ideological and political studies, Chinese, Mathematics, foreign languages, etc.). As in the case of Japan, the balance between the two could be determined according to the competence of teachers.

The concept of interdisciplinarity was conceived more as an approach to organizing science education. Israel has worked considerably on this concept, trying to design and implement a Science, Technology and Society (STS)) approach, aiming at teaching science and technology in an integrated way, emphasizing their relation with society at large. This approach relies on science and technology teachers who choose their curriculum from the subjects included in the syllabus (such as energy, information, communication, ecology, etc. for elementary schools) and decide how to integrate them. Netherlands follows a quite similar scheme at senior secondary level.

At this level, science teaching starts from themes such as energy, food, health and other issues; the relevant concepts and principles for gaining insight into these themes are drawn from different disciplines. The overall objective is for students to get used to drawing on concepts in an integrated way. Traditional subjects such as physics, chemistry and biology are only taught as optional courses. Participants made a distinction between the concepts of 'intended curriculum', 'implemented curriculum' and 'attained curriculum'. France noted that the texts defining curricula are interpreted differently by different teachers, and that the way pupils and students understand the teaching they receive varies considerably as a function of the individuals concerned and the school environment. In other words, one can observe significant disparities between what is set by official texts, what is taught at school level and what is actually learned by children.

This has important implications for all aspects of curriculum development, in particular the methods used for curriculum design and assessment from different disciplines. The overall objective is for students to get used to drawing on concepts in an integrated way. Traditional subjects such as physics, chemistry and biology are only taught as optional courses.

Participants made a distinction between the concepts of 'intended curriculum', 'implemented curriculum' and 'attained curriculum'. France noted that the texts defining curricula are interpreted differently by different teachers, and that the way pupils and students understand the teaching they receive varies considerably as a function of the individuals concerned and the school environment. In other words, one can observe significant disparities between what is set by official texts, what is taught at school level and what is actually learned by children. This has important implications for all aspects of curriculum development, in particular the methods used for curriculum design and assessment.

Options and Policies

The variety of conceptions about science teaching prevailing in different countries and of methods being used to put them into practice at school level clearly demonstrated the diversity of aims and missions of scientific and technological education worldwide, and of the values attached to it. A number of diverse options and policies as regards science and technology teaching were identified. One choice is between decentralizing or not decentralizing responsibilities regarding content and curriculum from the central government to local authorities and/or the school. In the 1990s Hungary went from a state-controlled curriculum to a school-based curriculum. Schools are now required to develop their own teaching programme (allocation of time for subjects, translation of content and objectives into subjects, formulation of local goals and objectives, sequencing of learning content, etc.) on the basis of the National Core Curriculum. The National Institute of Public Education has set up a Curriculum Bank to help standardize the way the curriculum is prescribed. A private textbook industry has been expanding in parallel.

A second decision to be made concerns the development or non-development of diversified approaches in science teaching, according to target groups and areas. This question appears particularly relevant in large countries, such as China or India. In the case of China, a curriculum structure adapted to regional differences, the main characteristics of schools and students' individual particularities was set up. Diversified approaches also appear particularly relevant in multi-ethnic countries, such as Indonesia.

The 2000 Indonesian school science curriculum reform will provide national standards for basic competencies in science and technology, leaving each district responsible for adapting them to its own cultural characteristics. A third choice concerns whether or not to link science and technology education to local development. Sri Lanka recommended that education for the creation and application of science and technology on an 'industrial basis' be taken into account, in particular in the case of developing countries, in order to help them reorient and improve the productivity of their economies.

A fourth choice involves the extent to which a country's financial capabilities determine its education policy. Sri Lanka, for instance, has decided to give a strong priority to equal access to education, by providing free textbooks at elementary and lower secondary school (up to and including Grade 11) - which represents a heavy financial investment for public authorities, but also a firm policy engagement.

Strategies

Many countries have just undertaken or are about to undertake an in-depth reform of science and technology m of science and technology teaching aimed at counteracting the lack of flexibility of science teaching, the segmentation of content, the lack of practical knowledge, the poor capacity of teachers to manage change, inadequate textbooks, the isolation of science from its environment and unsatisfactory assessment of science learning. The strategies adopted can differ significantly from country to country but the alternatives confronting public authorities when setting up the reform appear quite similar.

One of these alternatives is the weight to be attached to scientific studies in teaching programmes. According to China, the curriculum structure should be balanced by means of establishing reasonable subjects or areas of study and their time allocation. Another alternative concerns selecting what constitutes the 'basics of science'. While it is generally recognized that in the face of escalating increases in scientific knowledge, comprehensive courses should be avoided, how to be selective still needs to be explored. It was recommended that, as is the case in literature courses, some 'classics' and 'masterpieces' in the scientific field be identified as reference for the analysis. A third alternative concerns harmonizing science teaching at various levels: the problem here is to ensure a continuity between primary, secondary and tertiary science and to determine when to start specialization.

Among the most important factors for any strategy of change, the time factor was very often mentioned. As the example of the reform undertaken in the Netherlands shows, for all the steps of the reform to be accomplished (i.e. the adaptation of the curriculum, the training of teachers and the modification of teaching materials) and for all the actors concerned to accept the reform (i.e. academics, parents and the society at large), a gradual approach is undoubtedly indispensable but also difficult, as implementation of the reform is linked not only to available resources but also to social resistance to change. The relation between the scale of reform and the time required for its implementation needs to be clear but it is difficult to predict.

Ensuring teachers' capacity to implement the reform also poses a difficult problem. The Indonesian pre-service training, for example, does not really impart the basic competencies needed by a successful teacher, i.e. a thorough understanding of the subject taught and well-developed skills in promoting learning. Most institutions Most institutions responsible for pre-service training are useful for improving teachers' mastery of subject content, but less so when it comes to improving practical school learning. Several strategies to improve the situation are being explored but have to be further tested in different contexts. Some of these include starting teachers' specialization at a later stage; teaching them the history of science; creating teachers' guidebooks and providing teachers with support services (New Zealand); designing new 'inquiry-based teaching materials' that would allow for more flexible and creative teaching methods (China); creating data banks that can help them in their daily work (Hungary); mobilizing 'agents of change', such as universities or regional advisers, to guide them in the implementation of the reform; relying on a body of regional inspectors (France) or of teachers' organizations (United Kingdom), to meet with teachers in the schools and explain to them the aims of the reform, give them examples of courses, show them examples of assessment, etc.; and providing teachers with funds to conduct research on improving teaching methods and materials, and thus contributing to their professional development (Republic of Korea).

Methods

Both Asian and European countries have developed innovative experiments during recent years, either inside or outside the school system, as regards the methods and pedagogy used in science and technology teaching. China, through the Zeijang experience, tries to change traditional pedagogic approaches, by insisting more on mastering than on understanding science. Malaysia has designed a 'model of scientific and thinking skills', which permeates science lessons in various stages, ranging from introducing scientific and thinking skills explicitly, applying these skills with guidance from teachers and, finally, using these skills to solve specific problems independently.

Sri Lanka has set up another model, called the 'Skigushi model', which attempts to systematize the mental process through which a conclusion can be formulated and is intended to develop the ability to think quickly and logically. Most countries are confronted with the difficulty of arousing pupils' interest and curiosity in science and technology matters. In that respect, China underlined the need In that respect, for teachers to emphasize the importance of the 'wonder aspect of science'. The Republic of Korea and Japan emphasized the role of play, and the United Kingdom called United Kingdom called for the use of a 'set of explanatory stories'. China and Indonesia described practices appealing to the local environment, such as the 'banana project', according to which bananas are used to study biology, chemistry, economy, etc. Pupils can be asked to write 'science papers' in order to help them draw precise conclusions from what they observed. The role of teachers in the latter case is crucial and quite different from that in traditional teaching settings: they have to 'coach' pupils and students throughout the learning process and develop context-specific learning activities and tasks.

Hands-on learning projects are being implemented in French primary schools and by the European Organization for Nuclear Research (CERN) to try to raise the interest of the young. These projects aim at familiarizing children with science by carrying out experiments and, through this, gradually assimilating scientific concepts and technological know-how. They have been developed in France at the initiative of Physics Nobel Prize winner Georges Charpak. Throughout their investigation, pupils are encouraged to reason, argue and discuss ideas and results in a very independent way. In the case of CERN, RN, hands-on activities are made available during school visits. Participating groups of children are asked to mimic the activity of conducting research. CERN is planning to record these hands-on activities in written and visual form written and visual form and make them widely available over the web.

Dutch schools follows a quite similar approach by proposing 'problems-based' and 'projects-based' science teaching. The idea is to replace learning the ever-increasing amount of specific principles and applications of scientific disciplines by learning to use the fundamentals in the situation in which pupils live and that are relevant for their future life as citizens and workers. Learning and working towards an outcome or product of educational activity helps raised the interest of the young. These methodological innovations have strong implications for curriculum design as well as for the assessment criteria being utilized.

The use of non-school resources for science and technology teaching was advocated as a complement to school courses. In the Philippines, visits to science museums, to science museums, to manufacturing companies and to industrial sites take place. In India, science exhibitions, science clubs, activities, debates, etc. are organized. In other countries, networks are being created with the help of local partners to support school courses. China has established some 'scientific circles', for instance, and Japan 'school-centred networks of science learning'. Part of the curriculum is devoted to fieldwork and, for that purpose, local existing social facilities, such as museums or private companies are used. Pupils use exhibits to show their research tasks to others. Learning is organized through networks: a network of the subjects to be taught, a network of school and out-of-school facilities, a museums-centred network, a nature observation network, etc.

Most of the innovative experiments described referred to science. The exception is the 'Smart School' project in Malaysia, which tries to capitalize on the introduction of new technologies in schools to create a stimulating teaching environment. Various issues were raised concerning the innovative approaches presented above.

Organisation and Management

A key aspect in the reform of science and technology teaching concerns new and innovative approaches in curriculum design, and the methods used to help the teachers find the appropriate tools to implement the curriculum. One of the issues raised is whether curriculum design should start with disciplines or subjects, for each of the levels concerned. In the case of Malaysia, the primary level science curriculum is organized around five subjects, namely the living world, the physical world, the material world, earth and the universe, and the world of technology. At upper secondary level, it is organized around disciplines, i.e. science, biology, physics and chemistry. The identification of attractive subjects is not always that easy. A second issue consists in identifying which disciplines are the subject/object of integration. Disciplines which are the subject of integration are bound to use elements and approaches borrowed from other disciplines; earth science for example, which appeals to physics, chemistry, biology, environmental science, etc., can be regarded as a subject of integration. Disciplines that are objects of integration are bound to be used by other disciplines; mathematics, for instance, as a science tool, can be considered as an object of integration. A third issue has to do with identifying the relation between different learning sequences and the aims of education. This is necessary to determine which courses are compulsory and which elective, at various levels. In Thailand for example, the secondary level curriculum distinguishes between compulsory core, compulsory elective and free elective courses.

At lower secondary level, general science courses are offered as core compulsory and elective ones. At upper secondary level, students are divided into science and non-science stream. For the science stream students, physics, chemistry, biology and environmental science are offered as compulsory elective and free elective courses. For the non-science stream, various units on physical and biological science are offered. A fourth issue is linked with the need to avoid overloading curricula - which exercises a great pressure on pupils-and to avoid the 'cumulation of knowledge' ' which leads to 'sediment-like curriculum'. The trend in various countries is to reduce the time allotted to science teaching, either to give time to the development of 'creative activities' (Republic of Korea), or as a result of the integration of disciplines (Japan).

A fifth issue concerns the 'operationalizing' of scientific contents, in other words in the methods to be used to put science into context and to encourage the understanding of society through science. In the Netherlands, at secondary level, more attention is given to relating science to the world outside school as well as to practical work in all science subjects. In Israel, the curriculum is being utilized to develop awareness on wise consumer thinking and behaviour by using the decision-making process when selecting a product or a system. It is also being utilized to prepare individuals to take care of the environment.

A final important point for the implementation of new approaches in the field of science and technology teaching is the profile and management of training of teachers. In fact, it is difficult to ask them to teach things quite different and quite differently (to help them 'coach' the education process) to what they have learnt themselves (Indonesia talked about 'new times, old players'). In various Asian countries, most in-service training in science education uses a 'cascade model', which helps to limit the cost of reform management and to train people in a short timeframe. Through this training model, a group of key personnel are trained (called 'master-teachers' in China); they in return train other users of the curriculum at regional and then local levels. Indonesia considers that this top-down model has little value due to the heterogeneous conditions of Indonesian teachers, resources and cultures. In Malaysia, it has led to a dilution of knowledge and, consequently, to the misinterpretation of the curriculum; it was suggested that a bottom-up community-based approach might be more useful for science development.

Assessment as Tools of Learning

Science assessment was presented as a key tool not only for evaluating and comparing pupils' educational results and, on this basis, for selecting a small elite, but also for monitoring the quality of learning, and above all, the success and the limits of implementation of a reform. One of the difficulties consists in defining precisely what has to be assessed-which has strong implications on what is being taught, as what is not considered relevant for examination purposes is usually not considered relevant for learning.

In Indonesia, assessment is focused on content; this results mainly in memorization and routine exercises, responsible for the failure of students to acquire real understanding as well as adequate problem-solving and critical thinking skills. In India, little importance is attached to the assessment of practical work, resulting in utter neglect of practical work in school education. In the United Kingdom, the testing of practical skills has been abandoned because of its high cost; this has resulted in teachers, who want their pupils to get the best possible results, putting less emphasis on the practical aspects of science. France has succeeded in imposing experimental science in classes and its proper assessment, after decades devoted to convincing decision-makers that practical work is worth the money, sensitizing teachers of the interest of it, and leading schools to build laboratories and buy equipment.

The evolution of science learning (in particular the attempt to increase the emphasis on the mastering of knowledge) requires an evolution of the assessment methods) used. The Philippines established an examination system based on learning competencies, which are assessed in national elementary and secondary achievement tests. It is applied through school-based assessment, with progress reports in science achievement shared with parents and other stakeholders. The Netherlands developed portfolios and dossiers with products produced by students and reflection on learning results and learning processes. France created a computer assessment resource bank in science.

The limitations of assessment are not always well understood. To begin with, assessment does not give clue to the attitude of the young towards science learning. In Japan for instance, according to the Third International Mathematics and Science Study (TIMSS), the achievements of Japanese children at Grades 4 and 8 are the second and third highest among the twenty-six and forty-one participating countries and territories; forty-eight per cent of students think that science is important in their daily life and twenty per cent want to get a job in the future related to science. The way to assess attitudes, inquiry spirit and curiosity has still to be found. In China, assessment fails to take into consideration multiple forms of intelligence and, consequently, the various potential of students, which leads to the academic failure of most students and damage to their self-esteem. In Hungary, the lack of assessment skills among the teaching force limits any attempts to reform the system.

In various Asian states, the pressure of international comparisons, such as TIMSS, compels public authorities to formulate their education reform policy on the basis of expected results, which limits any evolution of the assessment systems and, consequently, of teaching.

There exists a wrong perception of what a good eduction is, through assessment: in seeking to make the important measurable, only the measurable has become important. There were not many suggestions made to change the situation.

Secondary School Science in Developing Countries

Across the world, in developed and developing countries, science education is in a position of both privilege and peril. It is privileged because the political world recognise a relationship between quality research and development in science and technology, and economic stability and growth. In many countries, this recognition has resulted in additional efforts being made to support science and technology education at all levels

In addition, in many countries there seems to be a growing recognition that science education is important - not just for scientists, but for the majority of students, both male and female, who will never become scientists (or engineers, or mathematicians). 'Science for all is a rallying cry in many countries. Many of the problems facing humanity today will only be solved through the active involvement of a scientifically and technologically knowledgable citizenry. Agriculture, health, union, population control, environmental management, and industrial development are a few of the areas where a wider understanding of science and technology will lead to more informed decision-making.

However, when countries invest limited financial resources in science education and the impact is less than anticipated - or slower in realization - then there may be a backlash against science education that is as emerge in the negative direction as the current trend is positive. This comment does not imply that quality science education is vitally important for all students in all countries. It is simply a note of caution-a plea for realistic operation.

In most countries, the first wave of secondary science education reform, which began in the late 1950s/ early 1960s, was unsuccessful in reaching large numbers of students with scientific information. For some time, the prevailing wisdom has been that these highly academic courses are, at least, an excellent preparation for science studies at university. Now, even this belief is being challenged. However, there is no agreement on how to reform upper secondary school science courses for students who intend to major i sciences at university.

For the majority of students who will study no science after secondary schooling, the new definition of quality science education springs from the utilitarian tradition - important science knowledge is useful science knowledge, and vice versa. Science is considered one way of understanding the natural -world, rather than as solely the body of knowledge accumulated through this process.

Science is recognized as existing within a societal context. The students' need to know science is established through science courses that emphasize the connections between science, technology, and society (STS). Issues and applications (eg, use of fertilizers and pesticides, sound nutrition, healthy living, etc.) are used both to motivate students to learn science, and to think well of the scientific enterprise.

STS themes are introduced into science classes as either "enrichment' material in otherwise traditional science courses, or they may actually become the organizing focus of the course. Both approaches are found in developing countries, but usually only at the lower secondary Ievel, often in the form of an integrated science course.

At the upper secondary level the impulse toward science for all tends to become subverted by the need to pass a specialist examination for university entrance.

The new science courses are even more of a challenge to teachers because, not only do the courses tend to be interdisciplinary, they require a new pedagogical approach. Teachers who are uneasy with their subject matter Knowledge tend to teach almost solely through lectures. These teachers are being asked to change not only their teaching techniques but their whole concept of classroom management.

Role-playing, games and simulations, student-led discussions, and cooperative learning are strategies that are considered helpful in reaching more students with science knowledge. They can only be successfully introduced by a qualified teacher.- Not only may these techniques be unfamiliar to the teacher but they may threaten a given culture's definition of an appropriate relationship between teacher and taught - the student-centered classroom is an alien concept in many countries.

The desired qualification for teaching secondary school science in most parts of the world is typically a four-year degree/certificate after 12 years of education. In Latin America and Asia, this is often a joint degree in science and education. In Africa, at the upper secondary level this is more likely to be a bachelor's degree in science, with a teaching diploma taken separately a year later. At the lower secondary level, this is usually a three- or four-year teacher training certificate/diploma in science education.

In reality, secondary school science teachers in the developing world have a wide range of academic credentials - from little more than a 10th-grade science education and no pedagogical courses, to the equivalent of a masters degree in science education. The teachers may have a science degree obtained after 17/18 years of education but have received no instruction in pedagogy. Alternatively, they may have received a pedagogical degree after 15/16 years of education, but have taken very few science courses. Almost any combination is found.

In most countries, teachers at the upper secondary level are expected to have received a more extensive education in the sciences than teachers at the lower secondary level. On first reaction this makes perfect sense - · in many countries the science taught at this level can be quite complex This is especially true in those countries where students specially in science for two years before entering university. However, the result of this practice is that the teachers with the poorest understanding of science are found teaching in the pivotal lower secondary school years. These are the years when a student will decide whether or not to continue in the science stream.

These are the final years of exposure to formal science instruction for the majority of students in secondary school These are also the years when teachers are more likely to teach integrated science, or several different sciences. Science teachers at the lower secondary level need as strong a science background as teachers at the upper secondary level but with a much broader exposure to the range of science disciplines. There is world-wide dissatisfaction with many science teacher education programs because science knowledge and pedagogical knowledge tend to be taught in parallel rather than in an integrated fashion.

The connections between educational theory, science knowledge, and conveying this knowledge to students are not made explicit, or are not well-emphasized. This is very much a consequence of the institutional, intellectual, and attitudinal barriers between scientists and educators in most countries, developed and developing. Many secondary science teachers are teaching out-of-field. This is true especially for teachers of integrated science, who tend not to have the wide content background needed, and physics teachers who may have qualifications in chemistry, mathematics, and engineering rather than physics.

Teachers with a strong background in physics content (and, to a somewhat lesser extent, chemistry) can often find employment in other sectors of the economy. The status of secondary school teachers of all disciplines is low in many developing countries, but especially in sub-Saharan Africa and Latin America, where the secondary teacher often have to take more than one job to survive economically.

Secondary school teachers in many Asian countries appear to have a higher status in their society than do teachers in Africa and Latin America - teachers in Korea are especially favoured in terms of both prestige and pay. Where teachers have status, there is a great deal of competition to enter teaching and the candidates art better-qualified.

Teachers who have already obtained at least the minimally required qualifications receive superficial continuing education only to support the introduction of new textbooks, equipment, etc. There appears to be a lack of recognition of the level of effort necessary to prepare teachers for reform - especially those who are poorly prepared already. This lack of understanding appears to be the most common reason why science education reform is so difficult to achieve in both developed and developing countries. When reform attempts to work around the teacher (programmed kits, so-called 'teacher-proof curricula, radio and TV instruction, etc.) it will always, ultimately, fail

Laboratory instruction is still considered an essential component of secondary school science classes in most countries it is easy to suggest that problems associated with implementing the laboratory component of science classes result solely from inadequate facilities, and a lack of equipment and supplies - if this were true, then simply providing facilities, equipment, and materials, would solve these problems.

However, too often, laboratories are used only as regular classrooms: equipment remains on the shelf unused to prevent breakage, or broken equipment remains unrepaired, consumables are not resupplied; and teachers are not shown how to use and repair equipment. Many of these problems are, at least partly, a consequence of teacher insecurity with the subject matter, and a failure to include adequate teacher continuing education in implementation plans. Laboratory skills may, or may not, be included on the examination which is driving the curriculum.

Assessment in the developing world tends to concentrate on student selection and certification, rather than be viewed as an opportunity to determine what does or does not work within the system (formative assessment), and then make appropriate adjustments.

Participation in a national comparative studies of science education provided the few developing countries which have participated with valuable baseline data from which to introduce informed change. It is unfortunate that more countries have not the resources, financial or otherwise, to take part in future international surveys.

The relationship between the curriculum and the standardized examination distorts the system, making curriculum reform an especially hazardous undertaking. Just as the teachers are an essential component of science education reform, so is the examination. The assessment system is so important that it has even been suggested that the ideal curriculum will follow the ideal examination, not proceed it.

In most developing countries, science education reform should begin by concentrating on ways to improve the continuing education (in-service and onservice) of secondary school science teachers. There are larger numbers of unqualified teachers already within a given system, than enter teaching each year. Many of these teachers are young, and likely to remain in teaching for many years.

Lower secondary school teachers should be considered a higher priority than teachers at the upper secondary level if this choice must be made. This continuing education should include both science content and pedagogy. Continuing education should be viewed as an ongoing necessity for all science teachers - both those who are poorly qualified and those who are defined as well-qualified. The former group should be given the first priority when resources are scarce. T

he use of well-qualified, and specially trained, secondary science teachers to run in-service education programs for less-qualified teachers (through, eg, 'cascade workshops) addresses the needs of both groups, and should always be considered.

This effort needs to proceed from: an action plan that includes both quantifiable goals, and a meaningful evaluation system. The goals should specify the numbers of teachers to be reached per year of the action plan; the number of contact hours of instruction to be provided; and the educational outcomes anticipated. These outcomes should be expressed in terms of teacher redentials and teacher classroom behaviours, as well as student enrolments in science classes, and student achievement

The evaluation should be formative and ongoing, and used as an opportunity to refine the action plan as dictated by experience AU efforts to provide in-service education to secondary science teachers should include a well-funded, and educationally meaningful evaluation component.

In many counties, there is a need to re-evaluate the content of teacher preservice education. A knowledge of both science and pedagogy is necessary for effective teaching but the balance of each component may, need adjustment. It is important to broaden the teacher's science knowledge to cover more than one discipline, especially at the lower secondary level and to purge the superficial from the pedagogical component of the program practice teaching under the direction of a 'master teacher can be of special value to novice teachers.

At the lower secondary level, the curriculum needs to develop a more utilitarian focus. It is probably sensible to begin by gradually adding remnant societal content to set-in courses, since this is a strategy which can be implemented relatively quickly, and with less expense, than a major rewrite of the syllabus. This is also a strategy which is less threatening to teachers, and can be used to gin them writing experience.

While, in some systems, a complete overhaul of the secondary science syllabus may be postponed a few years, it will eventually become necessary in most countries if science literacy for all is to have any meaning. Few of existing secondary science course are designed to meet the needs of the students now taking these courses.

Teaching the pre-university science stream in special science schools is one option that could be cost-effective, and permit students to gain experience in project work and research, using university-calibre instrumentation and computers. Reform of science instruction at the upper secondary level will have to be undertaken eventually, but only in conjunction with changes in the first few years of science instruction at the tertiary level

The direction of change is likely to erode traditional discipline boundaries, and thus may be strongly resisted by the more conservative university departments. Thus, it is recommended that a separate study be undertaken of the range of instructional concerns in developing countries related to the school/university interface for science majors. Many countries need to change their assessment system so that it does not impede science education reform, but promotes constructive curriculum revision.

Laboratory Instruction

There is a need to redefine the role of laboratory instruction in all countries. Given the poor utilization of laboratory facilities and equipment in many countries, it is a waste of time and effort to continue to support the construction and provision of traditional laboratory facilities without a very careful review of proposed projects prior to funding. For example, there should be a known relationship between equipment requested and specific curriculum objectives; equipment lists should be developed by educators familiar with the curriculum; and teachers should attend workshops on how to use the equipment

However, laboratory instruction is an important component of science learning and should be retained in some fashion. Low-cost equipment of a sufficiently high standard for use in school laboratories gm be produced locally. Only rarely should it be necessary to import equipment because it is cheaper than local equipment. If inexpensive equipment can not be produced locally, then there needs to be both an educational and a management study conducted to find out why.

There are no sound pedagogical or financial reasons why extensive and sophisticated instrumentation should be purchased for demonstration purposes only. There is a need to analyse, on a country-by-country and course-by-course basis, the cost-savings possible through maximizing the use of low-cost equipment. Given the extraordinarily high costs of traditional equipment, this study could encourage many more countries to explore the low-cost option than do at present.

Teachers do not have the time to make simple equipment themselves and should not, routinely, be expected to do so. However, teachers do need to be able to repair the equipment they have; workshops should be provided to give them the simple maintenance skills necessary.

Laboratory skills should be included in examinations as part of a clearly defined, continuous assessment component, for which the classroom teacher is responsible and receives training. Ways will have to be found to safeguard the integrity of these examination results.

Some very poor countries may have a larger percentage of well-qualified teachers than some relatively rich countries; it depends on previous government policies, not comparative wealth. Most countries do need to consider systemic reform but, as indicated previously, through deliberate and sustained evolution not revolution. The time period for systemic reform is closer to ten years than five. However, the one issue which should be first addressed in most countries is the education of science teachers, especially their continuing education given the large number of unqualified young teachers now working in many systems.

2

Current Trends in Science Education

Indian schools follow an education system that has its genesis in the recommendations of an Education Commission appointed by the government in the year 1964. The first ten years of schooling are devoted to eight years of elementary education comprising five years of primary and three years of upper primary education, followed by two years of secondary education. The students then undergo two years of higher secondary education to complete school. This format is popularly referred to as the '10+2 pattern' of education.

The Indian Parliament adopted the recommendations of the Education Commission as its National Policy on Education (NPE) in the year 1968. The highlight of the 1968. The highlight of the recommendations was that science and mathematics were, for the first time, made subjects for compulsory study for all pupils as part of general education during the first ten years of schooling. In this context, the Commission went on to recommend that:

— In the lower primary classes, science teaching should be related to the child's environment. The Roman alphabet should be taught in Class IV to facilitate understanding of internationally accepted symbols of scientific measurement and the use of maps, charts and statistical tables.

— At the higher primary stage, emphasis should be on the acquisition of knowledge and the ability to think logiquisition of knowledge and the ability to think logically to draw conclusions and to make decisions at a higher level. A disciplinary approach to the teaching of science will be more effective than the general science approach.

— A science corner in lower primary schools and a laboratory-cum-lecture room in higher primary schools are minimum essential requirements.

— At the lower secondary stage, science, taught in terms of disciplines like chemistry and biology, would help students to grasp the distinct pursuits possible within the broader spectrum comprising 'science'. Such an approach would pay long-term dividends in this age of super-specialities. Experimental approach to the learning of science should, moreover, be stressed.

— Science courses at an advanced level may be provided for talented students in selected lower secondary schools along with the necessary facilities of staff and laboratory.

— Science teaching should be linked to agriculture in rural areas and to technology in urban areas. But the levels of attainment and avenues to higher education should be the same in both types of schools.

Primary or basic education	
Pupils enrolled (1996)	110,390,406
Teachers (1996)	1,789,733
Pupil/teacher ratio	47:1 (3)
Gross enrolment ratio (1996)	
-Total	100
-Male	109
-Female	90
Estimated percentage of repeaters (1994)	
percentage of repeaters	
School-age population out of school	28,564,000(4)
Secondary education	
Students enrolled (1996)	68,872,393
Gross enrolment ratio (1996)	
- Total	49
-Male	59
-Female	39
Third-level enrolment ratio (1996)	
Estimated adult literacy rate (2000)	
-Total	56
-Male	69
-Female	42

A national curriculum framework was designed in 1975 to 5 to translate the avowed policy into action. It was suggested that, at the secondary stage, the science syllabus could be bifurcated under the titles Physical science, covering physics and chemistry, and the Life sciences, covering botany, zoology and human physiology. An alternative was to offer science as a single integrated subject where concepts are developed as units without violating the parameters of the various disciplines. At the senior secondary stage, however, science could be offered as 'discipline-wise' courses in the academic stream. The new curriculum elicited the criticism that the content of the science and mathematics courses prescribed for Classes IX and X were inordinately taxing on the students.

In June 1977, a Review Committee under the chairmanship of Ishwarbhai J. Patel was appointed to examine the syllabus and textbooks recommended by the National Council of Educational Research and Training (NCERT). The Committee suggested the restructuring of the scientific concepts taught in Classes IX and X. The members also proposed that students be given the option of choosing from two equivalent courses in the secondary stage.

The first alternative was to offer the study of science as a single subject encompassing its various disciplines, while the second alternative was to offer a discipline-wise science course consisting of biology, chemistry, and physics, etc. Schools affiliated to the Central Board of Secondary Education (CBSE) gave their students an opportunity to pick a course of their choice from these alternatives. The authorities, however, soon realized that the two courses were not being perceived as constituting a choice between equally rewarding options. It was observed that students who had opted to take the 'discipline-wise' science course received preferential treatment while securing admission to the higher secondary stage. Thus the spirit underlying the Review Committee's recommendations was practically undermined. The CBSE schools therefore abandoned these initiatives and returned to 'discipline-wise' study of science at the secondary stage, as was the practice in all other schools.

National Policy on Education, 1986

A new educational policy was developed in 1986, nearly eighteen years after the NPE was formulated and implemented. Fresh assessment was necessitated by widespread belief that the system in prevalence neither met the needs nor fulfilled the aspirations of the people. The 1986 policy 6 policy reposed faith in the conviction of its predecessors that science and mathematics should continue as compulsory subjects in the first ten years of school education. Indeed, the teaching of science needed to be further perfected as virtually all aspects of growth and development in the modern era had their basis in scientific knowledge and as such, societies needed citizens literate in science and technology at various levels to ensure overall progress. Towards this end, the policy further enunciates:

- Science and mathematics will remain as core subjects in the first ten years of school education.
- In order to develop scientific temper and to attain other goals, it is necessary to define the objectives to be fulfilled through science education.
- Involvement of community, non-government and voluntary agencies are required to pool resources by establishing networks among different institutions. Efforts should be made to generate manpower at the grassroots level to spearhead the implementation of the ideas stated in NPE.
- Programmes with exclusive focus need to be evolved for the educationally backward schools and states in the country. They need to be designed to eliminate disparities and attain equal status for women.

Education status for women. Education of scheduled castes, tribes and other educationally challenged sections of society, besides rural, remote and neglected regions of the country require innovative and culture specific approaches. The challenges are manifold and need to be addressed with a certain degree of sensitivity and with the sense of immediacy they merit.

— To attain universal enrolment and to pre-empt dropouts, improvement in both the environment as well as the quality of education imparted are to be treated as a quintessential ongoing process. The learning process, being neither uniform nor mechanical, allowances need be made for individual students who may differ from the majority. Teaching and learning of science should be so designed as to respect the basic rights of each and every student. Science education at the elementary level should not overwhelm children with loads of information but should instead aim to open their hearts and minds to the joy of learning.

— Science education will be extended to the vast numbers who have remained outside the reach of formal education. This is to be borne in mind while planning for non-formal systems.

— Science and mathematics curricula for the secondary level should help inspire conscious internalization of a healthy work ethos. This will provide valuable manpower fuelling economic growth even while moulding ideal citizens who can adapt effortlessly to a society based on science and technology.

— Science curriculum for general education will be implemented in pace-setting schools with sufficient scope for innovation and experimentation.

— Science up to Class X should be treated as a combined subject. The laws and principles of science, operating in the environment, should be used for creating desired teaching/learning situations. The learning and teaching of science should be so prioritized as to lay greater emphasis on an activity-oriented methodology.

Aims of Teaching Science

The general aim of science education is to help develop science education is to help develop well-defined abilities in cognitive and affective domains, besides enhancing psychomotor skills. It helps to foster an uninhibited spirit of inquiry, characterized by creative, innovative and objective approaches. Educational programmes are designed to help unravel the mysteries of the interrelationship between science and day-to-day life, health, agriculture, industry, and indeed, the individual and the universe. Scientific wisdom, knowledge and skills are ammunitions that instil confidence and inspire the individuals to challenge existing beliefs, prejudices and practices. They work as a liberating force and serve as a reliable tool in one's search for truth, harmony and order in different aspects of life.

In Classes I and II Environmental studies is wholly devoted to the fundamentals of science. In Classes III to V. Environmental studies branches into two sections: one dealing with science and the other with history and geography that are taught together under the title Social studies. The objectives of teaching science at the primary stage are:

— To learn about flora and fauna, natural resources, the sources of energy and so on, through interaction with the immediate environment;

— To sharpen observation, inculcate the spirit of exploration; and

— To develop concern, sensitivity and the ability necessary for the preservation and protection of physical and natural resources.

At the upper primary stage, namely Classes VI to VIII, the student is expected to consolidate and strengthen the abilities acquired during the primary stage. The objective is to develop an understanding of the nature of scientific knowledge; certain physical, chemical and biological facts and their relationship to their manifestation in nature and in daily life. The student should be enabled to develop the capacity to use science to help solve problems and arrive at the right decisions.

Pupils are also expected to develop the skills required to operate ordinary laboratory/science equipment, and to design simple experiments to seek and find explanations for natural phenomena. At this stage, science education should help the pupil develop an understanding and appreciation of the joint enterprise of science joint enterprise of science and technology and the interrelationships of these with other aspects of society.

School education comes to a close with the secondary stage comprising Classes IX and X. The aim of teaching science at this stage is primarily directed towards the learning of key concepts that span all disciplines of science. At the secondary stage, the pupil should be enabled to develop a more profound understanding of the basic nature, structure, principles, processes and methodology of science, with special reference to its relationship with agriculture, industry and contemporary technology. The teaching of science at this stage should help pupils develop insights in health and environment. Greater emphasis needs to be placed on precision and accuracy while handling laboratory equipment and while engaged in procedures such as quantitative measurement, collection, presentation, analysis of data, and drawing inferences.

At the primary stage science is taught under the umbrella of Environmental studies. The contents are thematically organized into chapters titled: Things around plants; Animals and us; Our body and Food, health and weather. The syllabus concludes with a chapter titled: Man, science and environment. Science education imparted to the students at the upper primary stage ought to form part of a smooth and seamless transition from the 'environmental studies approach' to a more formal study of science. With this as the guiding principle, efforts have made to formulate content and approach. Accordingly, the organization of concepts in Class VI Class VI is somewhat similar to those of the lower primary. In Class VII and VIII, subject matter is dealt with at greater length. Themes like Science in everyday life; Things around us; Changes around us; Measurement; Separation of substances; The living world; The living body; Air, water and Air, water and energy; Balance of nature and The universe, make up the course material that engage the students at Class VI. This is followed in Class VII and VIII by more subject oriented themes such as Mechanics; Heat; Electricity; Magnetism; Carbon and its compounds; Metals and nonmetals; Life processes; Evolution, etc., Interdisciplinary topics like Health, Nutrition and Agriculture Agriculture also constitute integral part of the subjects taught at this stage. Science, at the secondary stage, is introduced around ten themes, such as: Matter, nature and behaviour; Motion; Force and energy; Ways of living; Human beings; World of work; Energy; Food and health; Environment; work; Natural resources and the universe. The time allotted for teaching science at primary, upper primary and secondary stage is 15%, 12% and 13% respectively of the total instructional time.

Some of the pressing problems facing India with regard to science education can be summarized as follows:

— *Curriculum load:* There is substantial pressure emanating from parents and the general public alike who feel that the school curriculum is excessive and needlessly taxing. It is widely believed the students are stressed out and this has in turn affected their normal all round development. The problem of curriculum load is a complex one and has its roots in many related issues. NCERT is presently revising the national curriculum framework in an effort to resolve this contentious issue.

— *Preparation of teachers:* Pre-services preparation and in-service training of teachers are major problems experienced during implementation of the curriculum. Given the huge number of teachers and geographical character of the country, management of in-service programmers is an intimidating prospect. Efforts are being made to address the problem through direct intervention at the institutional level as well as through distant mode l (and through tele-conferencing). A collaborative mechanism is being evolved by agencies like the

National Council of Educational Research and Training (NCERT), National Council for Teacher Education (NCTE), Indira Gandhi National Open University (IGNOU), along with State Councils of Educational Research (SCERT) and District Institutes of Education and Training (DIET).

— *Methods of assessment:* The attitude, approach, criteria and yardsticks adopted to assess and evaluate performances in the field of science are woefully inadequate. It in fact is emerging as a major stumbling block in efforts to improve the quality of the education system in India. Unfortunately, queries considered unlikely to rise at examinations are considered irrelevant and ignored by both staff and students. Methodologies adopted to assess performances are hardly conducive to the development of problem-solving skills among the pupils. To make matters worse, instruction is mainly assessment-driven in the country. Little or no significance is attached to the assessment of practical work, resulting in utter neglect of practical work in school education.

Recent Reforms

The latest reforms implemented in India are listed below:

— *Improvement of science education in schools:* To improve the quality of science education and to promote scientific temper, a centrally sponsored scheme: 'Improvement of Science Education in Schools' has been operational since 1987-88. Under the scheme 100% assistance is provided to the states/union territories (UTs) for provision of science kits to upper primary schools, up gradation of science laboratories and gradation of library facilities in senior/secondary schools and training of science teachers. The scheme also provides for assistance to voluntary organizations for undertaking innovative projects in the field of science education.

— *Environmental Orientation to School Education.* A centrally sponsored scheme by this name was initiated in 1988-89. The scheme envisages grants to states and 88-89. The objective is increase awareness about environmental issues. Review of textbooks on 'environmental studies' 'at primary and upper primary levels are undertaken with a view to update and enhance their quality. Strategies for imparting environmental education at upper primary level are worked out. Teaching and learning materials are being developed. Efforts are under way to organize innovative activities with a view to enrich the work experience so the teaching staff. To achieve these objectives, the scheme also has plans to seek out jectives, voluntary agencies for help and assistance.

— *Computer literacy and studies in schools:* The Department of Electronics, in collaboration with the Ministry of Human Resource Development, initiated a pilot project, 'Computer literacy and studies in schools' (CLASS) from the school year 1984-85. The LASS project was modified and converted into a centrally and converted sponsored scheme from 1993-94. The aims of the projects are:

— To provide pupils with an understanding of computers and their use;

— To provide hands-on experiences;

— To 'demystify' computers to young school goers;

— To familiarize pupils with a range of computer applications and with the computer's potential as a controlling and information processing tool. Meanwhile, the Information Technology Action Plan (1988), which makes significant provisions for integrating computers into the schooling process, has been adopted by the Government. As a consequence, the Ministry of Human Resource Development has launched a new school-computing programme CLASS 2000 from March this year. CLASS 2000 has the following three components:

— Computer literacy in 10,000 schools;

— Computer-aided learning in 1,000 schools;

— Computer-based education in 100 Smart Schools will become model centres for others.

NCERT developed the Blue Print for Smart Schools upon which the concept of computer-based education would develop. NCERT is committed to providing all possible on-line and off-line support to the above venture.

Innovative uses of Non-school Resources

In order to promote and popularize several out-of-school activities (using non-school resources) like science exhibitions, science clubs, debates, essay writing and quiz competitions are being organized by the NCERT, the Department of Science & Technology CERT, the (DST), the National Council of Science Museums (NC-SM), the Ministry of Non-Conventional Energy Sources (MNCES) and many voluntary organizations, such as: Vikram

Sarabhai Science Centre, Ahmedabad; Homi Bhabha Centre of Science Education, Mumbai, etc.

NCERT has been pioneering exhibitions in India. It has been organizing national level science exhibitions every year since 1971. The national level science exhibition is the culmination of a series of exhibitions organized at school, district, regional and state level every year. At the beginning of the school session every year, NCERT circulates to all states/UTs the main themes and sub-themes of the state-level science exhibitions for a particular year. In keeping with the central and state government's emphasis on improvement of educational facilities in rural areas and for economically weaker sections of the society, the main theme of national and state-level science exhibitions are infused with a distinct bias towards the felt needs of rural India.

The social aspect of science and relevance of science and technology for development are some other criteria, which are given due consideration indetermining the themes. The NCERT also provides detailed guidelines to the states for organization of exhibitions and outlines the criteria for evaluation of exhibits and the selection of judges.

The financial and academic support for the organization of science exhibitions are mainly provided by the NCERT and the state governments concerned. A list of exhibits selected for display at the National level with brief synopsis about each exhibit, a book titled 'Structure titled 'Structure and Working of Science Models' containing details about some selected exhibits and publicity folders about the science exhibition are published every year by the NCERT.

The National Council of Science Museums (NCSM) organizes a number of activities like demonstration lectures, mobile science exhibitions for rural schools, science quiz, science seminars, science fairs, Nature Study and Environment Awareness Programs. NCSM operates and contributes to science education of children at a mass level through its four museums located at Calcutta, Bangalore, Mumbai and Delhi, besides utilizing a number of regional centres situated in different parts of the country. NCSM has set up 301 school science centres in the states of West Bengal, Assam, Tripura, Manipur, Andhra Pradesh, Karnataka, Madhya Pradesh, Haryana, Punjab and Rajasthan.

The centre develops kits and teaching aids, conducts hobby camps, popular lectures, exhibitions, etc. Vigyan Prasar (an autonomous organization under the Department of Science & Technology) has established a Technology) network of Science Clubs (VIPNET) throughout the country to strengthen the science club movement and to co-ordinate with other existing clubs and agencies. Vigyan Prasar also contributes to learning of science through its Homepage started in September 1996. It offers daily science news pertaining exclusively to Indian science and technology (S&T) along with archived news, links to other related sites, an online popular science magazine, which features interviews with eminent scientists, S&T development stories and articles on topical S&T themes. Vikram Sarabhai Community Science Centre, Ahmedabad, conducts a mobile exhibition known as 'Science Circus'. In this project, all materials required for demonstration, participatory events as well as slides, a special bus takes around films, etc. At any chosen venue, these are displayed for the benefit of the public. Most of these activities are related to the prescribed curriculum while some others demonstrate the application of science in daily life.

The National Council is organizing national Children's Science Congress every year for Science and Technology Communication (NCSTC). In this programme, children in the age group of 10-17 years, take up scientific projects related to local issues. They work under the supervision of the teachers/science activists and report their findings at school/block or district level Congresses. Select projects are presented at the state and national levels. The National Bal Bhavan has been contributing towards enhancing the creativity among children in the age group of 5-16 years especially from the weaker section. It was established in 1956 and now operates throughout the country through its fifty-three affiliated state Bal Bhavans.

There is a library as well as National Children's Museum. It regularly organizes programmes wherein children can pursue activities of their choice such as in environment, astronomy, photography, science-related activities, etc. These experiences are enjoyable and memorable for the children, especially as they are predominantly from disadvantaged backgrounds. Thematic and general workshops are also organized regularly for teachers, trainers and adults in science activities.

NCERTs Effort Toward a New Curriculum

We have had the opportunity to observe and analyse the strengths and weaknesses of the National Policy on Education that is in prevalence since 1986. With the benefit of hindsight we can safely conclude that we need to critically scrutinize and revamp the content, process, and approach to education, in general, and science education, in particular. Greater dynamism needs to be infused into the school curriculum in order to enable it to respond to the fast changing priorities and long-term developmental goals of the nation. A number of important developments have taken place since the last revision of school science curriculum and these are bound to decisively influence the formulation, design and development of science curricula.

— Our understanding of 'how students learn science' has changed significantly. From process approach to science education, we have moved to constructivist approach.

— Last two decades have seen emergence of a new taxonomy of practical skills, which is now internationally accepted and widely used. These aspects have to be taken care of in design of learning materials for children as well as in the technology of teaching and assessment.

— The most significantly, development has taken place in the area of information technology. This is not only likely to considerably influence the end product, but also hugely impact the content and process of science education.

The National Council of Educational Research and Training has already started the process of revising the national curriculum framework. In the first phase, a document entitled 'National Curriculum Framework for School Education-A Discussion Document' has been brought out in January 2000. This document provides a curricular framework for all stages of school education. It has been evolved through a variety of strategies-by looking into theoretical and research materials, consulting and discussing various issues with faculty members, eminent educationists and experts.

In the second phase, workshops/meetings at national/ /meetings at national/ regional levels are being organized for extensive and intensive discussion in order to evolve consensus on various issues raised in the document. The document has been made available to all the stakeholders in education, i.e. other national and state-level institutions, school boards of education, state councils of educational research and training, directorates of education, parent/teacher associations, professional associations of teachers and teacher educators, and eminent educationists and educators. Their suggestions and responses will help enrich the final document. In the third phase, based on the guidelines provided in the new Curriculum Framework, syllabi, textbooks and other instructional materials for all stages of school science eduction will be designed and developed.

The progress and development of science and technology in India and the enormous potential it holds for the future have been comprehensively summarized by Prof. R.A. Mashelkar, Director-General of Council of Scientific and Industrial Research in his Presidential address delivered at eighty-seventh Indian Science Congress, Pune, on 3 January 2000 as follows: Let me sum up by recalling the new Panchsheel of the new millennium, that we should launch in the year 2000. It is simply:

— Child-centred education;

— Woman-centred family;

— Human-centred development;

— Knowledge-centred society;

— Innovation-centred India.

These principles, if put into practice, will help India to acquire a scientific temper, edge towards a 'learning community', realise national dreams of being a 'knowledge society' and leave behind memories of underdevelopment.

3

Science Education Development

One of the major challenges facing human resources planning is dealing with the uneven level of technological development in different countries.

The world has witnessed a huge scientific and technological explosion in recent decades; but not all societies have been equally affected by this process. Yet the ability to master and apply science and technology are indispensable to the process of modernization and development of economies.

Well aware of this fact as early as the 1960s, developing countries embarked on programmes to support the development of science education at secondary and higher education levels. Much has been achieved and the number of pupils and students enrolled in science courses has increased almost everywhere.

However, expectations have rarely been met and lack of science trained personnel at higher- and middle-levels continues to hamper the socioeconomic development of many countries.

The reasons for this state of affairs are many: well trained and motivated science teachers have remained in short supply in most countries; curriculum reforms have not been implemented as planned either because the necessary resources have not been available or because it takes time, in any case, for schools and teachers to change their habits and teaching methods.

More recently, science education seems to have particularly suffered from the economic austerity which has led to a decrease in real terms of the resources allocated to education in a number of countries. All these problems have been aggravated by lack of coordination between the numerous administrations and institutions concerned with secondary education and by insufficient planning. As a result, science education in a large number of countries is still in a critical state.

Over the last two decades many developing countries have invested heavily in improving access to, and enhancing the quality of, science education. Human resource development has become a central feature of most national development strategies and within this the emphasis has more often than not been on the acquisition of scientific and technological skills and capabilities. In many developing countries there is now more than two decades of experience with system reforms, curriculum development, and teacher training for science education at secondary and higher levels.

Though much has been achieved, the impact of these initiatives has not always lived up to expectations-labour shortages for scientifically and technically qualified staff have persisted constraining the development of new productive enterprises and hampering the growth of existing ones; teaching and learning practices have been slower to change than many curriculum developers anticipated; and increased access to science education has sharpened awareness of variations in quality and participation associated with urban and rural, and gender differences. What evidence there is of levels of achievement in science suggest that scientific literacy is still a distant goal in many countries, and that the achievement of students who specialise in science falls short of that which is desirable.

There are many reasons for the problems that have arisen. These include inadequate problem diagnosis, lack of skilled curriculum developers, insufficient resources for effective implementation, persistent shortages of trained science teachers, and ineffective planning. Most recently, in a good number of countries, economic austerity within the framework of structural adjustment programmes, has placed severe constraints on the resources available for education. Science education, as one of the most expensive areas of the curriculum, has become vulnerable to the effects of parsimonious resourcing. Radically new technologies of production and access to information are beginning to permeate the developing world. Greater and greater proportions of the labour force are being employed in occupations where scientific literacy is an advantage. Scientific competence and understanding is required for growing numbers of professionals.

Context of Science Education Development

Rapid expansion in school enrolments since the 1960s is a characteristic of the great majority of developing countries. In most the rates of growth have been higher at secondary level, where most science is taught, than at primary. Enrolment growth has been driven both by planned expansion for human resource development and by the exigencies of social demand for greater access to school systems. Science education has occupied a prominent position in the expansion process influenced by aspirations to industrialise, to localise expatriate cadres, and to take more control of production technologies. In the first instance much expansion built on existing science syllabuses or weakly modified them to remove some of the more obvious distortions inherited from the past with the simple ambition of extending these largely unaltered to greater and greater numbers of students. Little of what would now be called science curriculum development was in evidence in most developing countries during the 1960s.

In those countries with a colonial experience that penetrated the fabric of their education systems deeply, science educational practice shadowed that in industrialized countries. Syllabi were borrowed, or perhaps more accurately lent, with little more than cursory attention to local conditions. They closely resembled those to be found in the more conservative parts of the education systems of the ex-colonial power. Thus in the case of British ex-colonies throughout the world there are many examples of mildly modified General Certificate of Education (G.C.E.) type science rubrics for secondary schools current in the United Kingdom in the 1960s, and even those derived from the School Certificate which preceded G.C.E.. Commonly these courses were assessed by overseas examining boards bound to anglo-centric orthodoxies of content selection and standards of achievement. The latter had the consequence that science was a relatively diffficult subject, which often had a substantially lower pass rates than other subjects. Partly as a result it is common to find, in those education systems where standardization and norm-referencing is not used across subjects, that there is a hierarchy of difficulty with foreign languages and mathematics as the most difficult subjects to pass, with science subjects following close behind.

Science at secondary level in most education systems was generally taught to selected groups of secondary age students both because of the limited resources available and because of the prevalent beliefs that suggested that orgy relatively small proportions of the school population with a special aptitude for science could benefit. The science programmes were predominantly academic, descriptive, knowledge based and inspired by 'grammar school' traditions. They were introduced by colonial elites who wished to ensure that their children would have access to higher education in the United Kingdom or in other industrialized countries.

The extent to which the children of nationals had access to the schools that taught science varied considerably from country to country, with more or less segregation of access depending on the national politics. Primary provision rarely included any science education beyond that associated with nature study. Alongside the high cost institutions which typically used European languages as the medium of instruction and which represented the apex of many of these systems, vernacular schools were often allowed to develop. Frequently these had support from missionary societies and other non-government agencies.

Depending on the country and the culture, formal and non-formal learning systems often coexisted and predated the introduction of colonial school systems. In some of these science occupied a place in the curriculum, but this was the exception rather than the rule. All this is well known. Its significance is that in the majority of developing countries it was the curricula and the school practices of elite institutions that provided the basis for post-independence growth. Not only did these schools present models of high status educational practice-in the case of science education the fully equipped science laboratory, the prestige attached to studying pure science removed from its application, the denigration of practical subjects which involved the design of useful objects-but also they were often the ones in which the generation of post independence leaders had their formative educational experiences.

Unlike in most industrialized countries, there were few if any alternative images of science education to act as models. In the United Kingdom there was a long history of the development of science education. Admittedly this was also dominated by grammar and public school traditions that developed during the nineteenth century and reached maturity in the tripartite system established by the 1944 Education Act. This, amongst other things, enshrined the view that there were three types of student: "... pupils interested in learning for its own sake, able to reason abstractly, to appreciate elegance and culture"...." boys whose interests lie in the applied fields of science and art" who have "an uncanny insight into the intricacies of mechanisms".....and pupils who could "only deal with concrete things, needed immediate gratification and were interested in things as they are and the realm of facts". Hence the development, widely reflected in other countries, of academic, technical/vocational and general secondary schools.

In the United Kingdom however, unlike in many developing countries, there were established traditions which acted as a counterpoint to over emphasis on academic science, albeit with different levels of success in different periods. Technological and engineering orientated science education, as well as the tradition of general science provision for the non-specialized students were a nineteenth century legacy.

The experience of puffing science to work in the 193945 war and in the cause of industrial development was deeply rooted —not perhaps as much as in the education systems of Germany or the USA but it was there. So also was embryonic concern for the environment and for the social implications of science. These had been given impetus by the invention of nuclear weapons which spawned populist movements and were precursors to the growth of ecology and environmental concern groups which offered a counter balance to technocratic views of the development of science.

In the 1960s most developing countries did not have a scientifically or technologically competent cadre outside the minuscule numbers of nationals trained abroad and the expatriate experts who brought science almost as a cargo cult' with mystical properties that gave power over the environment and substantial salaries to those who possessed it. Science was an elite preserve of alien knowledge, the practical value of which was not close to the experience of most of the population.

Though high educational achievement provided some access to this strange world of the rituals of science, these were narrow conduits with small openings. To understand some aspects of subsequent development, and the continued attachment to externally determined images of the science, it is necessary to appreciate these aspects of historical experience. Though certainly different in detail in countries falling under the influence of different colonial powers, the imagery resonates across different systems.

Towards the end of the 1960s, many ministries of education took the first steps towards taking a view of the curriculum which was broader than the redefinition of syllabus consisting of a list of topics. National curriculum units or centres began to be established, often with substantial external assistance in the form of buildings, equipment and staff. Inevitably expatriate staff carried with them current orthodoxies of science education as cultural as well as professional baggage. Those trained abroad also absorbed the fashionable wisdom of the times and transposed much of it into local science curriculum development programmes.

Many of the initiatives taken in science education had their inspiration in the explosion of curriculum development in industrialized countries in the 1960s. It is significant that in many countries systematic curriculum development initially concentrated on science education, along with perhaps mathematics and language since these were generally regarded as key subject areas. Thus, for example, one of the first national curriculum development centres was established in Sri Lanka in 1963 with a brief specifically orientated towards the development of science education.

Projects, programmes and institutions emerged to support science education development in diverse forms and were supported by UNESCO and many bilateral donors. The African Primary Science Programme (APSP) developed and became the forerunner to the African Curriculum Organization (ACO); professional associations like the African Association for the Advancement of Science and Technology and the West African Association of Science Teachers (and their analogues in countries throughout Asia and Latin America) were formed and linked to existing international networks like the International Council of Associations of Science Education (ICASE).

Many of these developments were influenced by aspirations to see to what extent new approaches to science teaching developed in industrialized countries could be adapted for use in developing countries. A comprehensive review of those supported by the British Council is provided in Chisman and Wilson. The 1970s saw the coming to fruition of many science education development projects. Large numbers of these were derivative in the sense that they were orientated towards the adoption and, as time passed, the adaptation of what was thought to be good practice in industrialized countries. Thus programmes which drew inspiration from curricula developed in industrialized countries began to appear throughout the developing world.

As curriculum development institutions matured and became more self confident emphasis began to be placed on indigenising science curricula. This it was hoped would make science more accessible and relevant to national needs, would update antiquated material, and relate science education more closely to the needs of modernization and development. The reports of the Science Education Programme for Africa (SEPA) and of the International Clearing House on Science Mathematics Curriculum Development illustrate how widespread this activity was and how many projects had substantial international linkages of different forms. To take one example, Scottish Integrated Science, a programme developed in Scotland in the 1960s, formed the basis for many junior science programmes in Commonwealth countries in West and Southern Africa, the Caribbean, and South East Asia.

Frequently adaptation concentrated on modifying content without questioning very deeply aims, dominant views of the nature of scientific knowledge, and the prevalent conventional wisdom on teaching methods. Some adaptation and localization took indirect forms-when, for example, programmes were adapted for use in one country and these adaptations were used as the basis for adaptation in a third country. Thus, in Swaziland five curricula were reviewed from other countries and a decision made to adapt the West Indies Science Curriculum Innovation project which itself had a relationship to Scottish Integrated Science. Lee illustrates how in Malaysia curriculum reforms in science were the result of a complex interplay between international influences and the sociopolitical context of Malaysian educational development.

Bilateral assistance to promote innovations developed in the United Kingdom coincided with local pressures to revise science curricula. She argues that the more countries become integrated into the global networks of information, economic relationships and sociocultural trends the more likely they are to emulate the educational ideology of the industrialized countries. Secondary curricula typically took the lions share of curriculum development effort. Much of higher education seemed largely untouched by the flurry of activity at lower levels. Primary curriculum development was almost universally the poor relation to secondary with relatively few examples of substantial projects with a science orientation.

The explanation for this probably lies in two directions. First, where primary schooling has become widely available it is secondary school certificates that command access to modem sector jobs-it is at this level that competition is sharpest and demands for curricula improvement the greatest. Second, staff trained in curriculum development disproportionately tend to be drawn from the ranks of secondary teachers whose experience is with secondary level subjects.

Most attention was focused on the design of written materials for schools-textbooks, workbooks and less frequently teacher's guides. Curriculum development activity related to in-service and pre-service teacher training generally came a poor second. Public examining and assessment systems have generally changed more slowly than curricula -- often the localization of the examining system followed rather than preceded the institutionalization of curriculum development activity.

Though the content of examination items changed, their style and quality often fell a long way short of comprehensively assessing key aspects of new science curricula. As a result 'backwash' from examinations characteristically undermined rather than reinforced fundamental changes in teaching and learning and the consequences of the 'diploma disease' were widely noted in curriculum implementation.

By the end of the 1970s most countries had indigenized curriculum materials in schools and had locally designed programmes in widespread use. Several had already embarked on subsequent curriculum renewal cycles. To bring this schematic story up-to-date is to grapple with the problems of describing heterogeneous circumstances concisely. The account so far has been selective-it has not touched on major influences that some countries have experienced and it has not highlighted differences between the anglophone and francophone traditions. But it does provide an account that should resonate in a good number of developing countries. To bring this story up to date will probably commit similar sins of omission but here is an admittedly personal attempt.

The last decade has provided evidence that development is possible and that developing countries will not always be 'running behind'. Several countries, mostly located around the Pacific rim sustained rates of economic growth far in excess of the mature industrialized countries. Much of their growth depended on their success in producing and marketing products with scientific and technological elements.

Electronic products began to figure as more and more important in this process, accompanying the development of more traditional technology intensive products like motor cars. It may have been true that this process was initially supported by copying ideas developed elsewhere. It soon became clear that this was only part of the reason. In any case to argue this perjoratively sounded distinctly like sour grapes to those who studied the history of innovation and industrial development. Science education in the newly industrialising countries was in considerable demand and regarded as of higher status than other subjects.

There is another larger group of countries whose experience has not been so fortunate. In these countries sustained economic growth has been a frequently cited goal which has proved impossible to attain. The reality has been economic stagnation, increased rather than decreased economic dependence and, in a good number of cases, declining budgetary provision for education alongside growing demand. In these countries science education development has probably taken steps backward more often than forward.

The resourcing problems are clear, especially in countries experiencing structural adjustment programmes. High population growth rates, and enrolments rising faster than national income, have diluted per capita educational resources. Educational expenditures per child have declined to levels below that where anything resembling the science taught in richer countries is a reasonable expectation, except for a select minority.

The economic circumstances of these countries have encouraged those who are qualified in science and technology to emigrate to greener pastures. Often public sector hiring practices have contributed to this by maintaining patterns of recruitment and reward that favour the non-scientific, administrative cadres. Why study science, the aspirant youth might ask, when it is more difficult, expensive, time consuming and culturally alien than arts and humanities subjects and it is qualifications in these that are likely to provide a smoother path to the higher reaches of the public service.

Alongside these changes in economic climate, experience with innovatory science programmes has introduced more realism into attempts at curriculum reform. Optimistic hopes that science educational practice could be transformed in a decade or so have proved far more difficult to realise in practice than they had been to conceptualise in theory. With perhaps a predictable sense of deja vu, critiques of the implementation of new science programmes introduced in developing countries began to illustrate how difficult it was to change established traditions.

The emphasis in the new programmes was often designed to replace teacher centred pedagogy and the teaching of science as an accumulation of facts by more involvement of children in their learning, greater amounts of practical activity, less dependence on traditional text-books, and more concern for the intellectual skills of scientific problem solving. It soon became clear that many of the necessary antecedent conditions for this were difficult to meet.

New methods tended to assume well qualified, motivated teachers working with adequate resources who understood and internalized the new pedagogic techniques. Moreover they assumed that the enthusiasm for change was shared throughout the science teaching profession. This despite the fact that it was invariably difficult to demonstrate that the return on the effort necessary to adopt new practices was repaid in terms of gains in the most readily available indicator of success-examination results. It may have been that new approaches did offer better ways of reaching more comprehensive learning objectives in science education than those that they replaced.

But generally patterns of assessment did not change sufficiently to reflect these new learning goals. Crucially, where expertise was in short supply and where the teachers' established role was as an authority within a subject area, open ended questioning approaches making use of discovery learning techniques placed teachers in new relationships wish students that required deeper levels of knowledge and confidence in science than many possessed. These kinds of problems are widely documented. The 1980s was a period of consolidation in science education in many industrialised countries. The initiatives that were taken built on, rather than tried to break with, the recent past. The most radical departures came with the growing momentum behind introducing more vocational elements into science education and linked school science more closely with the world of work and practical skills.

Developments in the United Kingdom illustrate this with many such initiatives. The science education drama took on more of the quality of playing out the debates of the 1970's than of She dislocations of radical innovation. Research on science education during this period was heavily influenced by those studies that explored teaching and learning. These invoked Piagetian schema on the one hand to gain insights into childrens' conceptual understanding of science. On the other hand constructivist approaches stressed the centrality of the learner and their perceptions as a starting point. Though this research undoubtedly impinged on the thinking of generations of teachers, its impact, at least initially, on the recently introduced United Kingdom national curriculum was small illustrating the power of the political interests overriding curricula decision making by educationalists.

From the literature some trends in science education that seem most likely to impinge on developing countries in the 1990s can be discerned. These include:

— The tendency towards making science available to all secondary students will continue. This implies more integrated/combined/coordinated/modular approaches which balance content from the traditional disciplines.

— Teaching scientific skills and cognitive processes related to scientific problem solving and reducing emphasis on the recall of information will remain the curriculum development orthodoxy.

— Technology will form a new focus of interest in curriculum development complementing or even leading new science curricula with an emphasis on the skills needed to solve real life problems.

— Broader definitions of science education that absorb health education, nutrition, earth sciences etc. will become more acceptable as will links with other curriculum areas.

— Science and society, and environmental issues will appear more frequently in new curricula as their importance for the preservation of global equilibria becomes more apparent. These initiatives may be linked to attempts to reduce stereotyping of science with a view to improving participation of disadvantaged groups.

— Science teacher twining precareer / in-service / on-service will be enhanced as the teacher is given more emphasis in the light of increasing demands made on the science teacher.

— Science will feature more prominently in the development of primary curricula.

There is evidence for all these trends. They mirror those identified as early as 1979 in a review of integrated science education by Haggis and Adey. They still cover most of the likely agendas for science education development and suggest that the pace of change has been much slower than anticipated. This indicates that the problems of implementing these ideas demand much more infrastructure and gestation time than has been forthcoming. At least in some cases, that the innovatory zeal of the science curriculum developers to change the way in which science is taught and how it is presented has not been so vigorously shared by all the groups that have to collaborate in making ideas become a reality-gaps in perception and priority between the science education community and their ultimate clients-the parents, students, politicians and employers-have played their part in slowing down the Ate at which changes have taken place.

Several other points emerge from the analysis of the context of science education in developing countries over the recent past.

First, since this was a period of consolidation in science education the 'demonstration effects' were weaker than they had been in the 1960s. There was no radically 'new' philosophy or teaching methods to consider. And there were fewer science education development projects in industrialized countries which had natural spin-offs in terms of extension elsewhere. Those that developed were more clearly grounded in domestic concerns which were not seen to resonate so readily with problems in developing countries.

Secondly what was new, in terms of a new vocationalism at secondary level which stressed employment related and technological skills, was not new to many developing countries. Leaving aside the many colonial experiments in practically orientated and vocationalized schooling which were displaced into the shadows by the expansion of general secondary schooling, many countries embarked on diversified secondary school projects, curriculum development in pre-vocational studies and life skills and other related initiatives. The experience was already there of attempts to introduce a new vocationalism-it did not have to be borrowed or invented. So also was the appreciation of the difficulties of successfully implementing such policies. There were many precursors of this concern to move science education from the realm of sterile facts into the world of action and towards more technological inclined emphases which were thought to increase relevance. Thus UNESCO noted:

> "a shift towards greater stress on first hand experiences by pupils and their active involvement in the learning process through enquiry and discovery, and on the application of science while incorporating elements of technology". Yoloye and Bajah note the post-independence emphasis in many African countries on ameliorating unemployment through introducing more vocationally relevant material into school curricula. Thus in Uganda science education was to be orientated towards 'job-makers' rather than 'job seekers'; many countries adopted the rhetoric of education for self reliance first promulgated in Tanzania—technological skill formation for national self-reliance became a live issue in Nigeria; science education for production and the development of socialist ideals caught the imagination of left leaning regimes. A rash of projects were launched with the intention of increasing the relevance of science to the majority of pupils who experienced it.

Third, the participation of disadvantaged groups in science education has become a more important issue than in the past. The lower participation of some groups — girls, rural children, members of minorities— in science is both a concern from the point of view of equity and efficiency. Most education systems adhere to commitments to equality of opportunity though, in science, patterns of participation suggests these continue to be unevenly distributed. In countries which have a shortage of science trained human resources, low participation by disadvantaged groups implies under-utilization of a pool of talent that might ameliorate human resource bottlenecks.

Involvement of Girls in Science Education

The involvement of girls in science education, or rather the lack of it, has been a growing concern in both developed and developing countries. In the latter group, however, the problem is exacerbated by the under-representation of girls generally in enrolments, though the extent of the problem varied widely from country-to-country. In sub-Saharan Africa for example the differential between male and female school enrolments is not pronounced at primary level, but is high at secondary level with girls only accounting for 34 per cent of total enrolments. This figure may be compared with 39 per cent in Asia and 50 per cent in Latin America.

Although great progress has been made in increasing access of girls to secondary education, the trend in several African countries is not encouraging. As early as 1982 it was observed that there had been a decrease in female enrolment since independence in three former Portuguese colonies and stagnation in Benin, Burundi, Rwanda and Togo. Where schooling involves direct costs, and austerity has reduced disposable income, the probability is that family decisions to support children in school in many societies will favour continued enrolments of boys. It is difficult to find global data on the participation of girls in scientific subjects, but there are many indications that enrolment ratios are often lower and dropout levels higher amongst girls.

Despite numerous calls for improvements in science education for girls it is evident that education systems in many developing countries continue systematically to favour boys more than girls in education in general and in science in particular the proceedings of the Gender and Science and Technology Conference (GASAT) from 1981 collect together papers on gender related issues in science education and illustrate both the progress that has been made and the magnitude of the problems that remain.

In 1986, Ogunniyi, has reviewed the nature of science education in Africa and identifies constraints such as rapid enrolment expansion, scarce resources, limited teacher quality and high dropouts as critical. His review of various primary and secondary curriculum innovations of the Science Education Programme for Africa illustrates this. Among the trends in science education he identifies are a shift in emphasis from rote learning to enquiry activities and from teacher-centred approaches to student-centred approaches; more subject integration; more emphasis on problem-solving; increased student population and crash programmes for the training of science teachers; tertiary admission policies favouring science students; expansion in the teaching of primary science.

Yet despite these efforts progress has been hampered by poor teacher preparation, rapid rate of teacher transfer, shortage of qualified science teachers, lack of a reinforcing home background and the 'conspicuous absence of an active involvement of the scientific community'.

Ogunniyi is critical of poor planning and the absence of clear-cut policies and he attributes this to the lack of a scientific approach to planning. He calls for curricula which reflect contemporary and emergent needs of the diverse cultures of Africa; examination reform is needed to support the new emphasis on science as enquiry; more involvement of African scientists in science education; less esoteric tertiary science programmes. Major problems in science education therefore remain. The first international conference of the Forum for African Science Educators drew attention to the most important of these in 1982.

> "We are aware of the goal of education to produce human beings who are self reliant ... We are aware of the failure in many ways of our current science education programmes to prepare (the dropout), be it at the secondary school level or at the primary school level, for useful living..... we observe that most African governments have in no way positively supported and sustained action programmes to make science education more functional with a view to replacing or complementing academic preparation .... We recognise that our curricula are deficient of technology, and in particular appropriate technology, for the transformation of rural life. We recognise that our examination system is inadequate, to say the least, and yet has its stranglehold on the educational system. We note with regret governments often times institute far-reaching changes in curricula or educational systems at relatively short notice and sometimes without cognizance of professional opinions..."

In summary, the environment for science education development in many developing countries has changed in at least six ways:

(i) The external 'pull' exerted by science curriculum development in industrialized countries was less powerful as an influence on curriculum development in the 1980s than it was previously.

(ii) Localization of curriculum materials was no longer the highest priority; most countries have developed their own programmes.

(iii) The difficulties of implementing significant changes in teaching and learning in science have become apparent; there have been at least as many examples of failure, as measured against expectations, than success.

(iv) National curriculum development in science has become institutionalized and bureaucratized in specialized units with defined responsibilities.

(v) Science and technology have developed rapidly and, in some countries, have penetrated the social and economic fabric deeply changing expectations of what science education should provide. In other countries, where economic development has been disappointing and austerity has resulted in low and declining resources for education, this process has been very slow. The prospects for improving science education in these circumstances may demand some radical reappraisal of both goals and modes of delivery.

(vi) There is now greater awareness of disparities in access to opportunities to study science, especially amongst girls as opposed to boys, but also in relation to other apparently disadvantaged groups.

Educational Policies

An alternative perspective of the role of science and technology in development, which gained considerable currency in the 1970s, is to stress the qualitative differences in the development problems of the poorer countries and argue for the development of indigenous and appropriate science and technology that cannot come about simply through technology transfer no matter how efficient.

Proponents of this view stress that the research and development efforts of developed countries are often simply irrelevant to the needs of rural populations where even the simplest technology cannot be maintained and capital is much scarcer than labour. They point to the tardiness and under-funding of research on tropical agriculture as one of many examples of how the development priorities of rich countries have shaped the impact of science and technology on developing countries.

Much of the research that has been applied, they argue, is directed towards improving the production of cash crops for export, not meeting the needs of the local population. One of the most well known developments of this case is provided by Schumacher and his work has spawned a respected development agency (the Intermediate Technology Development Group) and a considerable literature. The provision of sufficient competent manpower is also a central problem in this approach.

The need is seen to be for those who can create and radically adapt scientific and technological knowledge for domestic application, not simply transfer it. They can then contribute to scientific and technological development domestically and internationally. Thus, for example, Goonetilleke attempts to show that there is a reservoir of unexploited ideas relevant to recent developments in such fields as artificial intelligence in developing countries that is often overlooked in the haste of conducting research and development in metropolitan countries. In this alternative view of development technological dependency can be replaced by a judicious mix of appropriate and indigenously developed science and technology which is grounded directly in the needs of the populations it serves and has value beyond it.

The world is never as simple as the common habit of constructing dichotomies suggests. Both views contain elements of truth and paint incomplete pictures. This is because the problems of development have both local and international dimensions and because science is in a sense universal. It seeks knowledge which is not bound by specific cultural contexts but the utility of its application (technology) is specific to context and need.

Strategies based on these different views demand an understanding of the room to manoeuvre that national economies have. Small countries with limited access to markets cannot hope to sustain a wide base of technological industries. Even medium and large size countries are unlikely to have the resources to compete globally in most fields. The only strategy that is really viable is to identify affordable technologies where there is a comparative advantage. The corollary of this is to emphasize the scientific and technological needs of the population as a whole first, and make special provision to support science and technology in carefully selected areas.

For a good proportion of developing countries it will remain much cheaper to buy highly specialized training abroad than develop local facilities for which the demand will be limited and the costs high. The problem of ensuring that expensively trained staff do contribute the fruits of their knowledge to the national economy that sponsors them and do not simply brain- drain themselves away remains, but it is an illusion to believe that training in national institutions prevents this.

Policy on science and technology in most countries is the result of a complex interplay between competing and sometimes contradictory aspirations. Its derivation typically spans several ministries which will each have different perspectives on policy and its purposes e.g. industry, agriculture, labour, defence, education.

The resolution of these in the political process will determine the extent to which science and technology initiatives are seen primarily as contributing to economic growth of the kind linked to the penetration of global markets for products with a sigruficant science and technology component; as lessening dependence on imported technology and meeting needs to become more self sufficient; as improving the employment prospects of the workforce through increasing knowledge and skill levels; as promoting strong defence capabilities without reliance on imported military hardware; as enhancing the quality of life of the mass of the people through better understanding of their environment and how to make best use of it employing scientific understanding. Which of these is emphasised clearly has implications for the nature of science education that can contribute to such policy objectives.

The issues discussed above highlight choices that are available in the determination of science policy that sets the framework for science education. There is another important aspect to the policy debate. Science and technology have developed at an accelerating rate. This has consequences for the gap between the leading exponents of a technology and those that follow in the wake.

Mature technologies change slowly with marginal increments in efficiency or quality. Patent protection is likely to have lapsed. Any differences in technical production efficiency are likely to be overshadowed by other factors-the organisation of working practices, the cost of labour, access to markets etc.

New technologies of production are the obverse of this -they represent order of magnitude improvements in productivity, are patent protected, secret, and competitively lethal to outdated producers. The greater the rate of changes of this kind the more likely the collapse of markets to technological monopolists with the likelihood of a retreat into protectionism by industrialized countries.

Innovation may also take place with new products as well as new processes. Profitability comes either from the lead years of new product marketing in the absence of competition, or in later incremental improvements in process technology. There have been attempts to analyse the world economy in ways which suggest the existence of 'long waves' related to concentrated bursts of new product innovation followed by movement into phases of mature growth characterised by process innovations driven by Schumpeterian entrepreneurs. Some argue that the existence of these cycles of economic activity makes it more difficult for developing countries to keep up with the quantum leaps of change embodied in new products. Others stress the opportunities that exist on the downswing for catching up using improvements in process technology.

The implications of this for planning science and technology education relate to willingness to carry the risks involved in new product development as opposed to the opportunities for process innovation. The kind of creative individuals educated in science who can conceive of new products and develop them to a marketable form may not be the same people as those who can systematically produce process innovations. To put it another way the kind of education and training that develops the insights that lead to new discoveries may not be consistent with that which promotes incremental improvements in existing technologies.

The latter needs the ability to 'search and assimilate' ideas to a greater extent than it may need novel research based on laboratory science proceeding from first principles. It may need flexible learning from a position of relative inferiority, holding in abeyance nationalist sentiments to devalue that which is 'not invented here' and the confidence of vision beyond "the role of humble technology consumers". More a spirit of wakon yosai (Japanese spirit with western ability) than one of dependent acceptance. The 'crippled minds' of Goonatilake need space to overcome intellectual subordination which may not only be served by the self respect that comes with original invention.

In the light of this framework of issues which influence science policy and development strategies it is now appropriate to consider how the aims and objectives of science education are selected and how they shape science education policy.

Aims and Objectives

The aims and objectives given in different national systems have a variety of sources. One of the simplest ways of classifying these sources is in terms of the kind of analysis that produces them. Rowntree has developed a typology that distinguishes three characteristically different origins. These are:

(i) expectations about future needs in society;

(ii) analysis of the activities of subject matter specialists;

(iii) analysis of the structure of the subject matter itself.

The first mixes those that arise from the science policy debate at the national level with those that reflect broader educational concerns with citizenship and broadly distributed scientific literacy. The second utilises a conventional view of educational practice that leans towards training and takes the activities that qualified scientist perform as the end in view. The third relies on epistemological and philosophical discourse to identify the inherent logic of a subject that requires certain selection of content, development of intellectual skills and sequencing of material. In so doing it draws on the work of Hirst and Peters and Phenix which argues the existence of "modes of enquiry" and "ways of knowing" that are thought to be embodied in different disciplines.

These different sources result in at least three different types of educational objectives-those concerned with life skills which are of general value to educated citizens (the ability to classify, the power to discriminate according to criteria); those which are methodologically defined (the processes of scientific enquiry, the skills of systematic observation, the design of experiments); and those defined by content objectives (specific content linked knowledge and skills characteristic of the discipline, e.g. taxonomies in biology, the periodic table in chemistry, Newton's laws of motion in physics). Behind these mechanisms for defining educational objectives in science as in other subjects is a long list of questions that need to be answered before the process of establishing aims and objectives for particular programmes or grade levels can be operationalized.

Since it is clearly impossible to try and examine how these competing perspectives have weighed in the formulation of educational goals in science in many different developing countries it is instructive here to consider selectively the debate on some key aspects of the debate on aims and objectives.

First in relation to aims that derive from the national policy making process it does seem possible to identify some trends from the most obvious place in which these are stated-national plan documents.

A study of 29 plans from 16 countries indicates how plans in the 1960s tended to locate educational aims related to science and technology very much in terms of manpower development rationales. Typically the purpose of expanding provision was seen to lie in the creation of more graduate level scientists and technologists. It is only in later plans relating to the 1970s and early 1980s that the rationales shift to include a broader range of purposes which encompass social as well as economic goals.

More commonly in later plans science education is argued to serve needs to redistribute employment opportunities and reduce educational disparities that have consequences for different social groups; in some countries female participation becomes an issue and this is often particularly located in science and mathematics subject areas; nation-building arguments also are used more frequently to justify investment in science education to strengthen local institutions and reduce dependence on imported expertise and technology; and within the economic rationales used science and technology education are broadened to include rurally relevant science, less academic orientation and more concern, at least in principle, for extending scientific literacy to larger proportions of the population.

Second, concerning those aims that derive from the activities of subject matter specialists the key question for science education in developing countries is which specialists? This problem has at least three dimensions. The first issue is whether the scientists that are taken as role models are those to be found in the research laboratories of institutions in the countries of the North working within a highly specialized, resource intensive environment and occupying themselves with the pursuit of fundamental insights into the nature of physical reality. Even this image is misleading as it is well established that most qualified scientists and engineers in the North do not have such jobs. More frequently they are to be found in posts which require technical expertise but where the nature of the job is fairly routine and removed from the image that 'pure' science has established for itself. They are more often the puzzle solvers of Kuhn's 'normal science' than the paradigm breaking geniuses of 'revolutionary science'. Routine problem solving is a much more common activity than fundamental reconsideration of basic principles most of which are taken for granted most of the time.

The second aspect of this issue is that even if subject specialists can be identified in what do they specialise? The dominant specialities familiar to school science (physics, chemistry, botany, zoology) are themselves early twentieth century artefacts which came to replace the traditions of natural philosophy of the early nineteenth century and before where science was more commonly studied as a whole.

These distinctions have begun to look even more arbitrary as science divided and subdivided into more and more specialisations, some of which have begun to impinge on curriculum reality in schools. Environmental science, after a false start in the 1960s is now reentering the curriculum in many countries; earth science is rationalised as linking with the 'other' sciences and integrating geographical knowledge into science; hybrid subjects —biochemistry, biophysics, biotechnology are increasingly at the centre of the development of new products which have direct-consequences for development strategies.

Which kind of scientist should be emulated if the main purpose is to prepare learners for careers in those fields? And if universities, which in most countries act to legitimate and define the nature of school subjects, are encumbered by colonial legacies of subject compartmentalization, what prospect is there of yielding genuine status to science education defined in ways other than the traditional three sciences. The strategy of 'counter-penetration' advocated by Masrui depends for its success on the development of a capacity to innovate independently which in itself requires the courage to challenge the existing structure of academic knowledge.

The final dimension of this problem is that the idea of subject specialisation presuppose that the 'realms of meaning' and 'modes of enquiry' really are separately distinguishable. As we shall see in the discussion of curriculum issues below this looks less and less compelling as an argument the more science is defined as a learning activity which results in process skills and enquiry strategies rather than content based knowledge.

Aims that are based on the 'logic of the subject' are familiar to science teachers worldwide. Basic understanding of the laws of motion is a prerequisite for more advanced consideration of the motion of projectiles or the importance of momentum; the periodic table allows order to be put into the properties of elements and compounds; taxonomic classification is necessary to explore theories of evolution. But there are many aspects of science that do not require the same kind of cumulative and sequential study that may be logically essential in some branches of mathematics.

Some content selection and the order of its teaching is relatively arbitrary-optics does not have to be taught before or after thermodynamics except where the two interrelate. It does not have to be taught at all-choices have to be made to include and exclude content on the basis partly of what serves overall learning aims best. Indeed optics, as traditionally taught with a strong dose of geometric optics has increasingly fallen out of favour as a school level topic as other fields have been considered more important-e.g. electronics. There has been lithe debate that geometric optics provided something of educational value for science that could not be achieved through other routes.

Another aspect of the debate on aims and objectives for science education addresses the question 'whose aims'. The problem here is evident and not easily resolved. Each group with an interest in science education will have different perspectives on purpose linked to particular interests. This is not to suppose that consensus is not possible, merely to remind the reader that the ease with which it is achieved is often greatly exaggerated.

Havelock and Huberman identified consensus as one of the three key elements in the determinants of success or failure in implementing educational innovations. Their accounts of unsuccessfully implemented educational innovations also identify lack of understanding of project goals as an important factor in contributing to failure. This may conceal the real problem; namely that the goals are indeed understood but are not accepted and internalized by those with the responsibility for putting ideas into practice. To unpack this problem a little it is worth elaborating on some likely conflicts of interest.

Governments have frequently seen science education as a vehicle for human resource development to meet scarce manpower needs. If this is in their interest the science education aims that will be emphasized are those which seem to offer most prospect of providing predominantly high-level graduates with international comparable levels of qualification.

Employers in the modem sector may share some of these concerns but often have at least as much interest in the basic skills that the bulk of the workforce bring to specific jobs that require some scientific skills and the ability to employ them in day-to-day production activities. Hence the complaints from employers in many countries about the inability of school leavers to perform basic tasks of measurement, observation, and use reasoning skills on-the-job. High-level scientific manpower can be bought, or licenses for technology acquired, often at marginal cost to the enterprise; the workforce cannot be substituted so easily.

Teachers and curriculum developers have other interests, not least their own professional identity which may cause them to emphasise aims which promote specialisation and the status that accompanies it, and which emphasises the intellectual and academic at the expense of the practical. Thus Adamu illustrates how aspects of the Nigerian science curriculum were ambitiously specified and often not fully operationalized in his study of science schools in Kano State.

Parents and students will have the mixed motives that are associated with schooling everywhere; the aims for a good number will be to ensure success through study which leads to access to higher grades, the substance of the study being less important than reaching an acceptable level of achievement. For some, no doubt, what is learned will be of importance independent of its value for selection, but the pressures arising from restricted access to modern sector jobs where these are scarce, may make what is learned of secondary importance.

Despite these differences in interests it is worth noting that at one level, the importance attached to different content in the sciences, there does seem to be substantial convergence. At least in the 23 countries sampled by the IEA study it appears there was general consistency in ratings assigned to the importance of different content at different levels. Some content tended to have consistently high rating and other content consistently low ratings. Moreover, they argue, that since ratings tend to increase from level to level content treated at one level is generally treated more intensively at the level above suggesting to them that 'concyclic' patterns existed across countries.

Orientation

The range of aims and objectives given for secondary science programmes in different systems is vast, as might be expected. The reports of the International Clearing House on Science and Mathematics Education list project objectives for hundreds of projects which cover as wide a spectrum as can be imagined. At the most general level themes recur about which there is a certain universality.

Typically science courses at the lower secondary level will include knowledge of basic scientific facts and some ability to apply them, the development of basic measurement and observation skills, some practice of the psychomotor skills involved in conducting experiments, and affective objectives designed to encourage positive attitudes to science. At the upper secondary level in addition to these there are more likely to be objectives which seek to develop theoretical understanding and formal reasoning skills, the ability to utilise physical and mathematical models, facility with experimental design and data interpretation.

The content intensity of programmes also typically increases in the higher grades with more material being included. The situation is made even more complex by the fact that the same aims can be achieved, at least in principle, through many different routes. Thus curricula which share educational aims in large part may differ considerably in how they are presented and taught. Though Swaziland Integrated Science utilises the bulk of the aims for the West Indian Science Curriculum (which was itself adapted from Scottish Integrated Science) there is considerable deviation in the materials produced. Malaysian upper secondary science materials developed in the 1970s shared many common goals with those of Nuffield programmes in the United Kingdom but the form of the materials that were developed differed considerably from the Nufffield courses.

Science education programmes at secondary level can be roughly classified into those intended for selected groups who will continue to study science to higher levels, those for whom science is thought to be an essential part of a general education but whose experience of science will terminate at or before the school leaving age, and those which attempt to satisfy the needs of both groups simultaneously. In making this classification we should not forget that a good number of education systems allow secondary children to give up the study of science at an early stage in favour of other subjects. In other systems although science appears on the curriculum throughout the secondary years, the form it takes limits in practice the nature of the experience for many students to minimal levels.

The dilemma in orientating science education to the needs of different groups of students is a fairly universal problem in planning science education and it mirrors a broader problem of the conflicts between early specialisation with concentration of a limited range of subjects and broad based general education that exposes all children to a balanced diet of educational experience.

This has been problematic in most countries whether industrialized or not. Thus it was an issue in the development of Science for Every Student in Canada as it was when integrated science was being introduced into Malaysia.

The most common patterns are for introductory science to be taught to all children in lower secondary programmes without strong differentiation between those who will continue to study science and those who will not. This usually involves treating science as a whole and attempting to develop the same range of basic skills and knowledge in all students through similar educational experiences. The main difficulties in this approach seem to arise from the pressures for selection that generally accompany the end of lower secondary schooling and the prestige and opportunity that are associated with the study of science to higher levels.

Five factors can be identified that have often orientated lower secondary science programmes away from emphasising their value to those who leave school and study no more science.

First, continuity in the curriculum creates pressure to see lower secondary science as preparatory for higher levels. 'Backwash' from the demands of higher levels of science study militates against the inclusion of material and learning goals which only have direct relevance to school leavers. Hence the inclusion of topics that prepare the ground for their subsequent study rather than topics related to the science aspects of common economic livelihoods.

Second, to incorporate much material which deals with the science of everyday things often has low status. The development of science historically was indeed often influenced by social and economic concerns, but the way this is understood often stresses the latest innovations and the concerns of 'rich country science' rather than those of pre-industrial societies.

Third, those involved in defining the subject are themselves successful products of science education in sofar as they have become professionally qualified and orientated towards modem science and technology. They have an interest in maintaining its status and part of this process is to ensure that the modem science is promoted.

Fours, science is an important selection subject in most education systems. Conventionally educational selection based on academic knowledge has found more favour than that based on practical knowledge. This augers in favour of the abstract and the mathematical treatments of science which are widely recognized as means of discriminating between pupils' abilities.

Fifth, the more relevant to the needs of school leavers science becomes the more it may be difficult to find within the existing cadre of teachers staff with experience, insight and expertise in the science aspects of traditional economic activities. Involving local practitioners in teaching is a widely canvassed solution to this problem but it may be resisted if it is seen to deprofessionalize teachers. Some forms of science knowledge that might be relevant also have an economic value that it is not in the interests of skill exemplars to share. Parents also may resist the idea that schools are places where students learn about the science of local production activities when parents have aspirations for their children which run beyond remaining in the same socioeconomic environment. Partly as a result it is rare to find lower secondary science programmes that are designed on the basis of any extensive exploration of the needs of school leavers for whom this experience of science education is terminal.

Though there have been many attempts to do this the resulting programmes run into an enduring contradiction. If they are genuinely terminal and include the achievement of aims and objectives of most direct value to those who leave school, those who achieve most highly on them are least likely to become school leavers. For them emphasis on rural science, science for living and practical skills of direct economic value are of less importance than selection. For those whose futures lie in the direction of employment or self-employment their experience of science is that of the relatively low achiever.

There are curriculum alternatives that go some way towards ameliorating the consequences of the contradiction outlined. Science basic skills can be taught to a wide range of students through examples which are locally based. Thus basic ideas in fluid dynamics can be illustrated using models of boats, kites and windmills rather than aeroplane wing surfaces; acceleration can be illustrated without using the experience of travelling in an elevator as a starting point.

At a more sophisticated level of curriculum organisation different pathways can be followed through curriculum materials that provide different learning experiences for students who progress at different rates and whose needs are different. Thus some curricula provide optional enrichment material available at the choice of the teacher depending on progress and local environment. But these require quite high levels of resourcing, organisational flexibility and teacher expertise.

If relevance and the orientation of science towards the needs of most students who leave school is a problem at the lower secondary level it can be even more so for upper secondary children. The extent to which it is, will depend partly on how many are selected to follow science at this level. The more restricted a group this is at the upper secondary level the more reasonable it is to define the curriculum in terms of the needs of those who will continue to higher levels since the majority are likely to continue if they have been highly selected.

Aims and objectives defined for upper secondary commonly assume that most if not all lower secondary science has been mastered. Unless selection is draconian this is unlikely to be a very secure assumption. There is a danger that 'cycles of cumulative ignorance' can develop where there will be many pupils selected who have achieved and internalised only a proportion of lower secondary learning objectives. As a consequence they may quickly drift out of touch with teaching at the next level since it starts from assumed knowledge and skills that are not possessed. The longer they attend the less they master of what is supposed to be mastered.

Upper secondary science education is also closer to university entrance examinations than the lower secondary school. Universities in most countries exert their own special influence on the science curriculum in most countries. As they represent the pinnacle of achievement for students, and reflect the ambitions of many parents for their children, their nature exerts strong effects on the science curriculum as intended, and the curriculum in action. And university entrance requirements, and university undergraduate courses, tend to have a direct relationship with international conventions on standards and content for different science subjects. This cap on the system favours conventional academic definitions of science rather than those relevant to school leavers below university entrance level.

No neat solution to the dilemma posed between the needs of specialists and the general population has been identified yet this is a critical area-meeting the needs of the non-specialist majority are likely to be at least as significant as ensuring an adequate supply of graduate scientists.

Commentators like Layton see the relationship between two types of outcome—trained specialists and a scientifically literate population — as inherently conflicting and not compatible pulling the curriculum in opposing directions. Fensham has argued for a three stage policy to resolve the tension and create a balanced science curriculum which can meet the conflicting demands. He argues first for containment, where elite, academic science is deliberately restricted to upper secondary grades for a selected proportion of the population most of whom will study science to high levels. Below this containment level science should be taught to all students in an accessible way which is not over academicized.

Second, because academic science is restricted to selected groups it needs to be intensive and it should not be placed in direct competition with 'second class science for the rest of the student population. It should be clearly distinguished as science for those intending to pursue occupations with a scientific base.

Third science should continue to be taught above the containment level to non-scientists in ways which provide clear differentiation from academic science curricula. They should not simply be watered down versions of academic science. Though these suggestions do go someway towards a constructive response to the dilemma Fensham does not really address the problems of changing the preconceptions that are likely to block changes of this kind. Parity of esteem is an elusive chimera when academic science is an important selection subject. Containment will only offer assistance if boundaries are maintained and this may be difficult in many systems.

The science education debate over the relative importance of aims and objectives that are more or less knowledge or skill orientated is long standing. Some aspects of it have already been touched on. The historical experience of the development of science as a school subject generally placed more emphasis on science as a body of knowledge with the 'scientific method' raised on a pedestal in the background as a mechanism to achieve such knowledge rather than as an end in itself.

The development of many guided discovery, heuristic and pupil centred programmes which swept through the science education community in the 1960s shifted the emphasis at least at the level of intent away from a view of science based securely on facts to be learned towards one where the process of investigating the natural world was to be given pride of place. Science education was to develop thinking skills that would provide learning which would endure beyond the usefulness of the discrete facts that enquiry might lead to. The debate over knowledge or skills is often framed in terms of process versus content or concept based learning. The former stresses the view that students should acquire scientific attitudes and problem solving skills as a priority and that concepts and content have a second order importance. Scientific attitudes include scepticism, curiosity, open-mindedness, suspended judgement until evidence is available.

Process skills include observation, interpretation of data, inference, testing of hypotheses, prediction, classification skills. This view of science learning values an inductive approach Harlen where students accumulate experience based on observation and analysis that leads them to generalisations that can be tested. Concept and content based views of science argue that science is essentially a body of knowledge which consists of the insights scientists have discovered about the physical world. Thus science students should be required to internalise these concepts first through encounters with specific content and examples based on conventional subdivisions of science knowledge-mechanics, acids and bases, photosynthesis. The emphasis is on the concepts not the means through which they were developed or can be understood.

The underlying approach to learning here is deductive-generalisations, scientific laws, principles are to be learned first and then hopefully applied. Since secondary education in many countries has been heavily subject compartmentalised the latter view has been the dominant one. Most of the new science curricula of the 1960s and 1970s promoted process views in one form or another but they have not been as fast to take root in practice as they have been in principle amongst science educators.

The IEA's attempts to classify process skill objectives and analyse the emphasis placed on them in different national systems conclude that the emphasis on process skills increases at higher curriculum levels. Of the nine process objectives they consider observation, measurement, problem solving, and interpretation of evidence have the greatest emphasis. Generalization, and model building the least.

The limitations of science, and the applications of science were also not weighted as emphasized much, the latter perhaps surprisingly so given increased concern for the technological dimensions of science education. They note that some countries in their sample had not considered process aspects of their curricula and therefore did not respond. Content does influence the use of process skills. A well known example of this occurs when students use microscopes to draw biological materials. What students 'see' and draw is very much dependent on the cues provided by teachers as to what they are supposed to see. If you are told two contrasting lines represent a cell wall then that is what you will label the image-but what is inside and what is outside 'might they be holes'.

In the classic Brownian motion experiment particles are identified that move under the random impact of air molecules-but that tends not to be the observation made by students when looking at this experiment unprompted-it is only when attention is drawn to this effect that it becomes apparent to most. For others the swirling of bright specks is as important, the drifting of particles in a similar direction, and the colours and changing contrast many be as noticeable.

More programmes are developing a reconciliation or balance between process and concept or content based approaches, and are by implication seeking to resolve the crude polarity between skills and knowledge. Scientific skills have come to occupy a central place in the rhetoric of science curriculum development. Most recently increasing emphasis on technological aspects of science has heightened this trend though some would argue that this is balanced by emphasis on 'back to basics' that is to be found in some countries. It is important to separate the aspirations of governments and politicians and curriculum developers, from what actually happens in the science curriculum.

It is important also to understand the conservatism of many science educators who see their first loyalty as to their subject and whose career interests coincide with maintaining the integrity of separate science subjects. The boundary maintenance required to differentiate physics from chemistry and from biology generally emphasizes content based differences rather than those related to the science skills involved.

There is another dimension to the debate over aims and purposes which is germane to the questions of knowledge and skills. Increased emphasis on the technological aspects of science education necessarily leads curricula to greater concern for skills, both intellectual and psychomotor as well as perhaps aesthetic. Technology defined in terms of the processes through which needs are identified, solutions to problems designed and artefacts created to produce durable responses to needs, essentially couples the skills of doing with those of conceptualising. Few would accord 'technological facts' with comparable status as 'scientific facts'.

Science learning that consists of the accumulation of isolated scientific facts is unlikely to lead to any durable internalisation of science constructs. Without procedures to select and employ relevant knowledge and adapt it to new situations the knowledge itself has little value. Simply rote learning the periodic table without a deeper understanding of its significance for the properties of elements has no particular virtue. Similarly, process skills cannot be taught in a vacuum.

Problems have to be meaningful and directed towards real problems if problem solving skills are to be applied to them. But there certainly remains a question of balance between the approach and it is widely argued that too much of what passes as science education in practice is dominated by the acquisition of facts that are not coherently related to conceptual frameworks-consequently this learning proves fragile once the immediate need for it is taken away.

Any review of secondary science programmes introduced over the last two decades will show increasing emphasis on aims and objectives related to values and attitude changes. There are several reasons for this.

First, the view that science as a school subject is somehow value free has become unfashionable. This of course follows on from the more academic discussion amongst philosophers and historians of science concerning the ways in which values enter into the activities of scientists. Though there are aspects of science that appear universal in terms of understandings of the natural world-the kinetic theory of gases as useful in predicting the behaviour of gases in the United Kingdom as it is in Zimbabwe -science does have values embedded in it and scientists as human beings have values. The things which are identified as of interest to science are partly culturally determined as the history of science shows very clearly; the uses to which science is put are very much influenced by the values of scientists and others. In the areas where science interacts with politics and religion values emerge as important.

Second, it has been increasingly recognized that the motivations and interests children bring to science education and develop through studying it are important in the extent to which they achieve in the subject. Head explores this in depth arguing that students subject choices are heavily influenced by social psychological factors bound up with the development of self identity during adolescence. He also reviews the literature on the images that students have of science and scientists. This displays strong stereotyping which attributes scientists with having to work long hours, being competitive at work, not being very sociable and having a conservative life-style-attributes that may not appeal to many adolescents in the United Kingdom. Successful science students at university were more syllabus bound, more conservative and less neurotic than students from the humanities and the social sciences. Personality factors do seem important in attracting students to, or alienating them from, science. Some have seen this understanding as creating opportunities to make science more appealing to students by changing its presentation to take advantage of aspects that are attractive to particular groups. This has been a theme in the literature on girls participation in science some of which makes suggestions as to how to make the teaching of the subject more 'girl friendly'. Duncan's study of gender-typing in Botswana found that school science was perceived as a masculine subject and that gender typing is considerably more salient in the achievement process for girls than for boys, through its influence on attitude to school subjects. Her study also found that girls who favor a divided family role and have a feminine self-image are more inclined to see science as a male area of activity and have less positive attitudes towards school science. Lin and Crawley studied attitude differences in relation to gender, ability group and school sociogeographic location among rural and urban junior high school students in Taiwan. In this case perception of learning environment was independent of gender or ability group. Students in metropolitan schools reported more positive attitudes towards science, but also reported highly competitive learning environments. Rural students were just as interested in careers in science as their metropolitan counterparts.

Third, science is seen in many curricula as a subject which can promote rational analysis and inductive and deductive reasoning. It represents par excellence a field of study in which evidence can be collected and interpreted according to explicit principles. To encourage this is to place a value on the development of these skills in the population-and by implication to subscribe to some of the ideas of modernisation theory. These stress the importance of changing individuals values in traditional societies from the parochial, the egocentric, and the concrete to those which involve seeing other points of view, which are universalistic, and are abstract and not bound by the experience of the present.

Fourth, although many programmes introduce affective elements into the objectives for science programmes few articulate this in ways that assist classroom teachers in converting these general aims into specific learning experiences. The danger is obvious-that the cognitive aspects of learning science take precedence on a day to day basis and that the cumulative development of attitudes relevant to science is ignored or down graded. It is important here to distinguish between those values that might be thought directly part of science-e.g. scepticism, curiosity, open-mindedness, critical scrutiny of evidence; and those that might be promoted through the teaching of science but which also have a more general character-honesty, respect for others, tolerance.

Important problems in relation to values and attitudes seem to circulate around two themes in particular. For a number of commentators 'western science' carries with it embedded value assumptions that are culturally bound. These values are thought to interrelate with social and economic aspects of development and thus carry implications for what science should be taught and how. 'western science' is variously categorized as being concerned with the problems of rich countries, fundamental science rather than that with direct utility, 'big' science not 'small' science. The implications of this need careful consideration in any development activity based on the adaptation of materials from one country to another.

In addition many studies in developed countries seem to show that children's attitudes towards science deteriorate as they move through school to higher grades-and circumstantial evidence suggests this may well be the ease in many developing countries. Thus in the United Kingdom physics and chemistry show steep declines in popularity from grades 9 to 11. Biology increases marginally in popularity as a result of increased interest amongst girls. This mirrors similar findings on attitudes to school which also show deterioration.

Insofar as children antagonistic to science will not be motivated to study it, this creates a problem for science education. The more values are seen as a cross curricula concern and the product of experience in different subjects the greater the challenge is to explore how discussion of values may be introduced into science education, and how substantial a dimension of the curriculum engagement with value issues should be.

Broadening of Science Curriculum

Many countries have embarked on programmes to provide a more balanced diet of science to secondary school students. This has several elements and is reflected in at least three types of development. These are concerned with movement towards broad balanced science; the inclusion of science and society issues and the incorporation of environmental perspectives; and the introduction of technology into the curriculum.

First, complementary to the adoption of more subject integration already noted, there has been a general movement towards seeing science as a whole and giving more equal emphasis to its component parts. Historically a good number of systems have emphasized the physical sciences at secondary level and given less emphasis to the life sciences. With the increasing importance of developments in bio-technology and the growth of agribusiness the case for redressing this balance has been strengthened. In those countries where choice between subjects is permitted it has generally been the case that biology has been preferred by girls and boys have opted for the physical sciences. The consensus in the science education community has moved towards considering this pattern unbalanced. The 'science for all' movement has embraced the idea of broad and balanced science, as have many developments of national curricula. 'Science for all' has formed part of basic policy in science education in a number of developing countries and is generally associated with the idea of balanced science. So also are programmes which stress 'scientific literacy.'

Second, it has been increasingly common to find science and society material appearing in secondary science curricula. This has been an accelerating trend though it has proved unpopular with some science teachers and policy-makers who have taken the view that this dilutes the science that is taught. Several reasons for this seem influential. The work on attitudes has suggested that environmental concerns are popular amongst children and introducing more of this material has been used as a device to attract more students to study science. Growing public concern with environmental issues has played a part as public participation in the debate over these has grown in a number of countries. Attempts to increase the relevance of school science to students, especially those who leave school during or after secondary education, have also led in the direction of including more of this kind of content. The Discussion of Issues in School Science Project (DISS) based at Oxford has been running for two years in the United Kingdom and is one example of the many programmes designed to contribute to increasing the public understanding of science which have been introduced in many countries. In a number of developing countries pressing environmental problems (erosion, deforestation, desertification, etc.) have resulted in the inclusion of environmental science in the curriculum (e.g. Environmental and Agricultural Science in Zimbabwe and Man and the Environment in Malaysia). Sawyerr has argued for increased environmental aspects to the science curriculum in Sierra. Leone. Ahmed also argues that in developing countries the social objectives of education must take precedence over those concerning the development of the individual student. With respect to science education this means greater emphasis on environmentally-based integrated science. Knamiller suggests the development of issues-based biological education in schools can help bridge the gap between purely academic schooling and education for relevance.

Science and society issues, though much broader than environmental concerns, have increasingly penetrated new science curricula and most innovations now include material of this kind. The development of environmental education has also been stimulated by realisation of global interdependence as issues like the depletion of the ozone layer have become prominent. Thus a number of authors have argued like Knamiller that mutual interests between the industrialised North and the developing South are satisfied by extending the environmental orientation of science. Concerns for more widespread scientific literacy have been repeatedly voiced. This has been defined in terms of a basic understanding of science in order to make informed decisions in daily life and to function effectively as a citizen which can be subdivided into:

(i) survival needs in a physical environment pervaded by science derived products, machines and devices; and

(ii) the need to participate responsibly in formulating policy and making decisions concerning public issues having technological components which involve a basic understanding of science.

Third, and perhaps most significantly for the next decade, there has been a resurgence of interest in technology as a school subject. Sometimes this has been expressed in terms of technologizing the science curriculum, and sometimes it has been seen as a separate subject. This perspective has been stressed in several recent publications and it seems to have a growing momentum. 'Privileging the practical' is one of the catch phrases used to encapsulate the thinking behind this. Many have argued the central importance of science with a technological dimension for development.

Technological skills take the process of problem solving from conceptualisation, through consideration of alternatives, the design of prototyping and their testing, to the development of artefacts to meet needs identified. It is thus very much concerned with the tasks of putting to useful purpose the skills towards which many science education programmes are directed towards. In principle, it provides an answer to critics who see academic science education as a sterile theoretical exercise that develops arcane intellectual skills but does not result in useful skills of making and doing.

Technological education is differentiated from the older practical subject traditions-woodwork, metalwork, etc. since it encompasses a broader range of intellectual skills and is concerned with a wide spectrum of types of problem. It may approach textile design and production as readily as it addresses the problems of water pump design. And much of the knowledge and skills which underlie it are scientific in character-fair tests of performance of prototypes have to be developed; scientific knowledge of the properties of materials is important; physical and biological principles are likely to influence design. Technology also has an aesthetic dimension since good design also incorporates ideas of elegance, attractive and functional products, and aesthetics which widen the attractions of the subject to a larger group of students. It may therefore be a mechanism to encourage more students to acquire some science concepts. It is also consistent with increased integration between subjects and the need for this has been explored in a variety of curricula situations.

The issue at the policy level is the development of a clear view of the role science and technology play in national development strategies so that implications for science educational policy can be identified. This has a qualitative dimension, as has been argued above, and is not simply a problem of getting the numbers right in filling available and anticipated occupational niches.

New balances may need to be struck between emphasis on design and discovery, and maintenance and incremental improvement that reflect strategic choices in economic and educational policy for science education. Implications can be identified for the planning process in relation to science policy, the impact of austerity, and the definition of aims for science education.

From the above several issues for planners can be identified. These are concerned directly with national science policy and requires the identification of those aspects of policy that have direct implications for science education These need to be analysed in terms of how these have been changing to reflect developments in labour markets, the technology of production in science based industries, and in the markets for the products of such industry.

It may then be possible to arrive at some reconciliation between developing an indigenous science and technology base and maintaining efficient access to science and technology developed elsewhere. Some dimensions of the policy problem with every likelihood of being relevant are:

— What are the basic assumptions of science and technology policy?

— Is it directed towards establishing science based industry as a whole or in selected fields?

— Is innovation seen to flow from basic research or from borrowing and adapting ideas?

— How important is the design and control of new technology seen to be and how realistic are aspirations to achieve these things?

— How, if at all, are the developments of new technologies seen to affect policy and the needs for changes in the education and training systems for science and technology?

— What is the policy orientation for science and technology?

— Is it that of the 'leading edge consumer' which allows the use and adaptation of technology developed elsewhere; or is it an orientation towards new insights from fundamental research that will have spin offs that will increase agricultural and industrial productivity?

— Is there any evidence from the recent past that the policy employed has resulted in developmental gains or losses? If so why?.

— How is overall policy on science and technology related to education and training policy?

— Is it logically consistent?

— Have changes in the pattern of provision for science and technology education at school level been a result of strategic decisions or have they reflected other considerations unrelated to macro policy e.g. social demand for places?

Science and technology education at all levels tend to be amongst the most expensive curricula areas to resource. Many countries continue to suffer from a lack of scientific and technological personnel. Shortages at the highest levels of qualification are often matched and exceeded at intermediate levels and these may compromise the impact of expensively trained professional staff at graduate level on development problems. Even where the numbers of graduates stand in a satisfactory relationship to demand the quality of individuals' capabilities in science and technology is often considered a problem.

The exigencies created by austerity require a reappraisal of priorities. This needs to explore whether conditions of budgetary stringency can be accommodated by new approaches to education and training in science and technology that would make better use of scarce resources and the pool of talent that exists within a given population. Possible options include:

— greater attention to equitable and efficient selection of those who may benefit most from science and technological education;

— assessing the feasibility and desirability of concentrating resources in well founded institutions when it is impossible to provide these for the whole student population;.

— re-examining the structure of incentives that may make it difficult to attract and retain science students in employment related to their special skills;

— exploring reasons for aversion to the study of science where this is a problem;

— establishing more efficient ways of developing science based skills in the education system and through job related training;

— ensuring that opportunities to acquire science based literacy and numeracy in the population as a whole are not over shadowed by the needs of the minority who acquire specific high level skills in science.

The issues that arise for planning from the discussion on aims and objectives of science education can be summarised in terms of the need for:

— clear appraisal of the purposes of the science education curriculum; this needs to specify what is to be achieved, by which group of students, for which purposes. Only then can choices be made between curriculum delivery strategies;

— recognition that aims and objectives may not be shared by all the participants in the science education process in equal measure; without a degree of consensus on these implementation will be problematic;

— there are different pay-offs involved in selecting different emphases on aims and objectives; different mixes may be appropriate for different groups though the overriding trend is towards common specification for all students-at least at the lower secondary level;

— shifts towards integration, more recognition of the needs of those who leave school, the importance of attitudes and values, and the broadening of the science curriculum all carry resource implications that need careful consideration. These depend in part on pedagogical and epistemological questions about the nature of science and the nature of learning.

4

Teaching and Learning

There are now a very large number of studies on the factors that affect school achievement. Most of the earliest examples of these were conducted in the USA and the United Kingdom and were initiated by concerns to understand why children from unfavourable socioeconomic backgrounds failed to achieve comparable levels of performance to their more favoured peers.

They were thus heavily influenced by sociological analytical traditions and borrowed varieties of production function analysis from economic theory to partial out the influence of different factors on a dependent variable generally defined in terms of some combination of test results. These studies were accompanied by a developing literature which offered a critique of the methods used and which also became entangled in the debates about nature and nurture and socioeconomic background in the development of intelligence, school achievement and subsequent success in the labour market.

Much of the concern was to explore to what extent meritocracies functioned as such and to what extent educational achievement behaved as an intervening variable explaining why in these societies socioeconomic status of children continued to be linked closely to parents' socio-economie status. These studies tended to show that schools were less important determinants of scholastic success than home background factors. It was, however, misleading to draw the conclusion, as some popularisers did, that this implied that not much of importance went on in schools. It was differences that were being studied not absolute effects- as a weary commentator observed "students don't imagine algebra".

Neither do most of them independently establish Newton's laws of motion. Subsequently, studies have began to appear which extended the analysis offered to a whole host of in-school factors and these began to demonstrate that school effects were important. The studies also began to be extended in significant numbers to developing countries where the initial results seemed to confirm that school effects were more important than had hitherto been anticipated.

Heyneman and Loxley's study of science achievement in 16 developing and 13 industrialised countries examined a range of school variables and regressed science achievement scores against them. His study found relatively little variance explained by school factors in the industrialized countries but much larger amounts explained in the developed countries (27 per cent of the variance in achievement explained by school quality in Indian children and only 3 per cent by social class; 25 per cent by school quality in Thailand and only 6 per cent by social class).

Note however that the total variance explained in the cases studied was typically around the 20 -30 per cent level leaving much that was not explained. A priori findings that school effects are important might not be wholly unexpected in science since it is a subject which is removed from everyday experience and its systematic study is often only accessible through schools. The very large literature that now exists on school effectiveness is difficult to summarise. More than 50 multi-variate or experimental school effect studies now exist relating to developing countries.

Fuller's comprehensive review identifies several studies which have used science achievement as the dependent variable. However most school achievement studies use other subjects or a combination which includes science. We will consider the Second IEA Science study separately below.

The studies are methodologically diverse; vary in terms of the specification of the dependent and independent variables, use a range of sampling techniques, and have been undertaken in very differently structured education systems. The problems involved in research on factors which affect school achievement are well known. They include problems with the cross-cultural transferability of notions like social class; the difficulties in specifying the dependent variable i.e achievement-; the realization that often large parts of the total variance remained unexplained after the effects of independent variables have been accounted for, and the rarity of studies that are capable of controlling for the entry characteristics of students. Not surprisingly a universally applicable set of conclusions does not emerge from this literature.

Synthetic reviews like Fuller's and that by Schiefelbein and Simmons have additional problems of aggregation that make it difficult to decide what importance to give to findings that appear true in some systems and not in others. What can we conclude from the 11 analyses cited of school expenditure and achievement, six of which confirm a positive relationship, and five do not?; or of Hanushek's review of more than 150 studies which concluded that there was no systematic relationship between expenditures and student achievement; attitudes and dropout rates and reduced class sizes and more trained teachers were also unlikely to make much difference to achievement? Commonsense suggests that, in the limiting cases, level of expenditure must have some relationship to achievement; nevertheless it is unlikely to be a sufficient condition alone. And perhaps those studies that failed to demonstrate a link were in circumstances where systems were already well resourced and additional expenditure was at the margin.

Lying behind these difficulties we note that in any case these were not parallel studies; many of the parameters varied simultaneously between them. One of the earlier studies concluded that there was no relationship between expenditure per pupil and achievement at primary level but that there was at the secondary level. The latter was such that they claimed raising national examination scores by 5 per cent would require a 50 per cent increase in expenditures per pupil. This serves to illustrate the limitations of this kind of analysis. There are many ways of increasing achievement and each will have a different cost structure.

Simply redistributing existing resources towards the least favoured schools is likely to have a much bigger effect on those schools and little or no effect on those which already enjoy surpluses of qualified teachers, materials, etc. The incremental rate of return on investment to raise achievement in schools which have no books or facilities will be much greater than similar inputs in well-funded institutions. Another example of the kinds of problems that arise from taking a macro view of school effectiveness studies can be illustrated by the well publicized literature on the effect of textbooks on school achievement.

Fuller's review indicates that 16 out of 24 studies show positive effects of texts and reading materials on achievement-not perhaps as overwhelming a trend as might be expected from the fashionable wisdom on this subject. Again, though the general measure was textbooks/student the independent variables that were controlled for in the studies varied.

But perhaps more important is the lack of insight into whether the studies related to the first pieces of reading material available or the additions to an existing stock; neither is the qualitative relationship explored between the types of reading material and the demands of the tests used to measure achievement · do comics have the same effect as well constructed reading materials? Some of the violence done in the search for global generalizations is illustrated by the finding that the improvement in achievement attributable to book provision in the Philippines is twice the impact that would be gained by lowering class size from 40 to 10 students. But this finding uses evidence from an experimental study in the Philippines and data on class size effects from the USA. This presumes that the range of variation in class size considered and teaching methods are indistinguishable between the two systems which is unlikely to be true. Interestingly a more recent study fails to find any relationship between class size and student achievement in primary science in the Philippines.

Fuller and Heyneman have attempted to identify effective and ineffective factors that influence school achievement. These turn out to be:. Simple conclusions of this kind are dangerous. The effects of repetition on academic achievement are difficult to measure for a number of reasons. In many systems repeaters have a disproportionate tendency to drop out. The medium-term effects of repetition are then difficult to ascertain.

Since in most systems repetition implies just that-repeating the same material often with the same teacher without any special treatment · it might be surprising to find strong effects from repeating an experience of failure. Since few if any of the achievement tests are age corrected maturation effects will further complicate the interpretation of any achievement gains.

As a policy issue repetition is not a serious problem if it only affects the marginal student with particular learning disabilities. It represents a serious inefficiency in systems where repetition averages 20 per cent or more and this is really the policy issue, not what effect it has on achievement. It may be that within a wide band achievement is not related to class size but this does not mean there are no limits. Intuitively the significant factor is when teaching practices change-practical group work is difficult when class sizes exceed 40; it may not be practised below this number; a lecture is likely to be as effective with 20 students as with 80 if the space is available. And class size does interact with other variables -- if textbooks/pupil are correlated with achievement large class sizes given a fixed stock of books will diminish it.

Teachers' salaries, at the level of individual teachers, are unlikely to be directly related to achievement for the simple reason that achievement is unlikely to be the result of the teaching of a single teacher-students will experience several teachers over their careers in school. Moreover it cannot lead to the conclusion that paying teachers better is unlikely to have an effect on achievement-it may be that the most effective teachers do not get the highest rewards in a given education system; it may be that all teachers are paid so poorly that what variation there is not reflected in performance.

Given the fairly universal belief that income should be related to effectiveness the challenge is to change the reward structure so that they are. And the obvious comment to make about the effectiveness of laboratory provision is that if science achievement tests do not test the skills developed in laboratories it should surprise no-one that they do not have a large impact on achievement measured through pencil and paper tests that often emphasise recall and the abstract application of principles.

The reasons for incorporating practical work in science have been thoroughly explored by Haddad and Za'rour who argue its benefits whilst recognising the difficulty of measuring its impact. A study of university entrance examinations in China illustrates how the science papers do not assess experience of practical science in much depth. The most recent PEA study is complex to interpret on the subject of practical work and achievement; it does suggest that where students' views of teaching indicate more practical work probably takes place there is a positive relationship with achievement in five out of nine cases.

The weight of opinion seems to lie with those who are sceptical about the measurable benefits of laboratory science for achievement as conventionally measured, and who stress its high costs. The First IEA Science study noted positive effects of reported laboratory use in three of the four developing countries in their sample. Heyneman and Loxley's study found no such effect. Lockheed et.al., did find positive effects arising from teaching primary science in laboratories but note that the magnitude of this was much less than the effect of frequent group work and of frequent testing. That those who are tested frequently perform better on tests is perhaps not surprising. Whether the reasons why younger teachers make more frequent use of group work than their elder colleagues in an attempt to offset difficulties encountered by large classes, as is claimed, or whether it arises from other considerations remains an open question in the study.

A Nigerian study by Okebukola which examined achievement in chemistry did find that participation in laboratory activities was an important factor in determining achievement. In order of importance, student attitude towards chemistry, teacher attitude towards laboratory activities and availability of chemistry laboratory materials made significant contributions to the variation in achievement. Mutsune's study of the correlation between the practical and theory components of the Kenya A-level Biology examination found low correlation between practical and theory achievement which is attributed to lack of coverage of practical work by many students.

On the positive side length of time spent on instruction is reported widely as having an impact on achievement. Heyneman and Loxley note this in relation to general science in India, Thailand and Iran. Fuller counts 12 out of 14 analyses supporting this proposition. There are wide ranges between countries in the amount of time allocated to science at different levels-by a factor of two or more in the SEA countries.

Comparisons between countries are dubious since so many other factors vary simultaneously so the more useful comparisons are within the same system. The difficulty with this is that the largest variations generally stem not from official policy but from practice in the schools.

In some countries as much as 30 per cent of the official teaching days are not utilized for their intended purposes as a result of teacher absenteeism, school functions, excessive examination practice, natural events and casual holidays. Given that science is taught in lessons, clearly the more lessons there are the more is likely to be learned, but there is no reason to suppose that the relationship is necessarily linear and the most recent PEA data, whilst supporting the general proposition that time studying science is related to achievement, recognises limitations in its data that make more precise statements of the relationship difficult. It may well be, as Wallberg observes that 'Mathew effects' operate in education-such that initial advantages are multiplied. He argues that improved instruction may benefit all students but will benefit the more able most.

Feeding programmes are an established way of enhancing enrolment and increasing retention. A priori they will serve this purpose for science as much as other subjects. School libraries also offer the prospect of providing more relevant sources of information for teachers and students though the existence of these in relatively well endowed schools must not simply lead to the conclusion that they have a causative relationship with achievement. Those studies which relate use of the library to achievement do seem to indicate that frequent users benefit from the access they enjoy.

Pre-service teacher qualifications and training do show up in many studies as positively related to achievement. The magnitudes of the effects are often moderate however. They are in any case difficult to measure-children experience different teachers-should recent training be given the same weight as training ten years ago? -- and the number of years of schooling completed before training may be at least as important as the training itself.

One recent study suggests that other inputs i.e textbooks can be substituted for additional training since textbook use and training did not interact in their data and the effects of textbooks were greater Very little evidence exists on the effectiveness of in-service training. Those studies that do exist are generally positive but often have no means of controlling for the effects of training as opposed to the traits of the teachers who choose to take advantage of it-those involved are generally the more motivated and skilled in the first place. Of course it is also likely to matter what teachers are being trained to do and what kind of students they are teaching though this also is largely unresearched.

There is little doubt on the margin that textbooks do have a major impact on achievement in most subjects, and probably in science more than most since they are likely to be the only source of authoritative information relevant to achievement tests in poor school environments. Unfortunately, beyond the level of their existence in reasonable quantity there is little research to indicate at what point additional written material ceases to have an effect; or what the relative impact of different types of material is - - teachers' guides, student texts, worksheets, reference books.

And every teacher has opinions, often well founded, about 'good' and 'bad' books. Every textbook is not the same --. some have inappropriate reading levels, some are poorly structured, some contain factual errors, some are produced with poor quality and uninteresting design.

Four other observations are pertinent before moving on to discuss the Second IEA Science Study.

First, in an interesting study in Zambia, Mulupo and Fowler compared achievement, understandings about science and the scientific attitudes of learners at the concrete and formal levels of cognitive development. Subjects were an equally weighted sample of concrete and formal reasoners in 11th grade chemistry classes assigned to one of two teaching method groups for 10 weeks. Results showed that among formal reasoners discovery method teaching was more effective than traditional methods on understanding science; for concrete reasoners the mode of instruction made no difference; overall the traditional group outperformed the discovery group in achievement but the discovery group scored better on attitudes. This draws attention to the way the characteristics of learners are likely to influence the effectiveness of different inputs which is largely lost in most school achievement studies.

Second, Hamilton draws attention to how the attitudes to science of 11th and 13th grade Jamaican students influence achievement. Attitudes appeared to play a vital role in achievement, particularly as far as girls are concerned. This it is argued demonstrates the need for more role models for science achievement for girls and reinforces findings in industrialised countries. The importance of dispositions towards science is also rarely accounted for in the school achievement literature.

Third, Tuppen compares examination performance of secondary students in ten high schools in Papua New Guinea to an Index of Educational Opportunity (IEO) in the student's province of schooling. The IEO is defined as the percentage of the age group enrolled in high school. The study reports that the index, parental education levels and interest in schooling are important in explaining variation in examination scores. Some school factors were also found to be important. The study reports a 0 . 5-0.6 correlation between examination performance and internal school assessment in English, mathematics and science perhaps suggesting that the skills tested in different subjects overlap considerably.

Fourth, Maundu's study in Kenya explores student achievement in mathematics and science and relates it to parental education and occupation and to type of school. This study argues that socioeconomic factors such as family background are important in determining student achievement, but are reinforced by teaching and learning resources available which are interactive variables.

The most comprehensive data on science achievement are to be found in the Second IEA Science Study. This includes data from 24 countries of which China, Ghana, Nigeria, Papua New Guinea, Thailand, the

Philippines, and Zimbabwe can be clearly located as developing countries. Hong Kong, Singapore, and Korea might also be classified in this way albeit that their economic development has reached a different level. The IEA studies have been conducted on three populations, broadly speaking 10 year olds, 14 year olds and those in the last year of schooling before university entrance.

The interpretation of the IEA findings is very complex since various asymmetries arise in sampling, curricula emphasis, test participation between the samples in different countries, etc. These preclude the possibility of making simple comparisons between countries. At this stage it is only possible to draw attention to some of the main findings which seem to be of interest, especially as they relate to the developing countries in the sample. Even this is tentative since the variations in the data sets are important for any comparison between countries and all of the overall findings should really be contextualised in detailed ways which cannot be attempted here.

In terms of total score Ghana, Nigeria, the Philippines and Zimbabwe have the lowest total scclds on tile science tests. This is true in aggregate and in different subject areas. Other developing countries -. e.g. Papua New Guinea, Thailand and China have means that are comparable with industrialised countries like England, and the USA. Hungary and Japan score consistently well above most other countries. In general there is a high inter correlation between scores at the Population 2 level and those for Population 1 suggesting that low performance is compounded through the system. Though there are considerable changes in the ranking of mean scores by country at the Population 3 level, these are heavily influenced by the selection practices of different countries which, to a greater or lesser extent, concentrate resources on the most able science students.

In general, the proportion of schools scoring below the lowest school in the highest scoring country (Hungary) was high in the low scoring developing countries in the Population 2 sample (Ghana 64 per cent, Nigeria 88 per cent, Philippines 87 per cent, Zimbabwe 80 per cent). In these countries the performance of the lowest 20 per cent of students tested indicates that they have learned very little science. This is particularly worrying when it is realised that the Nigerian students were from a higher grade, and the Ghanaian students were from selective elite schools.

The LEA data suggest that the bottom 20 per cent of students in Ghana, Italy (Grade 8), Nigeria, the Philippines and Zimbabwe are 'scientifically illiterate' and that the United Kingdom, Hong Kong, Singapore and the USA are borderline cases. Interestingly the USA has a higher proportion of schools scoring below the worst school in Hungary than does Thailand.

Of particular interest is the finding that the teaching group or class that pupils are in is of considerable significance to the scores that they achieve in some countries. This effect is particularly prominent in Ghana, the Philippines, Italy and the Netherlands. By contrast in Japan and the Nordic countries at this level the effect is very low indeed at the Population 2 level. This changes dramatically in Japan at the Population 3 level, probably because of the increase in the number of private schools.

One of the implications of this appears to be that in some countries differences between schools are considerable and it does matter a great deal in which school or class students study science, in terms of their achievement. In other countries school and class effects are much smaller and have much less influence on achievement. This is not simply a function resource level; rather it seems to depend more on selection and streaming practices and organisational features of education systems.

The IEA authors have developed a yield coefficient that modifies the distribution of scores by the proportion of the age group in school. This is intended to indicate how many children know how much science. It highlights differences between countries and shows that yield coefficients tend to be much lower in those countries with the lowest proportions in school which are mainly the developing countries at Population 2 level. This raises a dilemma for countries with low yields wishing to improve them-should numbers enrolled be increased or should low levels of achievement be improved first? At Population 3 level in the IEA data inter-country comparisons are even more hazardous than they are at Population 2 level. There are wide disparities in the percentage of the age group studying at this level (from 1 per cent in Ghana and Papua New Guinea to 89 per cent in Japan). The average age of this population spans 23 months. There was a 2-year grade difference in the level to which the tests were applied. The average number of subjects studied varied from 3 to 9 or more with concomitant variations in the time spent on science.

Generally the United Kingdom, Singapore and Hong Kong and Hungary have the highest scores in Population 3 with some variations between subjects in this. These countries also have small numbers enrolled and highly specialised curricula. In general the IEA found no relationship between the proportion studying science and She achievement of elite students defined as tile top 3 per cent of the age group. There was no significant tendency for She number of subjects studied to influence science achievement except in chemistry. Positive age effects were noted wish older students scoring better.

The IEA study demonstrates Chat sex differences greatly favoured boys in the countries wish the lowest overall scores in terms of She performance of both the bottom 20 per cent and She top 20 per cent. Though in Hungary sex differences were minimal, in Japan, the other high scoring country, boys outperformed girls consistently at all levels of ability. Typically sex differences in performance are greatest in physics and least in chemistry.

A review of the Papua New Guinea School Certificate Examination reports shows significant difference in performance of males and females on the lower secondary science examinations. In this case male scores are typically about half a standard deviation lower for girls. The pattern is not universal however, in Trinidad and Tobago girls perform consistently better Than boys in all types of schools and at all class levels in science. Similar findings have been reported for African-Americans, and West Indians in She United Kingdom. Analyses of O-level examination results for Kenya, Zambia and Botswana demonstrate Chat girls perform less well Than boys in almost all subjects, but particularly in She physical sciences. And unpublished evidence from Sri Lanka suggests that differences in performance between boys and girls in science are generated largely from the performance differences between relatively low achievers-differences between high achieving students are small.

A number of factors have been suggested in an attempt to account for gender disparities in levels of achievement in science. Duncan and Eshiwani categorise These factors according to whether They relate to She societal context, the attitudes and aspirations of students, or to the school environment. The first group involves sociocultural explanations which are supported by the variations in magnitude of the disparities across countries, and socioeconomic explanations such as social class, family background and level of urbanization. The second group of factors suggested to explain under achievement of girls give rise to the hypothesis that girls hold less favourable attitudes towards science and have lower aspirations for science-based careers. This results in a lowering of motivation to work in science and a consequent reduction in levels of achievement.

Duncan in Botswana found that only six girls out of her sample of 650 girls aspired to technical occupations [outside medicine] which would require academic science knowledge. Eshiwani cites studies which show that in general girls find science more difficult than any other subject, a conclusion supported by the large number of girls who drop science at the earliest opportunity. Lack of self-confidence, particularly in laboratory work, was found to be a major factor contributing to negative attitudes towards science.

A number of research findings maintain that the school environment is a significant factor in influencing and reinforcing gender disparities in achievement. The staffing structure of schools may contribute towards gender stereotyping, especially in Africa where the vast majority of teachers in secondary schools, particularly in science, are men. Furthermore, women head-teachers or principals are extremely rare. In Nigeria women constitute a large proportion of the teaching force but a negligible number of them are in headships and only then in low status schools and girls schools. Of 150 secondary schools in Tunisia only 12 had female Principals and women were totally unrepresented in the inspectorate.

Biraimah in her study of a Togolese secondary school found that while the teaching staff appeared balanced in terms of numbers, men occupied all the positions that exercised authority and women were assigned to domestic or secretarial roles. Biraimah relates these disparities to a whole pattern of differential expectations and attitudes and argues that they convey female subservience especially to girls who view women teachers as role models. Gender stereotyping is also reinforced through teaching materials and textbooks of science which may rarely provide female characters or situational examples with which girls can identify. The type of school appears to be a significant factor affecting the performance of girls.

Eshiwani reports that in secondary schools in Kenya there were very limited opportunities for girls to study science, with several girls' schools having their laboratory facilities in nearby boys' schools. Coeducation is not necessarily the answer to this problem as Kutnick and Jules report that girls attending single-sex schools scored higher than girls in parallel coeducational schools. Similar findings are reported by Eshiwani who demonstrates that girls in single-sex schools in Kenya performed better in science than both boys and girls in mixed schools, and suggests that: "any intervention strategy for the improvement of science education among girls should steer clear of coeducation".

It is not uncommon to find single sex schools outperforming coeducational ones. Often this is partly a result of selected intakes -such schools are disproportionately drawn from those with a long history, established reputation, and elite urban catchment areas as, for example, in Malaysia. This in itself does not constitute a case for single sex schools in general. It should also be remembered that sex differences in performance exist in other subjects and movements away from coeducation may be detrimental in performance in these for boys or girls. In any case decisions on coeducation should not be determined by science performance alone. Great care should be taken to establish whether, in particular systems where single sex schools perform well, this is the result of intervening variable unrelated to sex.

It has proved very difficult to review the literature on achievement. It is massive and frequently contradictory. It often exists at a high level of generality with little accessibility to the detailed specification of which effects are being compared to which dependent variables. Aggregated reviews deepen the confusion by mixing together wide ranges of studies as if simply counting the direction of findings tell us of something of value to policy.

All the school quality indicators used in the various studies-material inputs, teacher quality, teaching practices, classroom organization, and school management practices -are measured in ways which prevent easy comparison or aggregation. The research results really only take on meaning in the context of the particular systems -- what is of critical importance for achievement in one part of one school system may or may not be elsewhere and that is what is of most direct concern to policy-makers in science education.

While the sincerity of the researchers who have painstakingly constructed the studies is not in doubt there must be reservations about the wisdom of attempting to package all these kinds of findings into easily digestible 'bind alleys and promising avenues' as if they were global prescriptions that are context free. For the reason outlined above it is not possible to arrive at a list of universally valid generalisations concerning the factors that affect science achievement. There are many different factors that, in different circumstances, seem to have causal relationships with achievement. Which ones are significant will depend on which characteristics of the particular system, school, teachers, students are of interest. Thus we can conclude that the kind of insights that come from achievement studies are important, but have to be approached with caution and full understanding of their derivation. They may carry important implications for planners if vigourously established and able to point the way to more and less cost effective strategies towards enhancing science achievement.

Theories of Educational Innovation

There are many reviews of the educational change literature which need no repetition here. Much of the early work developed in areas outside formal education systems and was based on the experiences that were beginning to accumulate in development projects which sought to promote planned change. Thus for example Rogers and Shoemaker, explored social system innovations cross-culturally using many examples drawn from different fields in the development literature. American perspectives on innovation and the linking of research and development with practitioners were heavily influenced by the development of the Land Grant Universities and agricultural extension practices.

Another strand in the innovation literature was inspired by psychological studies with a utopian, group participatory or psychoanalytic basis. Organizational psychology and sociology have provided other inspirations.

The most accessible educational change literature relates to experience with education systems in industrialised countries. Thus much seminal work reflects the organisational ecology and social system characteristics of educational institutions in the North. Case study accounts are often drawn from industrialised countries. As Havelock and Huberman note in their analysis of the problems of innovation in developing countries:

"These problems (of educational innovation) have given rise to a considerable theoretical literature in which research workers have tried to explain change phenomena in order to help practitioners better to organise for change. However, most of this work relates to industrialised countries, and tends to reach a degree of abstraction or complexity that reduces its applicability .... the case study literature and the empirical research that we expected to find in rich abundance were not really there ...".

Recently more studies are becoming available which address the problems of educational innovation in developing countries but the accumulation of experience based on independent evaluations of projects is still relatively thin. Chisman and Wilson are the last in a long list of academics who have commented on this lack of disinterested evaluation specifically addressing their comments to science education projects. There appears to be little or no independent development of theoretical perspectives which relate to science education innovations that is separate from that of the bulk of educational innovation theory.

Science projects may have special features related to the nature of the subject but the reasons they are judged to succeed or fail seem to fall largely into the categories that apply to educational innovations as a whole. Further, when surveying the embryonic literature on these problems in developing countries it becomes clear that few if any studies exist which chart the fates of a variety of innovations in science within the same systems where key organisational, infrastructural and cultural factors remain broadly similar. Any attempts to compare the importance of factors across these boundaries are problematic.

Many models have been developed for different phases of the innovation process. At the most general level there are those which identify over-arching theories encompassing initiation, development, implementation, and evaluation of outcomes. The models which have most currency in the literature and are most widely quoted are those related to the work of Havelock, and Chin and Benne. The former initially identified three dominant patterns in approach -research, development, diffusion; social interaction; and problem solving. The latter classified innovation strategies into rational-empirical; normative-re-educative; and power-coercive. This has led to several subsequent formulations and attempts at synthesis. Lewin in his work on science education development in Malaysia and Sri Lanka traces the innovation process through five key phases:

(i) project initiation;.

(ii) contextual constraints,

(iii) course development process,

(iv) implementation strategy, and

(v) examining and assessment policy.

Decisions and events in all these areas influence the way innovatory programmes are introduced into the schools and the extent to which they are put into practice as intended. Different styles are identified in the two case studies-internal and external initiation, science for all students or science for selected groups, writing groups involving extensive consultation and those involving little, phased implementation with a gradual build up or national implementation in all schools simultaneously, examination reform to reflect new curricula goals or minor adaptation of existing examining structures. These are used to develop some explanations of the effectiveness of implementation. In a later development of this work.

Lewin with Stuart identify six approaches to innovation with distinctive features. These can be characterised as systems, bureaucratic, scientific, problem solving, diffusionist, and charismatic. Systems approaches which view educational institutions as sub-systems which are part of a wider system that has formally specified goals. Innovation from this point of view is initiated as a result of a commitment to achieve these goals. The goals are generated by systems outside the education system and the innovators role is to design and implement programmes that will achieve these goals. Poor goal achievement requires remedial action to ensure that elements in the system behave as intended.

Bureaucratic approaches to innovation are directed by goals identified at the system level and are related to systems approaches. Unlike a systems approach they tend to have static rather than dynamic characteristics. In particular, directive circulars, rules and regulations, agreed procedures, and legal obligations provide the benchmarks against which innovation is judged and the needs for it are identified. As these change, innovations may be appraised against criteria which are more administrative than educational. Innovation then takes place to satisfy approval processes where the regulatory process is given prominence.

Scientific approaches to innovation claim that research and evaluation on the needs of reamers, the learning process, and curriculum effectiveness are at the centre of the initiation of change. The curriculum developer in this model must undertake basic and applied research on teaching and learning to arrive at the more effective design of learning materials and curricula. More sophisticated versions of this model have feedback built in to them so that formative experiments feature prominently and development is planned as a meticulous process of trial, evaluation and revision.

Problem-solving approaches offer a fourth alternative. In these 'organisational pain' and individual dissatisfaction are important. A problem may be experienced within educational institutions and the innovators' first task is to find out what problems have arisen and what their causes are. Alternatively problems may be recognized by individuals in their own practice. The problem-solver diagnoses the difficulty, searches for a solution which may or may not involve innovation, and then offers it to the organization, or applies it to their own practice for trial and refinement.

Diffusionist approaches place the stress on the processes through which innovations are disseminated and adopted. This is seen characteristically as the result of social interaction between actors existing within networks of communication that provide access to information. This model assumes that behaviour is heavily influenced by the social networks which actors are linked to; that position in these networks is a good predictor of acceptance of innovation; that personal contacts are central to the spread of innovation, and that diffusion of new practices win follow an S-curve of growth with early adopters and laggards.

Charismatic approaches are difficult to classify since their nature makes them unique to individuals and circumstances. Strong beliefs, convincingly articulated by those in influential positions, are often the initiating activity. When they succeed in carrying other people with them they can generate development activity which reflects their educational philosophy. Their motivation comes from conviction rather than research; their goals may not be those of the organizations in which they work but which they may seek to change.

Examples of an these approaches can be found in descriptions in the literature on science education innovations. Commonly elements of more than one approach coexist. Though lip-service is often paid to scientific and problem solving approaches, these are rarely used in a systematic way, with research and development and problem diagnosis often being short-circuited by the exigencies of political demands for rapid change.

Systems views of education systems tend to dominate much public decision making on policy despite wide recognition that system malfunctions may be so common that there is a wide gulf between what is intended to happen and what actually does. Bureaucratic structures are often very powerful in explaining the events that take place during implementation when responsibilities for change more from professional developers to the administrators with day-to-day responsibilities for school systems.

Many science education projects can be linked to charismatic 'curriculum entrepreneurs' who play key roles, especially in the initiation process. Much actual change takes place as a result of the planned and unplanned diffusion of ideas through the social and professional networks of practising science educators. There are a number of studies of aspects of implementation in science education which raise important issues. These include the work by Lillis and Lowe in Kenya. Early difficulties identified in the School Science Project (SSP) were seen as staff rather than course related. SSP was never truly localized because it did not begin with a needs analysis but assumed transfer from a western context and produced an inherent role conflict between the heuristic approach implicit in the curriculum and the rote-teaching norm in African classes.

There was insufficient sensitivity to the interface between culture and knowledge and between culture and pedagogy: .... "curriculurn development in the third world over the last two decades has assume(d) complete transferability in content and methods ...an atmosphere of cultural neutrality is assured." Warf earlier argued that there was a need for more effort to adapt science teaching to the classical ways of learning of the indigenous populations, so lessening the contrast between science and traditional culture. At a national level there is a mismatch between educational objectives and development activities; there is little merit in imparting a technology more rapidly than it can be absorbed into the economy he asserts.

Ingle and Turner reinforce this view suggesting that school science education in some developing countries has been closely modelled on that in the United Kingdom and USA. The wholesale adoption of syllabuses and textbooks also implies the transfer of objectives, yet these may be inappropriate to the environmental, employment, cognitive and pedagogical situations into which they are implanted.

Ogawa takes the problems of science education innovation cross culturally to another level suggesting that science education in most developing countries is a foreign culture to most non-westerners. He presents a model to explain conflicts between traditional views of man and nature and ways of thinking and the science education view. He goes on to suggest one of the aims of science education in non-western society should be to compare the traditional and scientific views of man and nature and ways of thinking, and to explore similarities and differences between them.

Amongst other studies on science education innovation are those which highlight human and physical resource availability problems, training inadequacies, gaps between intentions and curriculum reality, and the paucity of timely and insightful evaluation. Thus Lutterodt describes the evaluation planning undertaken for the Project for Science Integration in Ghana, which highlighted the limitations arising from characteristics of teachers, students, authors, materials, and finances.

Jegede evaluated the Nigerian Integrated Science Project and found that teachers were not favourably disposed towards some parts of it though the majority of students had positive attitudes. Low achievement was attributed to problems with textbook readability and lack of training to teach integrated science which were compounded by equipment shortages. Brophy and Dalgety scrutinised the implementation of a new science curriculum in Guyana. They found that there was a wide gap between practice and officially stated intentions. For instance, what were intended to be student-centred, laboratory-based activities were in practice teacher-centred and textbook oriented.

In-service teacher education involving the use of distance education methods was being used in attempts to improve the situation. Vulliamy discusses the lessons that might be learned for other developing countries from the Secondary Schools Community Extension Project (SSCEP) in Papua New Guinea, which included science curriculum development as part of an attempt to increase the relevance of secondary schooling to rural development. This work emphasized the importance of appreciation of cultural differences, the potential for using the examination system to support desired teaching and learning strategies, and the necessity for a careful planning and monitoring.

Chisman and Wilson in their review of the experience of 25 years of attempts to innovate in science education single out more effective evaluation as possibly the most important factor in improving implementation of new science curricula. As might be expected the international literature includes other studies which focus on the role of external change agents. Thus Nichter discusses some of the problems faced by technical advisers implementing projects for the improvement of science education in Africa. Reasons for these problems include institutional underdevelopment, underestimating the process of reform inadequate finances, personality conflict and lack of motivation, and opposition from key groups.

Lillis focused on expatriates and curriculum change in Kenya and explores curriculum interdependence; the complex interrelationships between local and metropolitan actors; and the assumptions of universality. He uses three perspectives-the adoption perspective, the implementation perspective, and the politico-administrative perspective to reflect on the Africanization of formal decision-making, curriculum decision-making and of the curriculum itself.

Maybury reviewed a range of science curriculum projects which have involved international aid through the Ford Foundation. He argues the most successful have been those where the foreign specialists were resident in the country and had acquired a wide knowledge of local political, social, economic and educational conditions. Crucial to success is the ability of the members of curriculum development groups to discern the world-view held by children, particularly those from the more deprived sectors of society. These kind of findings cannot be seen as definitive-if only because there are successful projects supported by international donors that do not involve foreign specialists on a large scale. There is very little literature that explores in depth the tensions that arise in technical co-operation and assistance related to science education and not much in general.

Leach's recent study is an exception which highlights the kinds of perception gap that may develop, the different organizational and procedural assumptions of key actors, and the strategies that project staff develop to accommodate these. In so doing she illustrates that many projects develop goals that go beyond those formally negotiated and these may have more importance for the actors involved than successful goal achievement of that originally agreed.

Zainal notes that in the reform of the science curriculum in Malaysia decision-making at the adoption and adaptation levels involved a very small group of key actors who were influenced by external change agents. The latter mobilized arguments to suggest that the planned changes would meet needs for continuity, feasibility and relevance. However, at the implementation stage, none of the planned innovations were fully implemented by classroom teachers. Pedagogical aspects in particular were heavily modified or rejected whilst content changes appeared more durable. The centralized decision-making system failed to appreciate fully the extent to which this would happen as teachers adapted the intended curriculum to reflect needs and constraints of particular teachers in particular schools.

Organization of Science Curriculum

It was only in the nineteenth century that science began to strongly differentiate into what are now recognised as the three main sciences-physics, chemistry and biology. Since the 1950s other specialities began to emerge at University level and filter down into schools systems which were subdivisions or extensions of these three sciences. Additionally the more prestigious science became as an activity in the curriculum the more substantial became attractions of making more scientific other disciplines. Thus geography and earth science increasingly became seen as sciences suitable for study at school level and environmental studies curricula moved towards environmental science. In terms of the origin of the science curriculum three broad patterns can be traced.

First, the classical tradition of pure science reflecting the development of the separate subjects and to a degree rivalry between them. Historically physics, closely allied mathematics had the earliest claims to be considered the core of science. The natural philosophers of the sixteenth and seventeenth centuries used mathematical and scientific concepts with their roots in antiquity to explore the physical world and it was these that largely defined science. This was a period when the nature of the cosmos provoked sharp debate and much scientific effort was directed towards problems of navigation and warfare. Subsequently the successful development of chemical concepts in the eighteenth and nineteenth century opened a new window on the world through the systematic understanding of the properties of elements and the ways in which they combined with each other. The economic implications of this became important as it became possible to synthesise new materials, starting most notably with synthetic dyes whose properties could be predicted. Chemistry became respectable and lost its alchemist's image. Later the biological sciences grasped the popular imagination in the Europe of the nineteenth century as the travels of Darwin and Wallace revealed the wealth of flora and fauna on the planet and began to developed theories with far reaching implications. The economic advantages of understanding how biological resources could be exploited by colonialists played an important supporting role.

The second tradition was utilitarian. There was a long tradition of useful science removed from academic science in the elementary schools of the United Kingdom. This always remained of much lower status than the real science which had more classical than utilitarian origins. Thus the 'Society for the Effusion of Useful Knowledge' in the nineteenth century in the United Kingdom was an early precursor of the general science movement of the mid twentieth century and the science for all movement of the late twentieth century. In this tradition the ideas of science were to be made available to a broad cross-section of society to assist them in their occupations and in everyday living. Thus elementary science was to be more concerned with the science of everyday objects and simple skills of observation, measurement and experiment, mixed with a modicum of basic scientific knowledge, than with the more profound investigation of the scientific laws, the nature of matter and evolution of species..

The third tradition that can be traced is technological. It appears most strongly in the nineteenth century in Germany as well as the United Kingdom and USA. The development of large scale industry and the infrastructure that depended on sophisticated engineering skills created a need for the technological skills of making and doing in the cause of new products and structures to serve particular purposes. Systematic knowledge of the strength of materials was required, design became important, and though trial and error remained an important feature of technological development with many economically significant developments depending on a certain amount of serendipity, there were comparative advantages to those who used scientific ideas to create technological artefacts. AU this stimulated the growth of technical institutes and schools, often of lower social status than academic institutions, that taught practical knowledge related to engineering skins.

All these three traditions have their current analogues in the development of science education internationally and have had an influence on the development of science curricula. Dominant have been the academic and classical traditions since these in the majority of school systems have continued to occupy the high ground of teaching in elite institutions which yield access to the most attractive jobs. Science for an, with its utilitarian emphasis has come to new prominence as more and more school systems teach science to most if not an of the school population. The intrinsic difficulty and lack of relevance of fundamental science to the majority of school populations has forced curriculum developers to consider providing more accessible science related to the experiential world of students. Most recently technological approaches to science have become fashionable as a way of teaching economically useful skills that takes advantage of some of the strengths of both of the other two approaches.

Organizational Patterns

The overall trend over the last two decades is clear. Most lower secondary science teaching has become integrated, at least in the sense that science is treated as a whole and not as separate subjects. UNESCO has been instrumental in encouraging this trend. The same trend exists at upper secondary though less pronounced. It is uncommon at the pre-university level. There is some evidence that these tendencies have been less pronounced in Francophone countries than in the rest of the world. It is also the case that the physical sciences are more commonly integrated than are all three traditional sciences. The IEA data also support this picture and shows that integrated or combined courses are most common below grade 9 in the 23 countries sampled. Above this single subject teaching becomes more common. There is no single commonly accepted definition of what constitutes integration beyond the practical consideration of whether science is time-tabled as one subject.

Integration can be conceived of as thematic, taking themes like energy transformations and examining them from physical, chemical, and biological perspectives; it may be topic based choosing a topic like water and similarly treating it from the three disciplinary perspectives in a coherently interrelated way; science may be conceptually integrated by stressing science process skills which are common to the three sciences and emphasizing these in the teaching of content located in the three disciplines. Examples of an these approaches can be found. What lies behind them are the philosophies of science education and curriculum development. There are practical reasons why integrated science has become more common as wed as those based on changing epistemological and pedagogical perspectives. Lower secondary school systems almost everywhere have expanded rapidly and schools have become less selective as greater proportions of the age cohort are enrolled.

At the same time in many systems more subjects have been introduced into the compulsory curriculum squeezing the time available for science. Rapid expansion also creates severe problems of teacher supply. The attractions of integrated science in these circumstances are clear -textbook production and teacher training can be simplified by concentrating on producing science teachers and materials rather than three varieties for each of conventional science subjects; science taught as three subjects is generally thought to require four to six periods a week for each subject-totalling about 15 in all. This time is unlikely to be available if there are seven or more other compulsory subjects.

Integrated science is usually allocated four to six periods a week. Integration might also be thought to reduce overlap in teaching between the three sciences and economise on scarce resources Laboratory space, equipment, trained teachers. De facto, therefore, integrated patterns of science teaching are becoming the norm at lower secondary level, with similar trends at upper secondary in many countries. The literature contains few examples of attempts to compare the effectiveness of teaching science in an integrated way with the teaching of separate subjects.

It is generally very difficult to find comparable groups that have a choice between single subject and integrated programmes; where they do single subject science is invariably allocated more time. Other common problems of this kind of research (e.g. variable teacher effects, interschool differences, non-parallel learning objectives) make it elusive to reach simple conclusions. It does appear true that, for example, students taught in integrated science are less aware of the differences between the sciences, but this kind of finding does not contribute much to decisions on whether or not to adopt integrated approaches.

The decisions are usually made for other reasons like the advantages noted above. It must be remembered that the relative attractions of single subject teaching rests largely on hearsay, casual empiricism, and the attachment of teachers to the disciplines that they were trained in. They are most frequently advanced in relation to students who may subsequently follow careers with a science base for whom in-depth knowledge is thought essential and who are in a minority.

The IEA Second International Science Study does suggest that the performance of those studying single subject science is not related to the overall percentage enrolled in secondary education, and it is negatively related to the proportion enrolled in science subjects. The latter might be expected as the size of the cohort following science increases and selection becomes weaker.

The epistemological and pedagogical arguments for specialization into separate subjects become more convincing at higher academic levels. Here, if conventional assumptions are retained about the depth in which science is to be studied, more time is required and some selection is inevitable. The differences in achievement across groups of students become wider and more prior knowledge is assumed to have been mastered.

If it has not, learning at the level of meaning becomes extremely difficult in science since the subject is cumulative in nature.

At lower secondary level however, the cognitive skills and assumptions of antecedent knowledge should not be seen as a barrier to integration. There -are examples of successful integrated science programmes up to and beyond upper secondary school and there have been many initiatives with interdisciplinary degree courses. The reasons why they have not become a dominant mode of provision probably owe more to the entrenched conservatism of science educators and organizational limitations on resources, than to inherent epistemological or pedagogical weaknesses.

Curriculum organization in secondary science has many other aspects in addition to the debate on integration. These include the interrelationships with other subjects; the balance between the sciences in the curriculum; the time allocation thought appropriate; the conditions under which science is to be taught and which groups are to be taught science. Practice varies widely on all of these. It is not difficult to find examples of curricula planned with scant regard to the mathematics curricula on which some abstract manipulation and data analysis are likely to depend. It is rare to find science curricula, except those with a conscious science and society orientation, that make direct connections with learning in history, social studies or languages. This is not a problem specific to science since similar things can be observed in relation to other subject areas.

Its significance is that where there is some interdependence coordination is obviously desirable; and where few links are made between science and other subjects the separateness of science is emphasized and this may discourage some children and reduce the appeal of the subject. Policy varies on science subject emphasis. If tentative generalisations can be made then biological content is more heavily emphasized at the lower levels and physical science at the higher levels. There is no great universality to this pattern however.

To talk of emphasis at higher levels is to be confounded by the complexities of option choice where different numbers of students take different subjects often in an unknown pattern of overlap, and this is further complicated by the differential allocation of study time to the different subjects.

In an exception to the common pattern in China biological sciences were virtually eliminated from the secondary curriculum at one time -reflecting perhaps the influence of Russian orthodoxies on content selection.

Physical science has been given most emphasis at secondary level for many years though this is now changing. But in many countries emphasis is more equal. It is also true that the only science subject that many girls study at upper secondary level is biology in those systems where a choice is available.

The time allocated to teaching of science varies greatly as the IEA data show. But so does total instructional time. If there is any consensus it appears to be that science should occupy between 10 and 20 per cent of curricula time for most secondary students-any less and it will be a shallow learning experience, any more and the competition for curriculum time with other subjects will become fierce but there is enormous variation in practice.

Most systems have ideal images of the conditions under which science should be taught characterized by graduate science teachers, well-established science laboratories, adequate textbooks and enlightened teaching methods. These conditions are not met in the majority of schools in developing countries. One consequence is that whatever the policy on streaming and tracking the common reality is effective science education for the few under appropriate conditions, and relatively poorly executed science for the majority.

Tracking and Streaming Policy

Tracking and streaming policy have both resource and pedagogical implications since it will determine how many students study science to which levels. It will also influence what types of science students experience in schools. There is an extensive body of research on the effects of different methods of grouping students. Most of this research has focused on primary and the lower reaches of secondary education where practice has varied widely within and between countries. Much less work relates to upper secondary where commonly some selection takes place, either as a result of student choice or as a result of schools deciding to treat more and less able children in separate groups. First we should consider the range of options that exist in organising groups of students at any given level. These cover a spectrum broadly defined by the following practices.

Options for grouping students streaming and tracking by ability:

— children are segregated into different institutions depending on achievement scores and/or

— children are divided into groups on the basis of their achievement and grouped into classes accordingly.

Setting: Groups of children electing to follow a particular subject are placed in teaching groups which are streamed so that sets in the same subject are of recognisably different achievement.

Banding: Groups of children electing to follow a particular subject are placed in teaching- groups that are broadly comparable in terms of achievement.

Mixed ability: Children are randomly assigned to schools and class groups independently of their ability and the full range of ability is represented.

The extent of homogeneity in achievement in teaching groups reduces from the first to the last of these options. The reasoning used to defend each of these practices differs. In its simplest form the argument in favour of streaming suggests that the narrower the ability range the more the class can be taught as a whole without losing contact with the very able or very slow. Opponents of this view argue that this is not convincing as all classes are mixed ability in some sense and that teaching methods can be devised that allow students to progress at different rates. What evidence there is generally fails to show consistent achievement gains for children in streamed classes over and above what would be expected of more able children in any case. In particular some studies draw attention to the negative consequences for low stream teaching groups on achievement and suggest that, if a view of achievement is taken which includes effects on the cohort as a whole, any gains that may accrue for the best students are likely to be compensated for by deterioration in performance of the least able. The phenomenon of the 'sink set' is a part of teacher folklore in many countries-failure reinforces itself as motivation falls and peer group subcultures begin to develop anti-school attitudes.

Another consequence of streaming which is widely recognized is that schools that stream students often stream teachers too. That is, the most well qualified, senior and effective teachers tend to teach the most able groups and the older students most of the time. This might partially explain the deterioration in performance of low stream groups. It seems undesirable unless the philosophy behind teacher allocation is unashamedly elitist. A recent study in Zimbabwe confirmed that teachers of Environmental and Agricultural Science of the lowest grades generally had the least number of years of formal schooling and the lowest level of science achievement. Those with the highest professional qualifications were concentrated in the highest grades. Where classes are streamed it is also often the case that the better qualified and more experienced teachers teach the most able students.

An ongoing research study in Malaysia also suggests that this pattern prevails. Though this ensures that the more demanding science constructs are taught by the most scientifically competent, it creates a situation in which the most competent teachers may spend a considerable amount of teaching time trying to overcome the effects of poor quality teaching in lower grades. Streaming by ability creates another dilemma since it always implies a mechanism to separate the more from the less able. Though it may be more fashionable to take a genotypic view of human abilities than was the case a decade ago it is still widely recognized that children's achievement is complex and not necessarily stable or unidimensional. Thus any selection process will risk misclassification- learners develop at different rates, especially during adolescence in the secondary school, and may be misclassified; the type of achievement on which selection is accomplished is usually based on a number of core subjects and/or attempts to tap an underlying general ability factor which may or may not correlate closely with science achievement.

As we have seen there is little unanimity as to what kind of attributes are especially suited to science education since the question begs the issue of what kind of science education we are talking of. Whilst there appear to be no convincing educational arguments that can be made across the board about the benefits of streaming for achievement there is more convincing evidence that streaming by ability has social consequences, at least in the industrialized countries where studies have been completed. Thus rates of delinquency, truancy and misdemeanours appear to increase amongst low ability children when they are grouped together. The peer group subcultures that form are antipathetic to school norms and to status acquired through school achievement.

Admittedly these effects may not be the same when projected cross culturally and where the calculus of reward for school achievement is very different to that in societies where alternative opportunities are available to those without educational qualifications that provide reasonable standards of living. There is a considerable amount of research on the interaction between teachers expectations of pupil's abilities, pupils self concepts and actual achievement. From this emerges a consensus that teacher's images of children are likely to create 'self fulfilling prophecies' which enhance the performance of favoured students and suppress that of the less favoured, though not perhaps in the simple way implied by Rosenthal and Jacobson. This is not the place to enter into this literature in detail, but it is worth highlighting some findings that emerge from research on grouping practices.

Pidgeon's analysis of the IEA pilot tests in 1970 showed that standard deviations on test scores tended to be higher in England and Wales than in other countries. This he attributed to streaming practices more prevalent in these schools than in those of other countries. The most recent IEA science study also notes that the proportion of the variance attributable to the class and school attended is much greater in some of the developing country samples than it is in most industrialized countries though there is considerable variation in this. Where it is high e.g., Nigeria and the Philippines (Population 1 data) and Ghana, Italy, the Netherlands and the Philippines (Population 2 data) it suggests that the class and school attended make a considerable difference to achievement in science.

A well known United Kingdom study compares performance amongst 12 secondary schools on an aggregate measure of scholastic achievement. This study indicates strong school effects after verbal reasoning score on entry and socioeconomic background have been controlled. The effect is so strong that the most disadvantaged students (lowest verbal reasoning, lowest socioeconomic background) in the most successful school are as successful as the most advantaged students in the worst school. There is no reason to suppose that these effects are not reflected in science in particular though evidence on this is not presented.

If generally true, these kinds of findings suggest that where there is a significant range in institutional types (as is the case where institutional tracking exists) there may be improvement of students in performance in favoured institutions, but this is accompanied by deterioration in performance of similar students in unfavoured institutions. This of course ceases to be an immediate problem from the point of equity if the achievement of concern (e.g. science) is not available to those selected out of elite institutions, i.e. the mass of the Population do not compete for similar levels of achievement in science.

In such cases equity tends to be defined more by fair competition for entry into selective institutions than by equal participation in curriculum options. The Second IEA Science Study indicates that the performance of elite students is unaffected by the proportion of the age group studying science, when examined cross-nationally. This suggests that elite students do not suffer in general from broader access to science. To what extent this may be a result of particular grouping strategies is, however, not explored.

There is another dimension to the streaming debate that turns to two strands of argument for its defence. On the one hand it is argued that some subjects have relatively high 'entry prices' and are cumulative. That is to progress with them to ideas that are of interest and can be applied, a certain amount of persistence and systematic study is required. Since some learning has to be sequential'y' cannot be understood until 'x' has been mastered-it follows that the subject itself requires differentiation of students since they will not all progress through these sequences at the same rate, nor will they have the motivation to do so. If the view of some psychologists is accepted, namely that what really differentiates learners achievement is not intrinsic inabilities to master concepts but differences in the length of time that it takes to acquire them, it follows that student groups should be subdivided to reflect these differences.

For some students the length of time will be so long as to be unavailable and they will never master the ideas- but this has different educational consequences than a view which holds that they could not do so under any circumstances. On the other hand cognitive development studies are cited in science which show that in school populations only a minority of students consistently perform at Piagetian levels of formal operations whilst in secondary education. If the view is taken that concrete reasoners find formal thought intrinsically unavailable to them this limits what kind of science can be taught effectively. Many of the ideas of science require formal reasoning. This then reinforces the previous argument that science students should be grouped to reflect their rate of progress towards the acquisition of formal reasoning skills.

Implementation Issues

One of the reasons why it is difficult to tease out common factors that lead to problems in implementation is that perspectives on what these are depend very much on the analytic framework employed and the nature of the innovation attempted. Thus those within a functionalist sociological tradition will take a very different view of the nature of problems, there causes and the action necessary to overcome them to those within the traditions of conflict theory in organizational analysis. What may look like the failure to communicate the purpose of an innovation in science education requiring better public relations from one perspective could be interpreted as the inevitable result of conflict in interests between different groups expected to implement the innovation which is not based simply on ignorance of purpose.

The six approaches to curriculum development identified- systems, bureaucratic, scientific, problem solving, diffusionist, and charismatic

— all have different implications for implementation strategies and their likely effectiveness which will be context specific. At the risk of over-generalization, some of the most important implications for planners arising from the analysis seem to be:

— The careful consideration of the source(s) of innovation.

— The identification of information needs to improve decision-making as the innovation takes shape. In particular, a tenacious pursuit of antecedent assumptions on which the implementation strategy may depend.

— The systematic appraisal of options to achieve desired ends, using wherever possible, realistic pilot projects that are capable of extension to scale.

— Flexible adaptation to evolving goals as events unfold and the limitations and possibilities of implementation strategies become apparent.

— Serious commitment to the aftercare of innovations designed to support durable changes and discourage regression to previous patterns of provision.

Organizational questions are clearly of importance to planners since they carry implications for resources and some options will be more expensive than others. However, from what has already been argued it is clear that the number of possible permutations is very wide and cannot be reduced to simple algorithms. This is because organizational decisions have to take into account existing traditions, and the established deployment of resources, as well as the nature of the goals towards which science education is directed. Often there are real choices to achieve the similar ends at different costs but inevitably not all patterns of organization are appropriate to different circumstances. In planning science education the resource implications, as well as the pedagogical ones, must form an integral part of the decision-making process.

Tracking and streaming policy in science education has implications for costs and internal efficiency. The evidence suggests that early selection does not have very substantial impact on achievement- especially when gains for the selected group are balanced against possible deterioration amongst those not selected for special treatment. The behavioural consequences of streaming seem a matter of concern, at least in those developed countries where these have been shown to be negative in character.

At higher academic levels some forms of streaming and tracking are inevitable for several reasons-the increased difficulty of the science to be learned, the preferences of students to study science, the difficulties of resourcing science adequately. What form this should take has no generally appropriate prescription and must be examined at the country- and school-levels.

Examinations and Assessment

The form and structure of examination systems are widely recognized as key determinants of educational practice. Well known expositions of the reasons for this can be found in Dore and Oxenham. Many others have commented on the significance of examinations for educational development and quality improvement. Wherever opportunities to enter modem sector employment are scarce and the rewards of doing so are great, selection mechanisms will adopt great importance in the minds of teachers.

Most commonly educational qualifications are used to regulate flows into career jobs and science is often a key subject for selection. In China the examination system is known as the baton which conducts the schools and this is a common perception in many other developing countries. The industrialized countries often exported and imposed their own national examination systems on their colonies and the traditions established by these boards linger on.

However, most developing countries now have their own examination systems without any apparent lowering of standards at least as determined by the percentages of candidates passing the examinations each year. Thus West Africa, the Sudan, East Africa, Malaysia, and more recently Cyprus and the Commonwealth Caribbean have instituted regional or national Public Examination

Councils. Local examiners have been substituted for expatriate ones.

The World Bank has shown a particular interest in the recent past in the use of examination reform to improve academic achievement and has invested in the strengthening of examination systems in a number of developing countries. As long ago as 1973 Fletcher warned 'the musicians were changed, not so the music', suggesting that localization of examination boards would not of itself overcome the criticisms of their effects on teaching and teaming.

Typically secondary level tests do not appear to cover the range of educational aims and objectives that are usually associated with secondary science courses. There may be both structural reasons for this and those which are concerned more with traditions within subjects as to what is examinable and what should be examined. The first observation is that since assessment in most secondary school systems in science is undertaken through written test this immediately places boundaries around what can be assessed. Further, much testing is constrained by the use of multiple choice formats which are very limited in the extent to which they can assess powers of expression, communication skills etc.

In addition multiple choice items may have a counter productive effect on teaching if the assessment pattern of the classroom mirrors that of the examination rather than that of the curriculum and its goals. The reasons assessment is often limited to written papers and to multiple choice items are practical as well as pedagogic. Written examinations and multiple choice in particular offers relative reliability, objectivity, economy, and ease of administration over most other methods.

These are also the methods that many teachers, pupils and parents have become familiar with. The restrictions placed on assessment of curricula goals by written examinations are well known and need no extensive development here. It is worth noting that some rather more subtle processes are at work in electing for such formats. Multiple choice examinations as conventionally constructed from pretested items, select items which have proven reliability, a restricted range of facility values, and which discriminate between students positively in terms of overall score. They will also be selected using a table of specifications that tries to ensure coverage of a range of topics across the curriculum tested at different levels of cognitive demand. Reliability is essential if confidence is to be placed in results for selection and the associated error score will be minimized in part to achieve this.

A technical reason for restricting the range of facility values for items is to ensure that discrimination remains high since the two interact—very easy or very difficult items cannot discriminate highly. Moreover, in selecting only those items that discriminate well the assumption is made that the attribute being measured is unidimensional — if an item measures an attribute on which performance does not correlate with overall score it will be rejected, though it might be a valid measure of that attribute.

Without delving too deeply into the technicalities of examining the point to be made is that different selection criteria for items could produce different patterns of performance. They could also convey different messages back to teachers as to what constructs and capabilities in science were most important. Emphasizing discrimination emphasizes those things where there are the largest differences in performance between candidates, not those things which may be most useful or fundamental to the understanding of science. To put things more concretely there is evidence from internal studies by various examination boards that both facility values and discrimination indices for items vary between sub-populations. There may be, for example, some items which are completed relatively well by rural students despite the fact that their overall performance is inferior to that of urban students. So for boys and girls, linguistic minorities, etc.

This is important since it implies both that a different mix of items might produce different patterns of performance, and because it illustrates that differences between groups may not be stable across the curriculum as a whole but the result of particular difficulties in certain curriculum areas. If the latter is so, planned intervention to improve performance and reduce disparities would be well advised to focus on those areas where differences in performance are most marked. And it also acts as a reminder that in principle, it should be curriculum goals, not assessment criteria, that should define the curriculum in action and that the assessment system fails in an important sense if it does not reinforce the full range of curriculum goals to which teaching and learning is intended to be directed.

There is little in the literature specifically on science examinations in developing countries. Kellaghan and Greaney provide a study of the examination systems of five African countries — Ethiopia, Lesotho, Malawi, Swaziland and Zambia. They identify a number of key issues in examination reform such as improving the efficiency of examination administration; improving the quality of examinations by reflecting more of the curriculum objectives; providing information regarding examination performance both for policy decisions at regional- and national-levels and as a diagnostic basis for classroom teaching. These writers also discuss the implications for examination reform.

In the early 1980s as part of the ILO Jobs and Study Skills Programme for Africa school examination papers were analysed in eight African countries—the Gambia, Ghana, Kenya, Liberia, Sierra Leone, Somalia, Tanzania, Zambia. These studies used the Bloom taxonomy to classify the skills tested in public examination papers in different subjects. The results yield insights into what were then common examining practices in science. Though practice may have changed in some countries since these reports were produced evidence from the literature suggest that many of the basic findings remain valid.

The general picture that emerges is of examining in science dominated by recall items that test the ability of candidates to reproduce factual knowledge about science. This is overwhelmingly the case for the lower secondary examinations analysed, and strongly but less emphatically true of the upper secondary papers. Other features of the examinations worth noting are the extensive use of multiple choice items in the format of public examination papers.

These are by far the most common approach used and few countries now examine science at secondary level without their use. Despite there being many excellent examples of multiple-choice items testing higher order skills there is evidence that they are perceived as being more associated with the testing of lower order skills. Lewin reports that 58 per cent of a sample of Malaysian students agreed or strongly agreed with the statement "to do well on objective tests all you need is a good memory ". A number of other formats are used which include blank filling, shorter answer items that require brief explanations or comments and interpretation, longer answer items that require substantial written responses for example describing experiments but these generally have declined in popularity.

Across all the papers analysed in the ILO study it was the exception rather than the rule to find many items which directly draw on life experiences, especially those of rural children, in their construction and situation. It is characteristic of most national examinations in science at secondary level that few if any attempts are made to measure affective outcomes. Yet affective objectives are included in most new secondary science curricula and are sometimes argued to be as important as cognitive ones. The ILO examination analyses showed that it was generally biology that had the highest number of recall based items, reflecting the way this science subject is often interpreted in the curriculum.

The more descriptive the treatment the more likely that its assessment will favour the recall of information. Physics tends to be the least recall dominated of the sciences, though this may be partly because the mathematical demands of it are generally more extensive. Most items that have a mathematical component are likely to require more than recall for their successful solution. Health science, agricultural science, home science and other electives appear in the examining systems of different countries. These subjects also tend to have a high proportion of items that appear to be directed at the level of recall minority of countries trends to reduce the number of recall based items have been apparent.

Thus the proportion of higher cognitive level items in the science certificate of primary education did increase from about 17 per cent to more than 70 per cent over the period of the 1970s in the Kenya Certificate of Primary Education. So also did the number of items with a rural bias which used material familiar to rural children as a vehicle to assess science learning outcomes. A recent analysis of secondary science examinations (grade 10) in Papua New Guinea showed that in recent papers more than 25 per cent of items were intended to operate above the level of comprehension and test higher process skills; the majority of the remaining items were testing comprehension, not simple recall.

Possibly foreshadowing a contrary trend Deutrom and Wilson expressed concern about academic standards in Papua New Guinea which seemed likely to lead to greater emphasis on more traditional science content in examinations. Low academic standards at grades 10 and 12 are attributed to the deliberate policy of 'containing' traditional science in grade 11 and above, and giving grades 1 to 10 a 'science-for-all'.

A Brazilian study of university entrance physics exams found that the level of attainment, as indicated by item facility indices, was very low, over a seven year period. This analysis revealed an overemphasis on mechanics problems and little attempt to present problems in an everyday rather than scientific context. It was also found that mean facility followed the hierarchical order for the taxonomy level dimension of analysis, with recap items showing the highest facility values and therefore being easiest for most students. Items which used a concrete context had higher facility values than those with an abstract scientific context. Lewin found average facility values in the Malaysian LCE/SRP Science examination of 60 per cent, 56 per cent and 52 per cent for knowledge, comprehension and application items, respectively, and comments that these differences were less than he had been led to expect from assertions that more higher level items could not be included since they would reduce mean facility values to unacceptable levels.

In another study of Chinese entrance university entrance examinations it seems clear that recall questions are common even at upper secondary level, though less so in physics than in the other sciences. Other types of item are still used in science examining in addition to multiple choice. These include various kinds of short answer and structured items, with or without graded difficulty within them, essay questions, and still on occasion the traditional description of an experiment followed by the calculation of some results.

Of the newer types perhaps the most widely used are short answer items with structured stimuli — graphs, diagrams, tables of results, photographs, etc.—and tasks to undertake based on the stimuli. These can test a wide range of skills though they are often time-consuming to construct. Though, with imagination and investment of suitable resources in training and development it is possible to test a much greater range of learning outcomes than is typically assessed in public examinations, the format itself is inevitably restrictive.

This may be one reason to encourage the growth of school based assessment where there are no contra-indicators that suggest that such developments will overburden teachers who do not have the skills or motivation to operate such systems effectively.

Practical examinations are no longer a feature of much public examining at secondary level in science. The costs and logistic difficulties of maintaining practical examinations have proved beyond the capabilities of many countries. Items are used in some countries which describe experiments and ask students to comment on what has been described in terms of the conclusions that can be drawn and/or the flaws in the experimental procedure described. Where practical examinations remain they are generally only held at the highest levels of the school system prior to university entry where numbers are smaller.

The recent movement towards more school based examining opens up the possibility of more assessment of practical skills. However, these developments are much more common in industrialized countries than in those developing countries with highly centralized examination systems. There are some alternatives to practical science examinations (the use of slides, photographs, thought experiments, critiques of experimental procedure, etc.) and there has been a lot of small-scale experimentation and many ideas about the best ways to test practical skills. They have not been widely adopted however since they generally require individual or small group working situations and multiple sets of equipment and are time consuming.

Certificate Examination which is locally set. Although there is no practical examination the syllabus emphasizes practical experiences -there are 29 such objectives, e.g. demonstrate how to wire a 3-pin plug -to be learnt by arranging an extensive range of simple practical experiences for each student in the laboratory. The new Zimbabwe O' level was to have included a practical examination consisting of a series of short practical exercises testing specific science skills with instructions provided to candidates and a circus style of test administration. Examiners are looking for evidence that candidates can apply basic skills such as handling apparatus, recording observations and displaying data in graphical form .

By circulating around a set of tests a balanced coverage of skills was planned and the possibilities of using teacher assessment are being investigated. However, the practical examination has so far not been implemented. The university entrance examination in China does not have a practical component in science. It does include a small number of items which describe experimental procedures and ask a series of questions about the reasons for the methods used and pose questions about the reasons for anomalous results.

Practical work by students is uncommon in Chinese schools and it is generally only in well resourced 'key-point' schools that there is sufficient apparatus to allow individual experimentation. Even in these most experimental work appears to be undertaken through teacher demonstrations. Where there are practical examinations, it is commonly the case that performance on them accounts for a small proportion of total marks -- rarely more than 15 per cent.

Moreover, the variance in students scores that arises from practicals is generally smaller than that on test scores as a whole. Thus they tend not to contribute much to the discriminating power of the test as a whole and may actually reduce it. Strategically practical examining is important since in its absence it is likely that teachers would arrange even less practical work than they currently do.

Life chances depend on educational qualifications in developing countries to a much greater extent than in industrialized countries. Because employers in the labour market use educational qualifications in the recruitment and selection of personnel students and teachers will follow strategies of learning and teaching which will maximise their chances of gaining the qualifications which will secure them a job, i.e. students and teachers will become exam-oriented.

Based on a secondary analysis of the 1971 IEA Survey of Science achievement data, Little reports on differences in exam-oriented teaching styles between countries. She reports a greater tendency in developing countries to view the education system in terms of examination orientation towards jobs in the modern sector, and discusses the historical reasons for this. Schools themselves belong to the modern sector resulting in a greater disjunction between what goes on in school and what goes on at home.

High examination orientation is characterized by frequent use of standardized and objective tests and greater importance of external exams and official syllabus as teaching criteria. The analysis revealed that the four developing countries in the study ranked in the first 6 out of a total of 15 countries on the frequent use of tests indicator, and in the top half on the exam/syllabus indicators.

For many teachers in developing countries examinations appear to be very important even at the primary stage. A hypothesized link between examination orientation and teaching which emphasized rote learning was investigated by analyzing sub-scores on the IEA achievement tests. Rote-learnable items in the tests tended on average to be easier than those testing higher order skills but the difference was insufficient to justify concentration by teachers on rote-learnable items.

Although recall items may not be that much easier for students to answer they are easier to teach towards, to revise for and to practice. The overall finding of the analysis is that factors affecting problem-solving sub test scores affect simultaneously rote-learnable scores. This suggests further thought is needed about the balance between rote and problem-solving items in exams given the likely backwash effects on the curriculum of the types of learning outcome emphasized in public examinations.

The Student Learning Orientation Group (SLOG) is investigating the hypothesis that highly examination dominated schooling induces in students certain values and attitudes which influence behaviour in the workplace. Six countries (India, Japan, Malaysia, Nigeria, Sri Lanka, the United Kingdom,) were involved in the study. The initial study was directed towards developing measures for describing profiles of learning orientation and planned to follow up with developing measures for workplace behaviour. Questionnaire items were developed to measure orientation to assessment, task interest, personal development, achievement and significant others of form 4 and form 6 students.

At the intra-country level of analysis assessment domination was clearly evident in Malaysia and Sri

Lanka but less so in India and Nigeria. At the inter-country level of analysis three main dimensions of motivation were evident: orientation to examination and assessment results, orientation to the task of learning for personal development, orientation to the expectations of parents, teachers and peers. The relative distinctiveness of the three dimensions was found to vary by country. These findings point to the need for more research on the classroom observation of science teaching to understand more comprehensively the nature of the link between teaching and learning orientation and achievement.

Assessment

Continuous assessment spreads out school-based assessment over a period of years and can thereby enhance the validity of assessment, improve the integration between the curriculum, pedagogy and assessment. It can also cover a broader range of assessable outcomes. Several countries have introduced various forms of continuous assessment into secondary schools to allow schools to play a greater role in assessment procedures and to take more control over the single most important determinant of teaching and teaming.

Pennycuick reports on the continuous assessment policies of Papua New Guinea, Sri Lanka, Seychelles, Tanzania, and Nigeria and finds a variety of practices including the total replacement of external exams, parallel and separate systems of continuous assessment and external exams, and systems where continuous assessment forms a component of final results, together with examination results.

In all the systems teachers are much more directly involved in assessment than in conventional public examining. But there has been a wealth of difference between the systems as planned, and the procedures adopted in practice as the Nigerian experience illustrates. She highlights major problem areas in the introduction of continuous assessment as inadequate conceptualisation by teachers, doubtful validity of test items, and inadequate structural and administrative support.

Though the planned system looks in many respects laudable its operationalization has been hampered by many unsatisfied conditions that are necessary for its effective implementation, not least the time for teachers to understand and absorb new practices and the timetable time to make it feasible to operate them. As well as teacher inexperience and increased workload Pennycuick identifies technical problems related to moderation.

Three moderation procedures are identifiable—statistical, visitation and consensus—the selection choice depends on context. Statistical moderation, for example using national test results to moderate school based ones, is probably the simplest assuming data are collected in a timely fashion since it can be accomplished centrally in an examination depart-ment.

Visitation and consensus require negotiation and agreement which may be both expensive in time and travel costs and may not be easy to achieve. School based examining moderated by national examinations has been tried in Papua New Guinea and this offers one possible solution to the problem of reconciling the need to locate assessment in schools if it is to be closely linked to curricula experience and the need to ensure comparable standards between schools. In this system continuous assessment occurs over the year and the national end of year test is used to moderate the continuous assessment scores, which count for 50 per cent of the final marks.

The extent to which school scores differ from rankings produced by national exams may illustrate that a wider range of attributes are being tested in school based examinations . Attempts to introduce continuous assessment schemes in other countries have floundered in the face of practical problems and the opposition of groups seeing few real benefits emerging and much extra work.

If school-based assessment related to the particular characteristics of curriculum at the school level is to flourish then its relationship to the national examination system has to be carefully considered. It does imply a degree of curriculum diversity, and local control over the curriculum, that is not common. Its advantage is that it can be more valid, and it can support local curriculum development and adaptation to make science more attractive and useful to different groups of students

In some national circumstances where a common curriculum is seen to be of over-riding importance, substantial variations at the school level in what is taught and assessed will not be attractive. Neither will it be where levels of teacher expertise are such that designing learning experiences in science and appropriate assessment tasks are beyond the reach of most teachers. But where it is possible it offers one avenue to reduce the adverse effects of examination backwash on teaching and learning..

Papua New Guinea provides an interesting example of a country which has recently introduced several examination reforms. It is relevant to examine this in a little more detail. In 1982 the lower secondary examination system changed from one based exclusively on internal school assessment moderated by external examination scores to one which combined moderated internal assessment scores with national examination scores.

As part of the changes the syllabus-free items which had been used in the moderating examination were replaced by items which were based on the science syllabus objectives. Internal assessment data are moderated according to school performance on the School Certificate Examination (SCE), held at the end of grade ten, and the results of both components are combined in equal weighting to give an aggregate score which determines final SCE rating on the basis of the national rating allocation; distinction grades are awarded to the top 5 per cent, credit to the next 20 per cent, upper pass to the next 25 per cent, pass to the next 40 per cent and fail to the bottom 10 per cent. Since the examination is norm-referenced the standardized score determining the various grade cut-off marks varies from year to year.

It is not possible to estimate changes in standards of achievement since the abilities of the population of candidates in each year cannot be assumed to remain constant, and the specification of papers varies considerably each year. The cut-off mark range for Upper Pass is between 50 per cent and 60 per cent. Detailed examination reports provide schools with school and provincial level results as well as analyses of the largely multiple-choice exam papers. However, there is little centrally organized follow-up to the report findings such as teacher in-service work on areas of weakness identified by the exam, largely due to lack of resources.

The annual Examination Reports published by MSU provide no information about the quality of school assessment, although correlation data are provided to show the relationship between the exam scores and internal assessment scores. The values for 'r' show wide variation across the country. For example in 1989, values for 'r' ranged from 0.54 to 0.87. Each year well over half of the schools have coefficients greater than 0.71, i.e. where variance in the school's internal assessment marks accounts for more than 50 per cent of variance in the school's examination marks. A high correlation, say of 0.8 or more, might suggest that a school had internally tested similar areas of content and skill to those tested by the national examination, perhaps even using similar forms of assessment such as written multiple-choice tests, or even old exam papers. This can be explored a little more by a further analysis of the inter-correlations for different schools grouped by overall achievement.

A rating index (RI) can be used as an indicator of overall school performance in science. RI is defined as the percentage of students in a school who obtain SCE grades of Upper Pass or better on a nationally examined subject. At a national level 50 per cent of students can be expected to obtain Upper Pass grades or better in science. Thus an individual school with RI of 50 has performed at the national level; while those with RI greater than 50 and less than 50, perform better and worse than average, respectively. Schools at the extreme ends of the exam performance spectrum were categorized as high performance and low performance on the basis of rating index in science.

High performance schools are defined as those whose Rating Index in Science is 70 per cent or more, indicating that 70 per cent or more of the students in these schools were awarded ratings of upper pass or better. In 1985, 11 schools were in this category. Similarly, low performance schools are defined as those with rating indices less than or equal to 30 per cent; in 1985, 14 schools were in this category. In each year except 1989 the low performance schools exhibited higher levels of correlation between the external exam scores and internal assessment scores.

School performance on SCE Science appears to be inversely related to the strength of internal: external correlation. Higher performance schools tend to exhibit lower correlation. The evidence from this analysis suggests that the more closely a school's assessment pattern matches that of the national examination, the less likely the school is to perform well overall. It is possible that schools in the high correlation group (and low performance) concentrate their efforts on the lower taxonomical levels using items from the national exam in classroom assessment.

Those schools which provide more practical work in science and provide more opportunity for a more analytical command of subject matter may test internally a different range of outcomes than those tested by the external examination. If this is true it suggests that teachers who test a variety of content and skills using different types of assessment techniques obtain better overall student results than teachers who confine assessment to the items which appear in public examinations. These observations are tentative since it has not been possible to verify through school case studies whether internal assessment does vary in the way suggested.

Papua New Guinea provides its science teachers with considerable assistance in the construction of classroom tests in science by including item banks of suitable test material in the curriculum package, teachers' guides for classroom assessment techniques, and a degree of training in assessment for teachers participating in annual item-writing workshops for the national examination. The examination reports provide schools with detailed information about item performance and overall examination performance each year at the system level.

Over the past decade a considerable effort has been made to ensure a closer matching of curriculum objectives and the examination items. The science examination now samples more of the content of the curriculum than it did ten years ago, within the restrictions imposed by its written and fixed-response format. There is much greater teacher participation in the final certification of students than there ever was as a result of the continuous assessment.

Yet, many problems remain. It is becoming more and more difficult to generate good quality multiple-choice items testing at the higher process level; written multiple-choice items reflecting the needs of school-leavers are difficult to design and are often rejected because they trial badly; the final selection of examination items after trials have be undertaken is still determined more on the basis of psychometric principles than on the basis of curricular validity; marking of open-response items is unreliable, and this limits the cognitive level at which such items can be set; opportunity to learn varies widely across schools; teachers have limited and training in assessment; the norm-referenced nature of the examination precludes its use in the monitoring of standards of achievement in science. Although teacher assessment contributes 50 per cent of the final student assessment in science the national centrally set examination still has a dominating influence on what is taught and what is assessed in the schools.

Examination systems represent low-cost levers for educational change. Experience from Kenya and elsewhere illustrates how curriculum reform can be reinforced by changes in examination items which closely reflect learning goals that are stressed by the curriculum. Conversely overlooking examination reform in implementing innovations in science education is likely to be counterproductive since, at least at those levels where there are public examinations, curricula in action are likely to reflect the demands of the examination for learning outcomes rather than the learning objectives contained in curriculum materials.

There are several avenues that can be explored to increase the match between examination systems and the curricula they assess and introduce positive feedback that reinforces teaching and learning objectives. These have been explored in the various publications of the Institute of Development Studies Education Project, and are listed below.

i) *Curriculum sensitive item writing*: There is a need to balance technical criteria for item selection with curriculum goals. Item writing is a highly skilled task which should involve teams of curriculum and examination specialists working closely with experienced teachers to develop item banks of examination material. The task is hampered where curriculum goals are poorly defined and where there is a rapid turnover of staff. Properly resourced examination development groups are essential to improving the quality of assessment instruments.

ii) *Provision of diagnostic information*: Examination performance analysis at the individual item level should be fed back to schools to indicate what types of items students are performing badly on. It is insufficient to merely distribute examination reports to schools which only contain data at the highest level of aggregation. Analysis of performance characteristics of low scoring schools and low scoring students can identify which elements of the curriculum are most difficult. It can be used in designing intervention programmes targeted at areas of special need.

iii) *School based examinations*: The introduction of school based examining can extend the range of types of performance assessed, particularly if combined with an appropriate moderation system. This requires careful appraisal of the antecedent conditions which need to be satisfied for this kind of innovation. The additional demands on teacher time and competence should not be underestimated. If statistical moderation is employed examination boards need resourcing for this purpose.

iv) *Regional examination groups*: The possibilities of supporting regional examination systems are worth exploration, especially in larger countries. This might reduce some of the difficulties associated with centrally set written examinations which by their nature cannot reflect regional variations in educational experience. Even where there is a national curriculum, in practice there will be variations in how it is implemented and which material is most valuable to different groups of learners. This could be reflected in different mixes of assessment items which could draw more heavily on the real life experiences of students and enhance curriculum relevance. The additional costs of moving in this direction are significant, but would be small compared to other recurrent costs. The benefits could be considerable.

v) *Standards*: Norm-referenced national examinations can provide little information on changes in standards of achievement in science. There is a need to develop systems for monitoring standards using a more criterion-referenced approach to assessment. Re-analysis of national examination data, where data are retained from year-to-year, has considerable potential in assessing the impact of attempts to improve quality and access in science education.

Teaching and Learning

Many science programmes have implicitly or explicitly adopted a view of science education based on emulating the activities of scientists. Some of the problems this has led to have been widely researched insofar as they arise from mismatches between the level of cognitive development of students and the tasks that they are asked to perform.

Indeed one of the major developments in research on the teaching of science has concerned the application of cognitive development schema to understanding the acquisition of science concepts. An example of this is the well known work by Shayer and Adey. This work developed from the Concepts in Secondary Mathematics and Science Programme at Chelsea College in London. In summary it takes Piagetian schema of cognitive development and uses them to classify different aspects of secondary science teaching in terms of their cognitive demand.

Amongst other things, this work confirmed the view of many teachers in the United Kingdom that the first generation of Nuffield 'O' level curricula were likely to be too demanding of students too early and that a number of specific concepts, like the Mole in chemistry, were shown to require reasoning that was unlikely to be accessible to most of the students that the programmes were intended for.

Indeed when science reasoning tests were applied to a sample of the British school population it transpired that even at the age of 16 years the majority of students were performing at late concrete operational rather than formal operational level in Piagetian terms. This observation reinforced the need to look again at the reasoning levels required in science curricula to ensure that difficulties were not arising from teaching material that was too demanding too soon.

A lively debate has ensued as to whether it is possible to accelerate progress through Piagetian levels through the use of specially designed intervention strategies which encourage students to make leaps in their thinking. This research has not been very conclusive so far. It has exposed some problems superficially interpreted as developmental which may be determined as much by language and familiarity as with terminology.

Thus students may understand the meaning of a variable in an experimental context without being able to use the correct terms to explain what they are doing. The ideas behind the research have been of significance internationally and many similar studies have been conducted in other countries. Adey extended his work to the Caribbean and confirmed that science curriculum development in the Anglophone West Indies has been largely an empirical process, lacking a theoretical psychological framework which might explain low achievement and guide the selection of curricular activities and objectives. His analysis of the West Indies Science Curriculum (WISC) determined the stages of cognitive development that seem to be necessary to succeed in each of its activities.

The data revealed that few of the students reached the stage of formal operations before the fourth year of secondary education, whereas many WISC activities seem to demand formal operational thinking. Nyiti, working in Tanzania with children in the 8-14 age range on conservation tasks on substance, weight and volume, found that while performance improved with age, surprisingly formal schooling had no independent effect. This could be as much a comment on the effectiveness of the schools attended in assisting the development of science constructs as on the stability of the underlying developmental process.

Some cross cultural studies illustrate how concept acquisition may take place at different rates between populations. Dasen worked with children aged 6-14 years old from Canadian Eskimo, Australian Aborigine and Ivory Coast African cultural backgrounds. He found that nomadic, hunting, subsistence-economy people develop spatial concepts more rapidly than do sedentary, agriculturalist groups, whereas the latter attain concepts of conservation of quantity, weight and volume more rapidly than do the former. Shea reviewed research dealing with problem-solving abilities amongst Papua New Guineans using individual intelligence tests, group intelligence tests, achievement tests, conservation measures, classificatory skills, and formal operational thinking.

Comparisons are made with the performance of Papua New Guinean children and adults with people elsewhere, and with foreigners resident in Papua New Guinea. Shea notes important differences within Papua New Guinea related in particular to schooling and language culture-group. By contrast to some previous conclusions about the cognitive skill development of Papua New Guineans, he concludes that while there are differences between some Papua New Guinean groups and groups from English-speaking countries in problem-solving performance, developmental patterns appear to be similar. Thus, educated Papua New Guineans achieve the highest levels of formal thinking though not necessarily at the same rates.

Otaala and Ohuche accumulated research on the cognitive development of African children and Petersen reports on a South East Asian project to establish patterns of cognitive development in the region. Others have examined science process skills and cognitive preference styles in Singapore and Malaysia, spatial ability and depth perception amongst Nigerian secondary students and the mental maps of Jamaican children to name but a few studies with links to the literature on cognitive development and science education.

The other prominent strand in research on teaching and learning develops from the work of 'constructivists' who argue that science education should start from the child's understanding of natural phenomena, not from attempts to emulate the reasoning of professional scientists, who have developed adult understandings of causality, formal reasoning etc.

The strategies and antecedent experience scientists bring to problem solving are unlikely to be the same as those mobilized by lower secondary children. Most of the research on students learning science suggests that students bring their own conceptions of science to explaining the natural world.

Ausubel's theory of cognition argues that: '... the most important single factor influencing learning is what the learner already knows". The conceptions that students bring to science education are often misconceptions. Moreover it seems that they are often resistant to direct experience which contradicts them and therein lies the challenge to teaching and learning. By way of example we might consider some common misconceptions that are held by many children-and adults.

Metals, glass and stone are generally thought to be colder materials than wood and fabrics with a lower surface temperature because they feel cold; pressure in liquids and gases is thought to act 'downwards'; electrical currents are thought to be 'used up' by devices in a circuit. The fallacy of these ideas is easy to demonstrate and many people who hold these views have seen this done. They have often also been taught the "correct' facts but the beliefs continue to exist because underlying structures are resilient enough to resist change.

In a recent evaluation of an environmental and agricultural science project in Zimbabwe one of the most difficult units identified was that which dealt with the Sun and the Cosmos. Why was this so difficult for most teachers? Part of the reason seems to lie in unfamiliar terminology; but another lies in strength of everyday 'commonsense' beliefs drawn from traditional cosmology that simply do not utilise the same frameworks to explain the changes of the seasons and the disposition of the planets. What the alternative conceptions of students are in different countries remains to be fully researched. Some literature already exists and is discussed in relation to cultural contexts.

Few countries have anything approaching a comprehensive research base that would be sufficient to design curricula that built outward from students existing understandings. It would be dangerous to assume these are the same everywhere though there are likely to be commonalties between countries. The constructivists have a powerful argument that this kind of research needs to be undertaken widely if learning difficulties in science are to be better understood and more effective teaching and learning strategies planned.

Approaches to Science Teaching

Statements of desirable approaches to the teaching of science can be found in many different official publications. Typical of the last two decades are statements like the following taken from teaching notes for an environmental science curriculum in Africa. Science should: "... develop an attitude of self reliance ...based on understanding skills and confidence in man's ability to solve problems himself. It is not the purpose of the course that pupils should be made to learn large numbers of facts, though basic knowledge is important. It is much more important that pupils develop an active and enquiring attitude towards their environment and this is only possible if the pupils do experiments, keep records of observations and draw conclusions from clear discussion sessions"..

But equally commonly criticisms are made concerning the persistence of recall dominated teaching and learning that stresses factual knowledge and largely ignores higher levels of cognitive outcomes. "Those of us who are concerned about education in Africa and indeed in the third world countries in general, recognise rote learning as our greatest set back in educational transactions". The intended stress on practical activity, on enquiry, on process skills and problem solving is clear.

Avalos and Haddad in their reviews of research on teacher effectiveness in developing countries claim that discovery learning approaches are likely to have a significant effect on higher levels of cognitive outcomes. Also of relevance is the finding from teacher effectiveness research that didactic methods of teaching seem to be appropriate for low level cognitive skills whereas discovery or problem-solving approaches are better for higher cognitive skills. If these things are so, there are important implications for science teaching.

There have been a number of attempts to research the use of discovery approaches in developing countries, and much discussion on the appropriateness of such methods in the context of preferred teaching styles, cultural norms and availability of resources. Little of the research seems to consider the relationships between teaching method used and the content of the science lessons however, nor is it usually able to reach firm conclusions about its relative effectiveness since adequate control groups are rarely available.

Even where it appears effective, the generalisability of the experience is often in question since most frequently it is selected groups of teachers who are involved in undertaking experiments with teaching methods. Some relevant studies relating to the relative efficacy of guided discovery and activity based teaching approaches are summarized below.

Mulopo and Fowler Compared achievement, understandings about science and the scientific attitudes of learners at the concrete and formal levels of cognitive development taught with different approaches in Zambia. Subjects were an equally weighted sample of concrete and formal reasoners in 11th grade chemistry classes assigned to one of two teaching method groups for 10 weeks. Results showed that among formal reasoners discovery method teaching was more effective than traditional methods for understanding science; for concrete reasoners the mode of instruction made no difference; overall the traditional group outperformed the discovery group in achievement but the discovery group developed what were judged more favourable attitudes to science.

Okpala and Onocha used experimental and control groups and ascertained that students taught physics concepts through active enquiry have less difficulties in learning the concepts than students taught the same concepts through vicarious enquiry methods. The authors recommended more active involvement of students in laboratory practical work.

In a Nigerian study by Ehindero which argues that the lack of formal operational thought in students might be due to a similar lack in teachers, compounded by expository styles of teaching. A sample of pre-service secondary science teachers were grouped into formal and concrete operators and observed. Judgements were made on how well concrete and formal operational sub-groups realized their teaching intentions in lessons involving concrete and formal concepts. The study found no significant difference between the groups with respect to the teaching of concrete concepts but found significant difference in favour of formal operational student teachers on the teaching of formal concepts.

Looking across 14 countries Kelly used scales derived from student responses to describe the science learning environments of 14 year-old students. He found that the best science achievement occurred in countries which combine exploratory and authoritarian teaching styles. Within countries, exploratory styles were again associated with high science achievement although the relationship was less strong. These tentative findings, the author cautions, need confirmation in an experimental study since there is a question over the reliability of the reported styles.

Williams and Buseri paint an all too familiar picture of contemporary science teaching. They analysed 54 science lessons in Nigeria using the Science Teaching Observation Schedule. It was found that an expository style dominated. An 18 category explanation appraisal schedule was developed-an instrument for the analysis of teaching effectiveness in the expository mode. Lessons were analysed in two clusters: the fast pedallers and the slow pedallers. The fast pedaller lessons displayed high incidence of what were judged ineffective attributes such as discontinuities in argument and vagueness in explanation, and were considered to be less coherent and less effective at exposition.

Aminah Ayob examined the use of group work in science teaching in Malaysia. She found that although group work is widely advocated and is often practised, there is little careful consideration of its purposes, and active management of classrooms, to ensure its effectiveness. As a result talk within groups was mainly task-oriented and at a low cognitive level and interactions were usually between two students, not amongst the groups as a whole. Those who took the most active roles were higher achieving.

Conflicts between the need to ensure that adequate content is mastered on the one hand and that problem solving skills are developed on the other recur. Razali's Malaysian study has argued that chemistry teachers feel that mastery of knowledge in chemistry was the most important aspect influencing students to continue to study chemistry; in contrast college instructors viewed the acquisition of traits such as study skills and strategies for learning as the most important factor.

Adi's survey of Indonesian teachers, administrators and teacher educators regarding the in-service needs of science teachers reports that while teachers and teacher-educators perceived 'mastery of subject area content' as most important, administrators perceived 'use and management of laboratory teaching for teaching-learning process' as the most important.

Mehl and Lockhead's report on a study designed to investigate the learning problems of disadvantaged South

Africans suggests that selective attention to particular concepts that are poorly understood is a teaching strategy that can pay dividends. The study was motivated by concern about the large numbers of students who were poorly equipped to meet the academic requirements of first-year university courses in science related disciplines. An analysis of interviews yielded a list of deficient cognitive capabilities. Techniques were developed to compensate for these deficiencies; the strategy required for the use of a specific concept was developed as the concept was taught. The new approach was trailed on a controlled experimental group of first year university physics students. Results for the use of the concepts showed a 30 per cent improvement in favour of the experimental group. The study concluded that there seemed to be three effective approaches to teaching scientific thinking:

(i) teaching thinking free of specific content;

(ii) integrating thinking skills with content by providing thinking strategies to give more meaningful access to the content of a discipline;

(iii) determining the requisite thought processes for understanding using concepts and laws, and then making these explicit in the development of relevant curriculum materials.

Chiang studied effects on achievement and growth of scientific ability of Taiwanese eighth grade students who were taught physics using an individualized instruction (II) format as opposed to those taught using conventional instruction (CI). Data were gathered using an IQ test, a reasoning ability test, a physics aptitude test, midterm and final achievement tests, and a follow-up test on the growth of scientific ability.Results indicated that II was superior to CI on midterm and final achievement measures and in the growth of scientific ability. Merebah compared the effects of a co-operative learning method called Teams-Games-Tournaments (TOT), and Traditional Teacher-centred method (TTC) on science achievement, attitudes and social interaction in random sample of classes in intermediate schools in Riyadh. It was found that TGT was more effective than TTC in enhancing science achievement and that this was independent of ability grouping. The problems with drawing conclusions from the literature are obvious. Without knowing a great deal more than is usually reported it is difficult to know how much confidence to have in the findings. Further what may be the case in one school system/school/ classroom or with one teacher and group of students is not necessarily replicable in other circumstances. Which is not to say that nothing can be learned from the examples above, but rather to urge caution, and the constant need for validation of findings for the circumstances under which it is hoped to apply them.

Practical Activity

The extent to which practical activity has been seen as an integral part of most new science programmes in developing countries is clear from the reports of the 9th and 10th International Clearing House on Science and Mathematics Curriculum Development. Haddad and Za'rour reached a number of conclusions amongst the most prominent of which are that practical activities in science are important, especially at primary level, and with less able students, and that they have a specific and limited role to play in the achievement of the broad objectives of science education found in most curricula. They argue that practical activities need to be selected and restricted to those areas which cannot be treated by more cost effective methods; that activities do not generally require highly sophisticated equipment and extensive laboratory facilities; that there are some teaching strategies that can substitute in part for some of the practical activity currently undertaken.

Not all these observations are uncontentious. Thus there is evidence that less able students in Malaysia do not find practical activity nearly so attractive as more able students and that it fails to motivate them. This in itself does not demonstrate that particular types of practical work could not be helpful in this respect, it does seem to suggest that the experience of practical work less able students have is not of a kind that stimulates them. Nevertheless, many of Za'rour and Haddad's suggestions are well made.

In countries which have severe resource shortages practical activity in a conventional laboratory environment is generally unsustainable. For example, Mhlanga's study of 12 secondary schools in Malawi found that because of the acute shortage of laboratory equipment about half of the practical work is carried out by the teacher and the other half by students in groups; classes are too large to see what is happening in teacher demonstrations and the groups are too big to allow everyone to have an opportunity to handle the apparatus. And this is in a system with one of the lowest transitionary rates from primary into secondary schools in Africa where total enrolment is a small proportion of the cohort. Where resources are more generously provided under-utilization is not uncommon.

It is not difficult to find upper secondary laboratories in use for a minority of the school day, for reasons divided between the availability of consumable material, the serviceability of equipment, and the willingness and capability of teachers to organise practical work. And to compound the difficulties much of what constitutes practical work is reduced in practice to demonstration, or large group experiments with very limited participation by most students, directed towards the completion of laboratory accounts in standardized form which require very limited intellectual input.

It is self-evident that practical activities have high costs compared to classroom based teaching both in terms of equipment and time. These costs are both capital and recurrent. It is also obvious that the effectiveness of practical activity will depend greatly on the educational outcomes to which it is directed as well as the manner in which it is conducted.

If assessments do not test the skins which are likely to be developed this does not mean that nothing is achieved. On the other hand little may be achieved if practical work is reduced to the ritualistic following of instructions to replicate well established results. Under these circumstances much of the value of practical activity may be lost if its purpose collapses into simply verifying expected outcomes. Students may learn to play the game of getting the right answer for the experiment rather than appreciate anything about the design of tests of hypotheses and the sources of error that need to be understood and eliminated before test results can be confidently accepted.

One aspect of practical activity to which much attention has been directed is the various forms of low cost provision of materials and source books of ideas for improvization, often using science centres to promote this approach.

These have been developed and tried in many countries with some measure of success. However it is still the exception rather than the rule to find large proportions of the equipment used produced by improvization. The reasons for this are related to teacher motivation and access to suitable advice.

They are also linked to problems of financing that often make it difficult to find even small amounts of non-salary funds at the school level. Where this is so and teachers' salaries are low it is difficult to stimulate much improvization if the costs fall on individual teachers. Other low cost options, like the Minilabs available in Sri Lanka, provide lower cost options than fully found laboratories, which enable a considerable amount of practical science to be taught.

Cultural Contexts

The cultural contexts for science education differ substantially and there has been a considerable amount of work on how science and scientific ideas are perceived in different cultures. Much of the earlier work is summarized by Wilson. Many studies on different aspects of culture are reviewed covering economic, social, political, religious and philosophical differences and their implications for the curriculum. This valuable bibliography accumulates material on variations in the assumptions and practices of science education that are to some degree culturally bounded.

In a seminal paper Horton has explored the interrelationships and misunderstandings that exist concerning the relationships between traditional and scientific belief systems in African societies. This thought provoking piece argues that the differences between African religious thinking and 'Westem' theoretical reasoning are often not nearly so great as they appear to some who mistake a language distant from their own as no language at all. Horton identifies key differences in reasoning which he locates around the concepts of closed and openness. These he elaborates in terms of:

"(i) differences connected with perception of alternatives, i.e:
  - magical versus non-magical attitude to words;
  - ideas bound to occasions versus ideas bound to ideas;
  - unreflecdve versus reflective thinking;
  - mixed versus segregated motives, and

(ii) differences linked to the interpretation of threats to an established body of knowledge i.e.:
  - protective versus destructive attitude towards;
  - established theory;
  - divination versus diagnosis;
  - existence versus non-existence of experimental method;
  - confession versus non-confession of ignorance;
  - coincidence, chance and probability;
  - protective/destructive attitude to category systems;
  - passage of time as bad or good."

These differences he argues are characteristic of different cultural perspectives that inform different ways of viewing the world. Their existence is of obvious significance to science teaching, since much curriculums development is predicated on the assumptions of a Westem rationalist perspective on the various dimensions. To the extent that this is not held by teachers and students, or at least not held consistently, there are likely to be misunderstandings, different interpretations of the same pieces of data, and difficulties in internalising concepts that contradict widely held belief systems. Horton's work suggests these problems are not confined to traditional belief systems but may be exacerbated by them.

Another very readable investigation of culture and schooling is provided by Musgrave though this is not specific to science. This explores culture and thinking, the social basis for rationality, the relationships between education and the social order and the implications on the curriculum. It demonstrates again how different belief systems can have profound implications on how curricula are received and experienced by students who do not share the same world view as that assumed in curriculum materials. Thus giving just one example Musgrave argues that gemeinschaft societies are very different to gesellsclut societies. In the former apparently 'irrational' beliefs can flourish since the mechanisms to undermine them are weak; in the latter reason has more powerful tools to explore the natural world.

Adu-Ampona has explored the difficulties of bringing Western science to African children whose traditional background places emphasis on myth and superstition, and encourages unquestioning belief in the statements of people in authority. Sawyerr deepens this discussion in a study of the role of traditional beliefs in the teaching and learning of science in sierra Leone. He suggests that traditional African world views, on such matters as causality and animism, strongly interfere with the learning of science and are widely diffused amongst secondary school pupils in sierra Leone.

Mundangepfupfu has examined the influence of magico-traditional scientific beliefs on science education in an attempt to reconcile their existence with rational thinking. She argues that students can learn science without rejecting magico-traditional beliefs, because science is understood through an evidential belief system whereas traditional magic is understood through a non-evidential belief system.

Ogunniyi has shown that literate and non-literate Nigerians often hold both scientific and traditional notions of the world and cosmos simultaneously. Holding both views was evident regardless of the status of the respondent, though persons who had taken a course in the history and philosophy of science were shown to have a preference for the scientific cosmology.

Kay in his study of curriculum innovation in Kenya, notes that new curricula encourage attitudes of individual initiative and personal decision-making which are strongly at variance with the collectivism and consultation that is fundamental to Kenyan children's cultural heritage. He argues that very little attention has been paid to this 'hidden conflict' by those responsible for 'modernising' Kenya's curriculum.

Another aspect of learning conditions that Maddock draws attention to where there may be cross cultural differences relates to the distance seen to exist between school knowledge and that in the community. High school students in Papua New Guinea predicted scores for uneducated villagers which were significantly lower than the scores actually obtained by the villagers. The students also thought that village people were ignorant and could not be expected to show a scientific approach to things. In later work Maddock argues that Science curriculum reform in developing countries must take a much more fundamental account of the cultural bases of the societies which they are intended to serve. The adaptation of curricula originating in another country is unlikely to be satisfactory if the cultural and linguistic gap between the two societies is too great. The starting point must be the preexistent knowledge, practices and belief patterns of the society itself.

Another aspect of teaching and learning that has a cross cultural dimension and has received a lot of attention relates to language issues. This has cross curricula and medium of instruction dimensions and also a concern with language in science teaching. For example, Gardner investigated non-technical vocabulary difficulties among high school students in three regions of the Philippines using word lists arranged alphabetically and by difficulty-level to establish to what extent misunderstood words hampered communication in science. Johnstone undertook similar work in Papua New Guinea and Isa and Maskill researched differences in science word meanings in Scotland and Malaysia where Scottish Integrated Science had been adapted. Prophet attributes observed discrepancy between curriculum-in-action and curriculum-planned to second language learning problems and cultural context in Botswana.

"The most striking aspect of the science lessons observed in the schools was the passive nature of the pupils. The majority of work involved 'teacher talk' using either a lecture technique, or a simple question and answer routine that demanded only basic recall from the pupils, often as single words or simple sentences".

Strevins surveyed the language problems encountered by science educators and by learners when the language of instruction is not the mother tongue, and describes a convergence of interest between science teachers who teach in a foreign language, and foreign language teachers who teach learners whose principal aims include the learning of science. He distinguishes between linguistic dissonances which originate from the system of language, and sociolinguistic dissonance

Keats, Keats and Rafael investigated the importance of language in the acquisition of the concept of weight with two groups of S-year old Malaysian children, one group being bilingual in Malay and English, the other in Chinese and English. The results support Piaget's contention that language plays only a minor role in the acquisition of cognitive structures. The National University of Lesotho (held a workshop convened to analyse language problems faced in schools where pupils whose mother tongue is Sesotho are learning in English. The report provides a Summary of the issues facing both teachers and pupils of science and mathematics in the context of English as a second language. Razak has explored language issues in science education concentrating particularly on textbooks and reading problems. This illustrates another strand of concern. His study attributes science learning problems to widespread reading difficulties which are compounded by inadequacies in textbook design, structure, vocabulary and editorial procedures.

Any discussion of cultural contexts should consider gender issues cross culturally. The disadvantages girls experience in science education, though fairly universal in their incidence, may not have the same causes in different societies. An interesting study from Botwsana by Duncan reports on the influence of gender stereotypes on science performance among adolescents at the junior school level. Botswana is in fact one of few countries in the developing world where female participation rates are higher than male ones. Her nationwide survey of mid-secondary students in 27 schools supports her claim that the school learning process not only encourages gender differences in performance, but also operates different characteristics as it impinges on girls and boys.

School science appears gender-typed by both boys and girls as a 'male' subject. This impinges on students' attitudes towards the subject and as a result on their performance. Girls who favour divided family roles and have a feminine self-image are more inclined to see science as a male activity. Girls who see science and/or school science as a male area of activity generally have less positive attitudes to science and perform poorly. The study found that gender typing was considerably more salient in the achievement process for girls than for boys. The study found no significant differences in the extent to which boys and girls in Botswana gender-type occupations. Only 6 (less than 1 per cent) of girls in the sample aspired to technical occupations (outside medicine) whereas 18 per cent of boys aspire to jobs requiring academic science knowledge. Two processes were claimed to influence occupational aspirations: socioeconomic factors which influence job status; and gender which supports distinctions in job aspirations. Duncan maintains that the gender dimension is more fundamental than class dimension and takes the view that male and female cultures should be viewed as separate cultures, representing distinctive group identities, adaptive patterns and world views. The implications that Duncan draws from the study are that changes in science teaching practice are needed to favour more participation of girls particularly in practical activities in mixed classes, more relevance of curriculum to family life is necessary and more encouragement has to be provided girls to take up non-traditional roles if their participation is to be improved.

It is probably more difficult to generalise about teaching and learning in science education than about almost any other aspect. There is no best way of teaching science, suitable for a multitude of different purposes with students from radically different cultural and linguistic backgrounds. There remain many areas where there are strong differences of opinion amongst educationalists concerning which methods are most likely to result in which outcomes. And always there is the problem that what may work with a specific combination of circumstances may not be generalisable at the system level across many institutions with all their idiosyncrasies.

— Whatever the variation between cultures the evidence there is seems to suggest that cognitive development patterns are broadly similar. To the extent that this is true they place real constraints on the rate at which students can be expected to master the basic ideas of science and progress to more complex abstract teaming. The fact that some children acquire these earlier than others challenges curriculum developers to design pathways to understand science that are sufficiently flexible to allow all children to progress at a rate appropriate to their level of cognitive development. It is the planners' job to ensure that this is feasible and all science students are not locked into programmes that contain too many ideas inaccessible to the majority at their stage of development.

— It is a compelling pedagogic stance to proceed from the mental schema of the child to build science ideas from the explanations and understandings that are already present, and to treat apparent errors as possible misconceptions that have to be understood and resolved, rather than mistakes that simply require rectification. To do this is time consuming, especially if it is followed up at the individual student level by teachers.

— The planners' problem is to consider how feasible this is and how much strategic support for curriculum development and research on students' learning can be used to improve quality and achievement. · Innovations in teaching and learning can make a difference. Encouraging some experimentation, and channelling resources towards it, can offer motivational benefits to groups of teachers as well as achievement gains for students. Practically, this will always be an activity for a minority of teachers. But they, and the school structures, the professional associations and informal networks that disseminate new practices can be supported at low cost.

— The role of practical work needs careful examination. If it cannot be provided in conventional form to the majority of students alternatives should be considered. This is a difficult teaching and learning problem for science teachers to address, particularly those without an imaginative approach to their teaching. It win always be difficult to attribute learning gains to the presence or absence of practical activity, especially where the quality of that practical activity is not evaluated. Pedagogically the case is strong, but far too little effort has been invested in linking learning outcomes to the kind of practical activity that is realistically possible.

— The problems of are clearly bound to the cultural contexts in which science education takes place. Thus, although the developmental aspects of cognition seem to have widespread relevance to planning teaching and learning it is dangerous to assume that research on these in one country is directly transferable to another. The conceptions and misconceptions that students bring to the study of science will also vary from place to place. What constitutes effective teaching methods will depend on the learning outcomes which are desired-it may be that the new methods detailed above are better for certain students, under certain circumstances given appropriate assessment of learning outcomes. But the didactic approaches that seem most common also have their merits, not least that they are the ones many teachers are demonstrably happiest to employ, and it is clearly not the case that such methods can or should be abandoned indiscriminately.

Teacher Eduation

Teachers are the most expensive element in the recurrent budget for school systems. It is therefore important to try to reassure policy-makers that money spent on improving the quality of teachers is money well spent. In the late 1960s and early 1970s influential reports such as the Plowden and Coleman reports and IEA studies raised some doubt about the value of teacher training in developed countries. Surveys commissioned by the World Bank echoed similar concerns for the developing countries apparently showing that teacher certification and academic achievement were unlikely to be important determinants of student achievement.

An updated study five years later conceded that teacher qualifications were only important at upper secondary in some subject areas. These findings prompted a flurry of research activity which appeared to come to opposite conclusions to the World Bank. For instance, teacher credentials were particularly important for subject areas requiring specialized skins and knowledge, such as mathematics and science. Heyneman and Loxley re-examined the International Association of Educational Achievement data on the relative importance of school and home influences upon science achievement in high and low income countries.

The effects of school and teacher quality on science achievement in developing nations were greater than previously demonstrated and that home background was relatively less important. Otewa investigated the contribution of professional qualifications to the teaching of Biology in 10 government and 10 Harambee schools representing 44 per cent of the secondary schools in one district of Kenya. The study used survey questionnaires administered to curriculum developers, head teachers, biology teachers, laboratory assistants and students in form four. Findings from the survey indicate that the more professionally qualified the teacher in a given school the better the performance of students in that school and the less difficulty the teacher has with the curriculum material. However, since all the teachers in the Harambee schools were untrained the differences observed could be due to school effects.

Guthrie's review of studies on the effects of teacher education criticized the research methods used in the World Bank studies but notes that it did stimulate a more careful analysis of teacher training than might otherwise have taken place. Husén et al., regarded the question of the value of training as having already been answered by the cumulative body of research but "... the question that remains unanswered is how, and because of what qualin'es and in what contexts do teachers make a difference ".

The latest IEA data suggest that more post secondary education, more preparation for science education, greater experience, subject specialization, membership of a professional association, and reading science journals are all associated with teachers who can promote effective learning.

The most recent studies of teacher education in developing countries notes that it is only recently that research has concerned itself with the deeper question oil how the training process makes a difference to teacher effectiveness . She posits that the reason there have been few studies is because of difficulties with research methods. For instance, with regard to social factors influencing teaching effectiveness it is possible that what counts as authoritarianism in one context may not be so classified in another .

Avalos and Haddad call for more research on the differences in social contexts within which the teacher operates and for teacher effectiveness research which makes fewer assumptions about the nature of the relationship between various variables, and which makes more use of case study research methods. Sharpes argues for a multidimensional approach to research on teacher education which stresses the importance of economic, political and social factors in understanding the relationship between teacher education and national development. Others see part of the problem as residing in the previous educational experience of those who become science teachers.

In their review of scientific and technological education in developing countries Husén and Postlethwaite contend that the discipline-centred, inward looking curricula offered at university level in many countries have an alienating effect on individuals with respect to the contribution they can make to national development. This has serious implications for potential science teachers who take such courses. They identify some attempts to include the history of science and the role of science in national development in science curricula at tertiary level to address this problem. Trends in curriculum development at school level imply a stronger role for teachers in the promotion of scientific literacy and environmental education than in the past. This in turn has implications for the way teachers are trained and the kind of science they study at higher levels.

The paucity of available research on teacher education is noted by Dove in her review of teacher education in developing countries. This is particularly critical in science. The bibliography to her review contains 362 entries, only three which are directly related to the training of science teachers. This is a particular cause for concern given the widespread dissemination of new views of science education related to deeper understanding of cognitive development and the interpretations and mental maps that students bring to science learning. This new view is filtering through the science education community and influencing future directions amongst the professional community of curriculum designers.

Without adequate infusion into the training of teachers and sensitive adaptation and development within the constraints of national systems there is a danger that the potential benefits will be lost as half understood, or misunderstood, catchwords. Curricular implications will remain in curriculum developers' rhetoric, but not teachers' practice.

The Second International Science Study (SISS) conducted by the International Association for the Evaluation of Educational Achievement (IEA) is providing a wealth of data on science teaching in developing countries which has implications for the selection and training of science teachers. Most countries apart from China (45 per cent), Singapore (38 per cent) and the Philippines (10 per cent) have a majority of male science teachers, reaching over 90 per cent in Ghana. Science teachers are most frequently between 30 and 40 years old, with between three and five years post secondary education with up to four years of that specifically focused on science. Teaching loads are about 14 hours per week, with about 80 per cent of that time devoted to science teaching.

Most of the teachers surveyed had only about two days in-service training per year. In most cases teachers claim to spend as much time on lesson preparation and marking as they do on teaching. While over 50 per cent of science lessons tend to be taught in the laboratory there is wide variation in the time allocated to practical work, especially in those countries where lack of science equipment is reported. Length of teaching experience is greatest in Papua New Guinea (14.8 years) and least in Ghana (6.3 years). Science teachers in this sample have between 0.8 and 3.9 years of post secondary science education on average. There are a number of studies which provide further information on the qualifications of science teachers. To cite just two, Jain presents an account of the qualifications of biology teachers in middle and secondary schools in India.

Middle school teachers are expected to hold a first degree and a one-year education qualification; however only 10 per cent actually have such qualifications. A total of 75 per cent of secondary biology teachers are either graduates or have post-graduate qualifications. Wilson, using IEA data for the upper secondary level (Population 3) notes that in 1983 the 'average' science teacher in National High Schools is expatriate, male, between 30 and 45 years old, with 10 years or more experience and tertiary qualification. These teachers spent 94 per cent of their time teaching science.

Most belonged to (foreign) science teacher associations. They teach classes of about 25 students and set about 5 hours homework each week (the schools are residential). The most popular teaching methods used by these teachers are reported as question and answer sessions and small group practical work, the latter occupies about one third of total class time, and assessment is largely by means of multiple-choice items. Thus there are wide variations between countries in teacher characteristics and, it must not be forgotten, within countries between schools and regions.

The indications from the IEA study are that there are generally more males amongst science teachers. However this is from a very small sample of countries and needs to be interpreted in terms of the proportion of males in the teaching force as a whole. Circumstantial evidence suggests that more often than not science teachers are disproportionately male, especially in the physical sciences. This follows from much smaller proportions of girls studying these subjects to high levels. It has been the experience of a number of developing countries that as economic development has taken place and created more job opportunities teaching has become a more female profession.

There is a large body of research that draws attention to the cultural interface between teachers in the culture in which they work. This raises issues of special significance for science education teacher training since science education is arguably culturally alien to the communities in many developing countries. Some significant dimensions to these problems are identified by the authors cited below and this extends the discussion of cultural contexts.

The first group of studies address the problems that arise from conflict between rationale scientific belief systems and traditional ones, and where teachers are expected to adopt teaching styles dissonant with their traditional roles.

Whittle contends that traditional tribal education in Africa was primarily for the preservation of society. But reforms in science education have meant that teachers have had to learn how to foster children's interest in science, and how to conduct an enquiry-based experimental approach, which is at variance with their own dominant role in the classroom that teachers, and the children, instinctively expect from their tradition and upbringing. This situation poses a major challenge to science education in Africa, he argues, which requires some radical rethinking of the cultural and environmental aspects of science teaching. Similarly, Sawyerr describes how the new science curricula in sierra Leone required new teacher roles and instructional approaches which were not sympathetic to existing traditions. Cole, also working in West Africa, has pointed to the failure of many government initiated development programmes to improve the health and social conditions of their citizens. He attributes this to the antagonism of the people, arising from conflict between traditional and 'scientific' culture. He argues that it is essential to bridge this gap by teaching science in a way that accepts, rather than seeks to discredit, traditional culture.

A recent study of Nigerian secondary students by Jegede and Okebukola found evidence that science instruction which deliberately involves the discussion of sociocultural views about science concepts engendered more positive attitudes towards the study of science. Rather than attempting to radically change traditional teaching styles Guthrie argued for being more realistic about using existing teaching methods in a more creative way. His study in Papua New Guinea on teaching styles, though not specifically concerned with science, found evidence from interviews with secondary school inspectors that a formalistic teaching style dominated at secondary level. He argues that there may be very sound cultural reasons for this preferred teaching style and, if so, the style anticipated in new curriculums materials should match the empirical reality of teacher behaviour, rather than the aspirations of curriculum developers and teacher trainers orientated towards external value systems.

Approaches to teaching and teacher education in developing countries are more widely influenced by historical practices than by grounded research on teacher capabilities and needs. An implication may be that radically new approaches should not be introduced without very careful consideration of the consequences of their misuse in terms of continued adherence to traditional teaching methods. There are political and religious dimensions to the problems of science teacher preparation that merit consideration. McDonald and Rogan describe the implementation of an innovatory science education project in the Ciskei region of South Africa at a time in history when the education department was held in disrepute by the majority of students and teachers. The project raises the political as well as cultural dimensions of change. In this case:

> "Teachers found themselves in a difficult situation, caught between the demands of their pupils for political change, SEP's advocacy of educational change and the government's resistance to political change and suspicion of having its authority diluted by outside educational change agents."

From a different perspective Sharpes has considered the training of science teachers in some Islamic societies. He argues that the spirit of scientific enquiry is at variance with the politics of social control in some Islamic countries. He suggests that the agnostic rationalism of Western science presents a threat to Islamic belief. In such countries education and science must therefore be protected and rigourously controlled through religious doctrine leading to possible contradictions as seen from Western science educators perspectives. In his review of the preparation of science teachers for the African environment Bajah argues the need for teachers who will become agents of social and economic change. He discusses the implications of this for the pre-service and in-service training of science teachers and how these need to change to overcome embedded resistances to transformation. Brophy and Dudley explore how the shift in emphasis from academic science to scientific literacy has met resistance from parents and teachers, partly as a result of perceived dilution of the academic curriculum to strengthen its vocational elements. The paper discusses attempts to overcome these problems in Malaysia and the Seychelles.

Yet another aspect of culture which impinges on teacher preparation is highlighted by Krishna. He draws attention to the historical development of India's textbook culture which ties the teacher to a prescribed textbook. He defines the term textbook culture as

(i) teaching in all subjects based on the textbook prescribed by the state authorities;

(ii) the teacher having no freedom to choose what to teach;

(iii) resources other than the prescribed textbook not being available;

(iv) student assessment being based only on material in the textbook.

Dominant expectations of the role learning materials play in science education may therefore also be in opposition to innovations that seek to place the learners understanding and needs at the centre of the lesson planning.

Issues on the interface between orthodoxies of science education and how to teach science, whether of a conventional or innovatory character, need to be absorbed into the teacher training process. Schools are generally associated with the modern sector in developing countries and science has perhaps the greatest potential of all school subjects to alienate students from their culture. If teachers are to be effective it will be their job to bridge the gap between value systems and interpret science ideas in a meaningful way to those with other value systems. This is difficult when consciousness of the problem is high, it win be unlikely to happen if training does not address the issues. This is not a new observation, the number of times that it has been made suggests it is still a problem that has not been solved. Thus Dyasi, as long ago as 1977, discussed the competencies needed by science teachers, particularly for the implementation of innovative curriculum projects associated with the Science Education Programme for Africa. He argued that the science teacher should be concerned with the relationship between the culture of science and the culture of the child, and teacher education should therefore help him or her to develop skins of operation in these cross-cultural encounters.

There has been considerable criticism of college pre-service training programmes in many countries. Amongst the most common concerns are curriculum overload, inappropriate pedagogical models, irrelevance, and cost. Rapid expansion has led to sharp increases in student populations which have resulted in crash courses for the training of science teachers. At the same time new school curricula imported and/or adapted from overseas have been making extensive demands on the skins of science teachers.

Among the problems he identifies relevant to teacher education are:

— the poor preparation of teachers who teach the new programmes;

— the lack of motivation among teachers;

— the rapid rate of teacher transfer;

— the shortage of qualified science teachers.

The new science curricula demand teachers who are capable of using instructional procedures that are supportive of the new emphasis on 'science-for-all'. This implies less discipline-centred pre-service training courses and less emphasis on university level qualifications. It would be better to prepare students for teaching using more realistic and relevant science courses closely matched to the abilities of students and the demands of the school science curriculum, than to staff the schools with dropouts or those who failed the more traditional science courses offered by universities.

Kamariah argues for closer collaboration between science educators and science teachers and more emphasis on increasing the relevance of training to teachers' needs. He compared needs expressed by Malaysian secondary teachers and by trainers and found discrepancies were helpful in understanding problems that currently arise in the training system. In the same vein Ojo offers a critique from the perspective of a college lecturer which calls for a change in the organisational structure of academic departments in universities and colleges in the direction of greater integration of instructional activity in the training of science teachers to reflect a much wider interpretation of science. Ojo is extremely critical of what he terms the parochial compartmentalization of teaching in many institutions and calls for less restrictive entry requirements and more emphasis on course systems based on schools of study rather than subject systems based on faculty or departmental training.

The debate on the balance between academic and pedagogic knowledge is extended by Guthrie who reports that secondary school inspectors in Papua New Guinea rated diploma trained secondary teachers high in instructional and classroom management skins but low on subject knowledge; whereas degree holders were rated high on subject knowledge but low on professional attitude. He reports much less attrition from the diploma course which supplies the bulk of secondary teachers, and argues for a modularized diploma course which could later be upgraded to degree level.

Bunker and Palmer note a trend towards moving teachers away from single subject training courses to more specialist training where science teachers can specialise in more than one science subject. Teachers not only have to have personal knowledge of subject matter but also they need to know how to represent that knowledge for others. Wilson et al based on research in the USA, argue that research on teacher knowledge has been inconclusive because of the inconsistency with which teacher knowledge has been operationally defined. These researchers are concerned with how subject matter is transformed from the knowledge of the teacher into the content of instruction. They call this the missing paradigm in research on teaching. Hashweh examined the influence of subject matter knowledge on pedagogical reasoning and found that knowledgeable teachers were more likely to reject textbook explanations which did not match their own understanding and were also more likely to detect student misconceptions.

Practical experience during pre-service training is very limited in some countries. In China, Lewin identifies teacher training, professional support, incentives and motivation of teachers among key issues in science education if school level science is to meet the challenges presented by national policy. The study concludes Chat more balanced training courses and less rigid discipline compartmentalization of subject matter are desirable. Training is currently heavily content orientated and not much more than S per cent of time is allocated to training in pedagogical skim Teaching practice is too brief and not supervised closely enough to ensure classroom skills are developed which are an improvement on those already employed. In an apparently contrary view Preece concludes that traditional concern of science teachers with the content of the curriculum, rather Khan with teaching methods, is probably justified in view of the small effects reported of differences in teaching style on learning achievement. The positions are not necessarily contradictory since they must be interpreted in context. Where subject achievement of teacher trainees is low, upgrading must be a priority, especially if science teaching materials require a lot of interpretation by teachers. Where subject knowledge is adequate training in teaching methods and supported induction into teaching strategies and effective classroom management assume greater importance.

In countries where entrants into science teacher training have low scores on school leaving examinations understanding science will be a problem for prospective teachers. Where teaching is an unpopular choice of profession such entry scores are not uncommon. Context is therefore important to strategies for teaching education some strategies for which are reviewed by Fraser-Abder who summarises research reported in over 300 papers on teacher education in general from 17 Caribbean countries. Yoloye writing in a Nigerian context, focuses attention on three particular problems faced by teacher educators in the training of teachers of integrated science:

— the problem of organising individualized instruction in large classes;

— the problem of selecting appropriate practical work which win bring about an understanding of the underlying unity of science;

— the selection of appropriate evaluation strategies.

Some possible new directions for teacher education were identified by an APEID meeting in 1982 which reviewed science education activities with a view to developing competence and creativity amongst teachers of science. Among the issues discussed was competency-based science teacher education in Thailand. Another meeting held three years later discussed the concept of 'open-competence' and identified the competencies and attitudes needed by science teachers and science teacher educators to cope with changes in science education.

Pre-service teacher education systems are the most conservative elements of the school system when it comes to curriculum reform. There are many examples of the introduction of integrated science courses that have not been accompanied by concomitant changes in teacher education. If they are there is often a time lag of many years. Part of the reason lies in the stability and organization of teacher training staff who typically have themselves been single subject trained at degree level and have no career incentives to retrain. Separate subject science allows three heads of department, integrated science has only one. Perhaps most disturbingly, it is rare to find primary trained teachers in primary teacher training colleges, the more so in science. This cannot be beneficial to the science education system. Pre-service education of science teachers is an under researched area.

Though not a complete backwater of neglect, there is a shortage, especially at the individual country level, of systematic attempts to trace the products of science teacher education through into the schools and evaluate the adequacy of otherwise of their training. It is also generally the case that what research is conducted on teaching and learning science is not located in training institutions as much as University departments. The gestation cycle of useful results may therefore be long and understanding of learning problems and curriculum issues may remain the level of casual empiricism in training institutions, not a good basis to adapt pre-service training to meet emerging needs. All this suggests that pre-service training methods do require reappraisal at the country level. They tend to be expensive in facilities, staff time and opportunity costs. They may not be less effective than in-service and on-service methods, or at the very least a different mix of full-time and part-time study than that which is current.

There are many possibilities, and many examples of different patterns of organization of training that can be culled for possible alternatives for particular systems. The first step is to obtain a better understanding than is currently demonstrated in the literature of existing patterns, their match with the needs of trainee teachers, and the reasons why teacher training institutions are so rarely centres of curriculum development and new insights into science education.

In-service Teacher Education

Like pre-service training in-service teacher education comes in many forms. These vary from short courses lasting from less than a day to several days, to longer vacation programmes, to sandwich type arrangements over a year or more where training and teaching in schools are concurrent. In-service training may be on site within schools, or in colleges or teacher centres. It may be part of regular teacher support. More frequently it has a temporary existence associated with the introduction of new curricula. There are several attractions to in-service activity:

— It may be the only way to reach serving teachers with information and training in support of new courses. Serving teachers will always constitute the bulk of the teaching cadre, since new entrants will be a small proportion of the total each year.

— It is likely to be cheaper in most cases than full-time training if it takes place with minimal interruptions to normal teaching regimes.

— It offers the prospect of reaching large numbers of teachers whose initial training may have been many years previously.

— It can be often be arranged at the local level using facilities that already exist.

An example of the use of in-service training to train new teachers Chivore examined strategies used to attempt to solve problems of the secondary teacher shortage in Zimbabwe following independence. Rapid educational expansion created an unprecedented demand for teachers. As a result, a 4-year teacher training course was introduced comprising of 2 years resident in college and 2 years full-time teaching under supervision. The course used distance teaching methods. Students chose one major subject such as science or two minor subjects and were required to take other courses such as socialist ideology. This system had considerable cost advantages over the previous 3 year pre-service college model and was able to train large numbers of teachers in a relatively short period. There appears to be no independent evaluation of the quality of the graduates it has produced however.

In-service courses are commonly used to support the introduction of new curricula. Brophy and Dalgety describe the implementation of a new science curriculum in Guyana. An in-service distance programme for teachers accompanied the innovation and was evaluated by questionnaire survey. This showed that there was an apparent gap between the intentions of the curriculum developers and actual classroom practices. What were intended as laboratory projects and student-centred activities in reality became teacher-centred, textbook orientated approaches. In another example, McDonald and Rogan report on an in-service strategy employed by the science education project in introducing its materials and methods into black South African schools. The paper discusses the in-service tactics used in the Ciskei region of South Africa. Teacher security is recognized as of paramount importance, and the importance of gradually increasing teacher freedom. The Science Education Project sought to provide security by starting from highly structured content and lesson plans and gradually relaxing the structure as teachers became more secure in their knowledge of content. Contrary to orthodox practice the aims of the in-service programmes were formulated after teacher involvement in the innovation. It was found that teachers lacked the content knowledge required to assist in the formulation of in-service aims.

The importance of long-term commitment to in-service education is recognized as well as the need to ensure increasing teacher participation. The approach taken has been to encourage teacher support through a zonal system of 'centres of excellence' from which gradual diffusion can take place. These centres provide a leadership role for above average teachers. The authors stress the importance of support from school administration and inspectors for an innovation. Sustained support comes across as critical to many in-service initiatives. Once the initial need is met the motivation to continue support sometimes evaporates. 'Exposure' courses to new curriculum may become the only training that most teachers receive. Dock reports on the establishment of science centres in-service courses, communications with teachers in Zimbabwe as part of the ZIM-SCI project for lower secondary introduced in the early 1980s. This system was apparently very successful initially but its sustainability now seems in question.

In-service models which depend on cascading information and new teaching methods from key personnel, through regional and district staff, to the school level of in-service work are widespread and have been used in Malaysia and Sri Lanka amongst many other countries. Their attraction is practical, in that this may be the only economic way to multiply training over a short time scale to reach large proportions of the science teacher population. The disadvantages revolve around the adequacy of the training at each level, and the risk that whatever the initial messages were, by the time they have filtered down through several levels they may become distorted. Good supporting materials can help reduce these problems where there is time to create these.

Distance education techniques are used widely for in-service support. Though they can be very effective and may be a relatively cheap way of disseminating information and developing skills they may also encounter problems. Thus Guy's general critique of secondary in-service teacher education in Papua New Guinea discusses the Advanced Diploma in Teaching offered as a means of upgrading teacher knowledge. The diploma provides a mixture of residential and correspondence contact.

Progress is affected by clashes between cultural preferences for collectivism and the individualism of distance study. The model has been reviewed in the light of these findings and the distance component has been strengthened through more interactive materials and increased levels of local support for course participants.

A survey of pre-service students in Zimbabwe, Chivore found that there was a difference between the kind of training students expected of colleges and the actual training which the colleges provided. Distance teaching was rated by student-teachers as the least effective of 19 teaching methods suggesting this aspect of programmes has to be carefully designed and supported. There have been attempts to develop structured methods of identifying training needs amongst science teachers. Zurub and Rubba report on the development and validation of an inventory designed to identify the needs of science teachers particularly the Arab countries. The instrument, Science Teacher Inventory of Need (STIN), consists of 83 items arranged under seven categories:

(i) specifying objectives;

(ii) diagnosing and evaluating learners;

(iii) planning;

(iv) delivering;

(v) managing;

(vi) administering instructional facilities and equipment;

(vii) improving science teacher competence.

Content and construct validity was determined by a panel of judges and factor analysis, respectively. Al-Mossa used an Arabic version of this needs assessment instrument together with interviews to identify needs in Saudi Arabia. Analysis suggested a significant relationship between the intensity of professional needs of teachers and the location of their schools (rural/ urban), teacher nationality, attendance at in-service programmes, and teacher educational level. Kamariah et al identified the most prominent needs of Jordanian and Malaysian science teachers using STIN. These fell into four categories: delivering science instruction; managing science instruction; administering science instructional facilities and equipment; and improving one's competence as a science teacher. There are similarities in terms of the nature of science education in both countries. Despite espousal of laboratory-based instruction in curriculum materials, teachers in both countries continue to use didactic teaching methods.

Given the diversities of purpose and context in-service support must be very varied in its forms. Some of the dilemmas are clear, the solutions to them often less so. For example, a common difficulty in organising in-service support is that the clientele is heterogeneous. Teachers participating may include those with much experience and those with little, male and female teachers with characteristically different areas of difficulty, those with good subject knowledge and those with imperfect understanding of the subject. Treating all teachers in such a group similarly risks boring some and exceeding the capabilities of others. A second problem arises when course providers see themselves as information givers, whilst course participants express their needs primarily in terms of the new teaching skills that they need to acquire.

Describing new teaching methods is not the same as developing the skins to use them. Whilst much can be achieved by suitable demonstrations of technique and explanations of the ideas behind a teaching method the in-service experience may be ephemeral for many teachers unless it is followed up by supported practice and refinement in the circumstances of real classrooms with real students.

It is continuing and timely in-service support that is often the greatest weakness in in-service strategies and it is in relation to this that most imagination needs to be exercised in designing methods that are feasible and cost sustainable. In practice this is likely to involve some institutionalization of staff development activity at the school- or local-level, through professional associations of science teachers, departmental in-service days, peer group support networks or similar arrangements.

The composition of the science teacher cadre varies considerably from country to country in terms of qualification level, years of schooling, sex, and age. The significance of this is bound up with other aspects of the development of the education system so no simple conclusions can be reached. Science teaching probably does require more systematic training than some other subjects that are closer to the everyday experience of adults, particularly in those countries where science and technology are recent introductions, but even this kind of generalization depends on how science is to be taught and for what purposes. What kind of teacher education system is most appropriate and efficient will depend on the responses to the issues raised below.

— There is some evidence that more highly qualified science teachers produce better student achievement in science but clearly there are likely to be interaction effects with school level factors. Given the complexities of measuring both science achievement and teacher competence it is not surprising that some studies do not show strong effects related to training for science teachers. It would be wrong to conclude from this that training makes no difference for a number of good reasons.

  First, the effects of training must be related to the quality of that training and few attempts have been made to discriminate between different types of training experience.

  Second, the mismatches between the emphases of assessment systems and those of science curriculum might reasonably be supposed to dilute the training effects that may exist.

Third, those who have been involved in teacher training, and who can stand at a distance from immediate self-interest, can identify many ways in which systematic training can shorten the learning curie for new teachers which simply working on-the-job does not provide. Students are not expected to learn science on their own initiative without support; we should not expect this for science teachers.

— Most of the studies examining teaching methods favour new styles of teaching which make more use of discovery methods, practical work and student-centred learning. Despite this, didactic approaches continue to dominate indicating a preference amongst many teachers for them. Some of the reasons for this reside in familiarity and convenience, some may have cultural origins, some arise from resource constraints, and some reflect lack of change in the attributes that are assessed which have not changed as rapidly as advice on pedagogy. There is a need for more comprehensive research on the factors which influence teachers to adopt particular teaching strategies and to ascertain how these can be made more effective as well as to introduce gradually new methods.

— Research on cognition seems to point to the need to match more carefully the cognitive demand of science curricula to the capabilities of teachers as well as students. If science teachers have not reached formal operational levels of thinking they are unlikely to be able to teach formal concepts in science other than by rote. This could be another reason for the preference for exposition. There is some evidence to suggest that many science teachers may attach more importance to the content and concepts of science rather than the processes used in scientific thinking. This reinforces the need for teacher effectiveness research which examines teacher cognitive demand, and the understandings of science that teachers bring to the teaching of science—which can be used in designing more effective teacher training. This seems almost totally absent in the current literature.

— Because of the special role that science is perceived to have in development, in many developing countries the science teacher is excepted to be an agent of social and economic change. Governments keen to vocationalize science curricula require science teachers to implement plans which may be regarded with suspicion and as lacking in relevance by parents and students, and which are outside the direct experience of teachers as relatively successful academic scientists. This requires careful thought about appropriate training and support. So also does the emphasis on scientific enquiry skills in cultures unfamiliar with conflicting expectations of pedagogic roie and epistemological validation. Prescriptive textbooks and teachers guides may be an asset for poorly trained teachers and resource starved schools. The challenge is how to encourage initiative and creative approaches to science teaching where circumstances demand detailed guidance for those teachers lacking in confidence and knowledge to go beyond it.

The pre-service education of science teachers has been the subject of relatively little research and much debate. Whereas curriculum change has been rapid in many school systems much less change seems to have taken place in pre-service training approaches. Much teacher training is subject-based not pedagogically-orientated and moves towards more competency based training that stresses teaching skills and learning needs seem to have been slow to take root. The match between training experience and the day-to-day demands of science teaching could be improved in many systems. Similarly, in-service support appears often to be piecemeal and unlikely to exist as part of a long- term development plan; rather it is concentrated around periods when new curricula are introduced and tends to be one-off in character with limited or non-existent follow up. Yet the new skins teachers are expected to acquire are often complex and demanding and require much longer gestation periods. There is considerable scope to improve these support systems through creative use of new delivery systems like distance education and correspondence courses, which may be cheaper than conventional residential programmes, and stimulate on a much more widespread scale professional self-help groups of science teachers who can pool expertise and provide mutual support and guidance at the school- or local-level.

5

Skills in Science Education

For many school science teachers the assessment of scientific skills and processes is a major worry for several reasons. First, the sheer practicality of assessing every pupil's scientific skills and the sheer logistics of measuring the 'scientific process' of individuals in full classes is a formidable task. That task could have been made practically easier and more philosophically satisfactory by additional resources in either equipment or human terms. Unfortunately those resources have never materialized in the majority of schools despite the new system of examining.

As a result of practical problems teachers are faces with an unsatisfactory style of practical assessment, whereby sheer practicalities determine the form that skills assessment must take for busy teachers in a science laboratory. If specific skills are to be assessed and marks placed against them they need to be itemized, that is to have a number placed against them. In taking such an atomistic approach to skills assessment teachers will necessarily divorce scientific skills from their content and their context. Skills assessment has thus become for many teachers and isolated and contrived event, separated from other aspects of science teaching.

For few teachers does it become an integral and continuous part of their curriculum- it is an arranged appendage rather than an integrated activity. Woolnough consider fully the 'deeper' worries of many teachers about the nature of the whole exercise of practical assessment and its effect on the school science curriculum. Fairbrother offers detailed discussion and sound advice for those faced with the present realities of skills assessment. In addition to practical concerns and worries over the validity of the assessment exercise, teachers are also drawn in by the temptation of 'teaching for the tests'. This is a well-documented phenomenon which cannot be considered fully here although it is particularly topical with the advent of the national curriculum and increased testing.

Conscientious science teachers will inevitably prepare their pupils for the assessments awaiting them and will therefore attempt to develop and teach scientific skills and processes. This raises two fundamental issues which are considered in various ways by contributors to this volume. What are scientific skills and processes? How do they differ from the same skills and processes applied in other disciplines? More generally, what is scientific method'? Can scientific method be taught? Millar in particular takes a strong line on the latter issue.

In reality, teachers are faced with a working definition of 'scientific process' imposed upon then from the outside. In a sense, therefore, they do not have the opportunity in their day-to day teaching of critically questioning the implicit assumptions of examining group on the nature of scientific processes, their development, and their assessment. This book takes that opportunity in the hope that teachers and indeed all those concerned with science education will share it. If science skills and processes are to be afforded a central position in science education at all levels, their nature and status need critical examination.

Some of the key issues involved in determining the rightful position of skills and processes in the science curriculum. The arguments commonly proffered for a curriculum which is process-led are considered below as a starting-point for the discussion which follows in subsequent chapter of the book.

Process-led Science Curriculum

Few would contest the claim that science education had traditionally been dominated by the transmission of accepted knowledge as the principal teaching mode, and factual recall as the main mean of assessment-although Jenkins provided and important historical perspective on this claim.

Many practising teachers argue that, as a result, a vast number of pupils in the past have been' turned off' by science; they are uninterested, poorly motivated, and in extreme cases totally baffled by it. Concern for the lack of appeal of school science has led to numerous publications and initiatives which cannot be documented here- this book focuses principally on the resultant shift towards process science as a response to a so-called knowledge-led curriculum.

That move has received widespread support and is to be welcomed not only for providing a fresh approach to science teaching but also for opening up a whole new debate on the nature of science education and of science itself. The process 'movement' is now making its mark most obviously at lower secondary level in terms of new curriculum projects adopted wholesale by certain schools, or off- the -shelf potted versions in others- much as the Nuffield projects were either adopted of adapted in earlier years. The aim of this book is not to examine any project in detail but to analyse critically the notion of processes and skills in science and the idea of a process-led science education.

Numerous arguments have been put forward for a process-led curriculum in national meetings, conferences, publications, and in school staffrooms. The five main arguments are summarized and perhaps unfairly caricatured below. Comment is given on each argument with reference to further examination by other authors in this volume.

Content-led Approacn

Science teaching has been dominated by the transmission of facts, the 'tyranny of abstractions' and the clutter of 'inert ideas' according to its critics. The failure of this approach is expressed eloquently by Simpson. If content-led science teaching had been successful, pupils would have acquired the intended understanding of public scientific knowledge and would have been able to apply this knowledge effectively in familiar contexts and creatively in open-ended problem-solving situations. They reality was otherwise.

The majority failed to attain the level of mastery of school science which would allow then to proceed to certificate course; of those who did, some failed to achieve levels which would allow any recognition of attainment, and many were awarded certificates on the basis of performances which, if described in criterion referenced terms, indicated that 50 per cent of their expected knowledge was either faulty or non-existent. Rote learning was widespread. Only a tiny minority of pupils gained the meaningful understanding which allowed them to use their knowledge effectively and creatively and there were justified complaints that even pupils who apparently knew a lot could do very little. This is a strong argument for the necessity of change. It does not, however, imply that change should be processled.

A second argument, which follows from this, does have that implication. School science can be made accessible to a much wider range of ability if it becomes less content laden and less abstract. This widening of appeal can be achieved by emphasizing and teaching skills and processes:

> If not everyone can understand scientific ideas, almost everyone, it seems can be taught to observe, classify or hypothesis. This vies is countered by jenkins himself by arguing that scientific knowledge, if presented in an exciting and interesting context, can be equally appealing and accessible. In addition, the simplistic notion that all pupils can be taught to observe, classify, and hypothesize is strongly criticized by Millar.

The belief that the processes of science are in some way simpler and more accessible to pupils of lower ability is based on a mistaken conception of science which is followed up later in this chapter. In brief, this misconception of science is based first on a belief that science proceeds inductively, that is from the concrete to the abstract, from the particular to the general; and second that scientific observation, classification, and so on is independent of theory. Both beliefs are wide open to criticism, as several authors in this volume point out.

With the development of new information technology, facts can be retrieved from data bases with increasing ease- the role of science education is to develop 'the ability to access, use and ultimately add to the information store when required' It cannot be doubted that education should respond actively to developments in information technology which provide new devices for the storage and retrieval of information, and that the use of IT should be an integral part of the curriculum.

However, to adopt the collection, retrieval and handling of information as the dominant model in education is surely mistaken for at least four reasons which are outlines briefly below.

— It is an obvious fact, but worth stating, that thought involves far more than the processing of information. This model of thought appears to be gaining credibility, perhaps by accident, with the growing literature and discussion of artificial intelligence in it. The idea of the human brain as an information-processor forms a poor basis for a curriculum or an education for the future. The regard the brain solely as an information-processor is to debase human thinking.

— Thought is a creative, imaginative, and above all a personal process. This point was best expressed by Michael Polanyi in Personal Knowledge. Polanyi presented the notion of tacit knowledge joins together that we know with what well feel and experience - only this can lead to full understanding. In other words knowledge is personal, involving a mixture of feelings, emotions, and responses to previous experiences. Two simple examples of personal cricket strokes. Both types of knowledge are personal, and often harmed by attempts to verbalize and analyse them (for example the test-match cricketer who tries to analyse his own batting technique). The tacit or personal knowledge descried by Polanyi is one of the curriculum and education. Yet it will remain untouched by an education based solely on information skills.

— Learning and education do not involve the passive handling and acquisition of information. Human beings are not information absorbers any more than they are information processors. Active and meaningful learning involves selecting, interpreting, and transforming information according to the learner's previous experiences, present needs, preconceived ideas, knowledge, and hypotheses. Information handling is not done with a completely open mind any more than scientific observation. Information retrieval is theory laden. So in addition to so-called information skills the learner will require these previous ideas, experiences, and hypotheses. These are the true concern of science education. An educated person will also require the ability and previous knowledge to think about the information itself, and the ability to examine and question the source of that information.

— A sort of hierarchy having data and information at the bottom with knowledge and wisdom at the top is suggested by an often-quoted piece of T.S. Eliot's poetry:

Where is the life we have lost in living?

Where is the wisdom we have lost in knowledge?

Where is the knowledge we have lost in information?

The question of what knowledge is of most worth has never been answered, but it is clearly not the ability to handle information. A consideration of the question should surely from the basis for any curriculum planning. Perhaps Gilbert Ryle should have added a third category to his knowledge how and knowledge that; knowledge why.

1. Knowledge that - facts, 'happenings', phenomena
2. Knowledge how (to) - skills, processes, abilities
3. Knowledge why - explanations, models, analogies, frameworks, theories.

A 'Better Science' education will not focus on one of these Three categories at the expense of others. My suggestion is that science education - if it is to be 'broad', balanced, better, or indeed fulfill any of its expectations - could usefully employ these categories of knowledge in determining its future by concentrating equally on knowledge how, knowledge that, and knowledge why. Let information skills form an essential element in planning the science curriculum of the future, but let's remember how limited these skills are when seen as part of a general education, and where that lie in Eliot's hierarchy. The weakness of using the information explosion as an argument for no longer teaching facts is followed up by other authors in this volume. Jenkins, for example, points out that the inability of any one person to know more than a small fraction of existing knowledge is not a new problem. Other contributors discuss Polanyi's notion of tacit knowledge and its importance for science education in more detail.

The processes of science learnt by pupils remain after the facts have become out of data or forgotten:

> It could be said that the most valuable elements of a scientific education are those that remain after the facts have been forgotten.

These two arguments are based on three assumptions, all of which are open to question.

- That scientific knowledge is of a provisional nature and becomes out of date within a short period. This is hardly true of any of the science taught at school level, much of which has been with us for a century or more. This applies to virtually all the laws and theories taught in the three separate sciences and in particular physics. Admittedly motion is not longer taught along Aristotelian lines but it is taught largely within the framework set be Isac Newton 300 years ago. It could be argued that if the scientific knowledge of the twentieth century were taught in school science, the subject might have broader appeal. But if science education is to be relevant to the outside world it must be accepted that Newtonian mechanics should be taught- after all its application helped to put people on the moon. Similar examples can be found throughout the physical, biological and human sciences.

— The argument relies on the belief that although scientific knowledge is provisional, scientific skills and processes are not. This belief has little philosophical or historical evidence to support it. The scientific method adopted by Desecrates in his search for certainty bears little resemblance to the processes and skill of Galileo. In fact Desecrates' approach is perhaps most similar to the 'thought-experiment' scientific method of Einstein in the twentieth century. Similarly the nature of current scientific activity with the traditions the 'learned gentleman' scientific fraternity of the last century.

In short then, processes of science are at least as provisional as its products.

— There of no empirical and little intuitive evidence to support the belief that skills and processes are retained more readily that knowledge. Certainly if the skills and processes learnt in school science are never subsequently used or allied. Pupils are unlikely to retain them any more than they will retain isolated facts, disconnected knowledge, or 'inert idea's.

Generic and Transferable Skills

This is often bound up with the view that the provision of skills is an important part of a young person's vocational preparation for 'the world of work which will wait then. Similar statements on the purpose of education can be found earlier in Callaghan's notorious Ruskin College speeds of 1976 and later from, for example, current advocates of 'process science': ' any preparation of young people must take into account the transferable skills which they will need to succeed in the twenty-first century' The belief that science education should provide relevant transferable skills for a future society is, in my view, a highly commendable one but at the same time contains three extremely problematic notions.

There are the notions of relevance, of transferability, and of 'skills for the futures. Those notions can only be examined briefly below but the embodied ides, in particular of relevance and of transfer, are consider by subsequent authors in this volume. The notion of 'relevance' is one so widely used in all areas of discourse that the world 'relevant' on its own has lost its descriptive value, It is merely a term of approval. The word on its own has no factual content- it is simply part of a value judgment in the same way as the terms' good', 'marvelous', or 'excellent' would be.

The words does have meaning however when it is used in a relational sense, that is 'relevant to.....' Thus we may sensibly talk of science education being 'relevant to the needs of industry', ' to the pupils' everyday life', ' to life in a technological society', and so on. But even this relational use of `relevant' is of little value in planning the science curriculum. How can we know the needs of industry? Does a statement of needs not itself depend on a value judgment? If we talk of the pupils everyday experience their `life in society' or even `the world of work which waits them', then the issue becomes even more problematic. Decisions on whether a curriculum is `relevant' will depend on: the age of the pupils their stage of development the ability level of pupils the area region of the country and the time what relevant in 1988 may not be relevant in 1990. In short may argument is that 'relevance's in essence no more than a term of approval. Any attempt to give it descriptive sense or suggests that one approach is more 'relevant' than another is fraught with problems.

Thus the suggestion that the science curriculum should be relevant is in itself of no more value in guiding curriculum choice than the statement that it should be 'good',' worthwhile' or valuable. It lends no more substantive support to the process-based science education than the statement that 'process science is goods. Indeed it could be argued that a content-based science course is most relevant to people who with to succeed in 'Trivial Pursuit', 'Mastermind', and the plethora of quiz games which now abound. The 'skills for the future' argument so closely bound up with pleas for relevance could also be discussed at length here by the reader is referred elsewhere for extensive analyses, both empirical and conceptual.

Suffice it to say that the commonly used notion of skills for the future is like assertions of relevance of little value in guiding them curriculum. First there is increasing evidence that few employers state their personnel requirements in terms of 'skills' and 'skill ownerships. Aside from academic qualification employers are far more likely to state their requirements in terms of personal qualities and general attitudes such as motivation willingness to learn and enthusiasm.

A process-based approach to education may indeed foster these qualities indirectly but the output of people with specific scientific skills is not a directly stated requirement of employers. Indeed how could it be? Almost by definition we cannot predict skill needs for news technologies. How could anyone forecast the skill needs for any genuine innovation? It could be argued that education and training should therefore aim to develop transferable or generic skills. However the belief that skills are transferable has little psychological evidence to support it and this is conveniently ignored by those who advocate transferable skills as an aim of education.

Skills such as thinking reasoning problem solving observing and inferring have been labeled as generic skills and the assumption is made that such skills can be divorced form the knowledge, experience, attitude, concepts, and even theories to which they are inestricable bound, that is that skills are detachable or transferable. This assumption is based on tenuous evidence to say the least. What can be said is that skill transfer is most likely to take place under two condition; finest when the domains in which skills are acquired are closely related; and second when transfer is explicitly taught for example when the general nature of the skills being acquired is brought out by the teacher. These constraints impose severe limitations on the notion of transferable skills as a broad aim for science education. In summary therefore my argument is that the aim of promoting transferable skills relevant to the twenty-first century is exceedingly problematic and in concrete terms of little value in determining the science curriculum.

1. The content-led approach has failed.
2. 'Science for all abilities' necessitates a process- based curriculum.
3. The information explosion has made the teaching of facts highly questionable.
4. Scientific facts date too quickly to form the basis for science education.

5. Skills, particularly transferable skills, are more relevant to pupils than knowledge.

The main arguments put forward for a process-led science curriculum and to begin to examine those arguments in some detail. My contention is that a science education dominated and unbalance by and overemphasis on skills and processes is neither required by employers or a 'future society', nor is it based on a total misconception of the nature of science and the activities of scientists could be greatly damaging. The nature of scientific skills and processes is the theme of the nest section of this chapter- a theme which is explored more fully by subsequent contributors.

Mirroring the Processed of Science

It cannot be doubted that in the past science education has overemphasized the products of science that is its laws its theories it knowledge at the expense of its processes. But if this balance is to be redressed it must surely be based on an accurate account of the processed of science. Some may doubt that such an account could ever be offered:

> Ask a scientist what he conceives the scientific method to be and he will adopt and expression that is at once solemn and shifty-eyed solemn because he feels had ought to declare an opinion shifty-eyed because he is considering how to conceal the fact that he has no opinion to declare.

The late Sir Peter Medawar's scepticism in this quotation is tempered in a later work but it does raise the issue that few practising scientists can make explicit the processes that they themselves are engaged in. What chance therefore do science teachers have of accurately mimicking or assessing the real processes of science eve if such and educational aim were desirable? Hodson points to empirical studies which indicate that science teachers have predominantly inductivist views of science. Such a view which also seems to prevail amongst examination boards leads to totally false conceptions of many of the 'science skills' currently being taught and assessed nationally. It is therefore of rather more than philosophical concern. Take the example of observation a skill which is central to the syllabuses of all GCSE boards. As Hodson points out current philosophies of science have at least three important implication for the practice of science teaching and its assessment:

1. Observation do not constitute a starting point for scientists.
2. Observation are theory dependent and theory always precedes observation.
3. Competing theories may give rise to non-identical observations when people observe the same phenomena.

Another scientific skill which has been openly questioned but which forms the corner stone of most people view of science and the process approach concerns the control of variables is ever a feature of genuine scientific research by quoting Fisher.

> It is often supposed at least for purposes of exposition that to establish controlled condition in which all factors except one can be held constant and then to study the effects of this single factor is the essentially scientific approach to an experimental investigation. By contrast in the state of knowledge

> or ignorance in which genuine research intended to advance knowledge has to be carried on this simple formula is not very helpful. We are usually ignorant which out of innumerable possible factors, may prove ultimately to be the most important if the investigator in these circumstances confines his attention to any single factor we may infer that he is the unfortunate victim of a doctrinate theory as to how experimentation should proceed.

Two specific examples of the supposed cornerstones of scientific method that is observation and systematic control of variables have been examines briefly above and are considered further by later authors in this volume from their own perspective. But there is also more general confusion over the terms 'skills' and 'process' and derivation form them such as 'process skill". This lack of clarity is discussed later by Millar who offers a distinction between skills and processes.

A broader definition by Harlen defines a process-skills as any cognitive process involving interaction with content. Fairbrother takes a totally pragmatic approach by suggesting that 'there are certain things we want students to do' and calls them 'ings' — focuses on the ways in which these 'ings' can be assessed. However, while this paramagnetic approach is valuable for this purpose of assessment the confusion over the terms 'skills' and process' remains a serious thorn in the side for advocates of a process-led curriculum.

6

Science Education: Constraints and Opportunities

Social and technological changes require constant updating of the general populations' knowledge and skills. Developments in science and technology are tangible realities affecting any member of society.

Science education has become so important that many consider it necessary to strengthen considerably science teaching in all educational systems and to allow scientific literacy to develop.

It is particularly important for developing countries to develop their own capacity to evaluate, import, absorb and improve the scientific and technological knowledge that would be suitable and would contribute to their autonomous development.

The World Conference on Education for All, convened and sponsored by UNESCO, UNICEF, UNDP and the World Bank, charted in March 1990 a World Declaration on Education for All. The Conference stressed the need to respond to the impact of scientific discoveries and technological change on the content and process of education itself.

Many developing countries see science education as an important and effective agent in the development of national human resources. For example, five South-East Asian countries ranked science education third in importance - right after literacy and numeracy. It is assumed that better understanding of science and technology leads not only to more informed decision-making in science and engineering, but also in many other areas. Environmental management, industrial development, agriculture, health, nutrition and population control are only a few examples. However, traditional investments in science education can be a heavy burden for developing countries with limited financial resources.

When the impact of the investments is less or slower than anticipated there may be a backlash against science education. Science education is not partaking as it should of the local environment, the socio-cultural background and the occupational patterns prevalent in the country. The negative experiences which many developing countries have had with imported curricula show the necessity of designing the curriculum so that it promotes the socio-economic and cultural development goals of each nation.

The scientific skills developed could be applied to the problems of his personal life as well as to the social welfare of the community." Educational reforms in developing countries are in many cases coupled with a substantial expansion of the educational system. For example, secondary enrolment ratio in years 1980-1988 almost doubled in Ethiopia and Indonesia, tripled in

Uganda, while the increase in Zimbabwe was over six times. The success of such reforms depends on many factors. For science education one of the important ones is provision of adequate instructional materials.

Practical Activities in Science Education

There is a widespread belief that in the design of practical activities, local relevance and applicability to problem situation in the real world should be promoted together with the understanding of scientific concepts and the world of work. A process of development of the objectives of science curriculum can be recognized in recent years. There is a trend of change from traditional acquisition of knowledge to scientific inquiry, problem solving and application of science. Recent curricula in some developed countries place also practical activities on a new level.

Traditional approaches can be summarized as teacher demonstrations to illustrate scientific principles, combined with students' work in laboratories following 'cookbook recipes'. The 'modem' approach is characterized by inquiry and discovery methods, decision making, 'learning by doing', and 'hands-on' teaching. These approaches were first widely adopted in smaller countries, but are now fast gaining ground in larger ones. An example from the USA is the ChemCom project of the American Chemical Society. A need to implement similar approaches is recognized also in some developing countries.

Students carry out research appropriate for their level of understanding of science. Nevertheless, the results are in many cases quite impressive, particularly where state-wide competitions are organized. In the USA, the National Research Council is preparing National Science Education Standards. The main intention is to assure 'science for all', meaning that every high school student should participate in at least one science course. The project has several components. One of the proposed objectives is building the inquiry skills, which includes:

— formulating questions,

— planning experiments,

— making systematic observations,

— interpreting and analysing data,

— drawing conclusions,

— communicating, and

— understanding of inquiry.

Equipment for Science Education

The term 'equipment', as used to covers all the support material for science teaching excluding textbooks, other printed materials and the usual classroom materials and facilities, such as chalk, blackboards and furniture. It may also include perishable items (e.g. glassware) and consumables (e.g. chemicals).

Practical activities at different levels of sophistication are present in the majority of school science curricula at the primary level and particularly at the lower and upper secondary levels. Practical activities usually require special facilities and equipment. Although fully equipped laboratories and sophisticated equipment are by many considered essential, it is not necessarily so. It has been argued that traditional laboratory facilities are not needed at the primary level, but are desirable at least at the upper secondary level.

In many countries, science education is suffering from a lack of appropriate facilities and supporting materials, including the equipment. Modern curricula and textbooks based on discovery learning are sometimes used, but in the absence of practical activities it is questionable if the students receive a better understanding of science then they did when books and curricula were based on lecturing and blackboard teacher demonstrations.

To improve the situation, many national, regional and international projects have been launched, emphasizing labs and equipment. However, their success was in many cases far below the expected. The World Bank has supported secondary school science in over 100 projects; generally the equipment components were a substantial part of the total expenditures. In Bank evaluations, almost half of the outcomes were assessed to be negative.

In some cases the equipment provided was not used at all, and it was possible to find twenty years old equipment kits still in their original packages. There are many possible reasons for equipment supply projects to fail. Some of them are listed below:

— *Technical unsuitability of the equipment*: Climatic conditions in some developing countries are very hard on equipment. High temperature and humidity cause corrosion of metallic parts and make particularly sensitive (and often expensive) electronic equipment unusable. Lack oft or unreliable water, gas, and electricity supply are sometimes not taken into account. Precision electrical instrument's tolerance for current oscillations is in many cases lower than actual oscillations in public network, resulting in breakdown of the equipment.

— *Educational unsuitability of the equipment*: The equipment is not always relevant to the curriculum. In other words, it is designed for experiments that do not suit the curriculum. Envisaged changes in the curriculum are sometimes not taken into account in connection with equipment purchase, even if they are supposed to happen in the near future. On the other hand, in practical implementations of the curriculum there is sometimes little or no time allotted for practical work. Another possibility is that the educational value of the experiments is low because they fail to demonstrate scientific concepts convincingly, or do not illustrate the connection between scientific principles and the real world. The reasons might be use of unfamiliar materials, practical work following 'cookbook recipes' without real understanding of the process, or use of 'black boxes' - unexplained and unfamiliar equipment where input and output do not have any apparent connection.

— *Procurement procedures*: In many cases equipment lists are prepared by people unfamiliar with the curriculum. Lists are sometimes prepared on the basis of the suppliers' catalogs instead of the practical work as defined in school programs. Equipment lists are often based on out-of-date understanding of what a well-equipped science laboratory should contain. Long-range plans to support maintenance and replenishment are rarely included since procurement is usually considered to be a one-time operation. Suppliers' warranties which promise spare parts and service, e.g. within the first year, are often not used.

— *Cost of equipment*: Investments in equipment for all students at a given level are a heavy financial burden for a developing country. Essential follow-up procedures like teacher training in the pedagogical and technical use of the equipment, provision of maintenance, and replenishment, etc., are sometimes not accomplished because of the lack of funds. There is another risk in connection with the high cost of equipment. It is sometimes safely locked up in the school and not used at all, because the teacher is afraid that he/she or the students might break it and that he/she will have pay for it from his/her own pocket.

— *Teacher training:* In pre-service training, future teachers often get work experience with equipment they are not likely to use after graduation. They are not trained to work with the kind of equipment which is actually in use in schools, or to work with little or no equipment at all. They are seldom taught how to use and improvise with local materials. Maintenance and repair of the equipment are rarely included in pre-service teacher training. The future teachers do not develop managerial skills in selecting and acquiring equipment and consumable materials, although they in some countries are responsible for that, using the school budget. Proper in-service training is often not available when new equipment is supplied to schools. Although well-prepared manuals and teachers' guides may be supplied, they are frequently not enough to ensure efficient use of the equipment. In-service training is particularly essential when new equipment is accompanied by changes in the curriculum.

— *Incentives*: Teachers are often not motivated to put additional effort into the preparation of practical work. The social status of science teachers in many 10 developing countries is low, as well as their salary. They are frequently forced to take second jobs. Final examinations are reported to be very strong incentives for both teachers and students, particularly in African countries where access to universities represents a major goal for many upper secondary school students and their parents. If the final examinations include practical work, it is likely that it will be more carefully carried out also in science teaching.

— *Distribution*: In some cases, purchased equipment has not been supplied to schools, but has been stored in a central warehouse for a very long time. Reasons may be different, ranging from bureaucratic procedures to physical inability to distribute the equipment across the country. Another kind of problem is connected with the relative inflexibility of supply and distribution schemes. It often happens that the same standard sets of new equipment are distributed to all schools, even when the existing supplies vary considerably. It might also happen that certain items are not included in the pack, because the majority of schools already have them. The result is that a number of schools will never get that particular piece of equipment, while other schools will get equipment they already have.

— *Supply of consumables*: Consumable materials (for example chemicals) represent a significant part of the total costs of science education in developing countries. They are necessary for utilization of the equipment. However, the funds for consumables are not always available. This is particularly true if they have to be imported (i.e. must be paid in foreign currency). Distribution problems occur also here, similar to the problems encountered at the distribution of equipment. Many countries are still using hazardous chemicals in secondary school classrooms. These chemicals are now no longer used in most developed countries at this level.

— *Maintenance, repair and replenishment*: Teachers and laboratory technicians (where available) are rarely trained properly in maintenance of the equipment, either in pre-service or in-service training programs. If the equipment is in use, it will eventually break down. Teachers and laboratory technicians should be able to carry out simple repairs, but the necessary training is seldom provided. Centers for more complicated maintenance and repair are organized in some countries, but generally they are not available.

Low Cost Equipment

Import of school science equipment to developing countries has a series of negative side-effects. Foreign exchange is usually scarce, while the equipment is rather expensive, considering the large number of schools. This results in uneven and only partial supply of schools. Moreover, spare parts also have to be imported, as well as some (or almost all) consumables. If the equipment does not suit the existing curriculum, it may not be used in the teaching. If teachers' training is neglected, the equipment might not be used anyway.

Even if the teacher knows what to do with the equipment, he/she might be reluctant to use it out of fear to damage expensive apparatus. In the best case he/she would use it for demonstrations, and would not allow students to work directly with it. Some schools have 'graveyards' of equipment that require minimal repairs, which the teacher or laboratory technician have not been trained to carry out. When the necessary repairs are more complex or require a spare part, centralized repair and maintenance services are often not available. In some cases equipment is not used because of lack of necessary consumables.

Foreign aid in the form of equipment sometimes has negative effects. It rarely meets more than a small part of the demand, and often a developing country may have a variety of equipment received from various donor countries, each in small quantities. This makes it difficult to equip all schools evenly with uniform equipment. High cost and sophistication of the equipment do not necessarily mean high educational value. Commercial instruments are sometimes designed to cater for multi-purpose needs of industry and research, while an instrument often can be significantly simplified, according to the educational needs. Sophisticated equipment is not always comprehensible to students, and often not even to teachers.

Many sophisticated pieces of equipment come as completely enclosed units, and their function can usually not be understood by the user. Relying on the results without any understanding how they are obtained decreases the value of the practical work. One of the approaches to overcome the problems in supply, maintenance and use of equipment for science education is development of low-cost and/or locally produced alternatives. It must be emphasized, that low-cost, simply designed equipment is not necessarily synonymous with second-rate science education. It is possible to design low-cost equipment and experiments that are relevant to students and that lead to understanding. The main point in school science is to define the most appropriate equipment.

Many types of equipment can be developed at a low cost and still retain the precision needed for school science. It is important to determine what precision range is actually needed for teaching. Too sophisticated equipment is sometimes used, producing data whose accuracy is incompatible with the other measurements taken during the experiment.

Local production of equipment for science education, particularly at a low cost, has certain important advantages, some of which are listed below:

— *Cost*: The cost of locally produced equipment is often, but not always, lower than of imported equipment. That makes supplying a large number of schools in a country more feasible. However, every piece of equipment can not be produced in every country. For smaller countries, regional cooperation might be the answer. When calculating the cost of the equipment, some factors should be kept in mind. They are:

  — durability of the equipment (expected lifetime),

  — additional installation costs,

— estimated costs of spare parts during the lifetime of the equipment,

— estimated costs of consumable materials,

— service costs, and

— costs of teacher and technician training.

It may be assumed that the equipment will be used fully during its lifetime, as long as it is kept in mind that the most expensive equipment is that which is never used.

— *Maintenance and repair*: If the equipment is simpler in design, teachers, laboratory technicians and local craftsmen are more likely to be able to carry out small repairs. Teachers would hesitate less to open or dismantle the equipment in order to maintain it, if it is made from familiar parts and materials.

— *Replacement*: It is generally much easier to acquire spare parts from a local producer. Some parts can also be made by local craftsmen, if the designs are provided, and the materials are readily available.

— *Relevance to the curriculum*: In practice, developers of low-cost equipment are often at the same time involved in curriculum design or implementation. In many cases they are employed at universities, teacher training colleges, or secondary schools and are well acquainted with the existing syllabus or the one in preparation. They tend to prepare manuals and experiments to be needed for use of the equipment. They may also organize teacher training, which is more likely to be highly relevant to the new equipment.

— *Higher local content*: Equipment made of parts and materials familiar to the students is more likely to help them to understand the underlying scientific principles. Students are able to identify applications in their own environment and are better able to use them in their later life. There are numerous examples of everyday activities in rural communities, which are closely related to scientific concepts. For example, a four-part pottery distillation apparatus, which is in use in Kenyan villages to distill a local liquor from sugar cane beer, was replicated in Germany for student use in school project on the preparation of aromatic oils from plants.

— *Self-reliance*: Local development and production of the equipment for science education are seen as a method to cultivate confidence and expertise of educators in a developing country. The dependence on local materials is another aspect of this. It may also be a way to develop new small-scale enterprises and to employ handicapped personnel and school dropouts, as is the case in India. However, it might take some time to reach adequate production quality and quantity.

— *Flexibility*: Addition of a few new pieces of equipment, or modification of existing equipment together. with some teacher training, can facilitate the introduction of new topics in science teaching. A recent example in many countries is incorporation of environmental education in school syllabi.

Supply Strategies for Low-cost Equipment

Some parts are available at very low prices on the international market, for example electronic components. Some are not economical to produce in relatively small quantities. Developing a given production line might require substantial investments in infrastructure or training of workers and it might be more feasible to import those products.

Often, the best selection of equipment for science education in an educational system is a blend of low-, medium- and high-cost, locally produced and imported equipment. To implement national or local production of low-cost equipment, national and local conditions should be taken into account.

To enable teachers and/or students to build the equipment, detailed designs should be distributed. They should include description of necessary parts and materials and their availability in local communities, and should be carefully chosen and tested. In some cases, training of teachers in the form of seminars, workshops or science camps (together with students) is organized.

Sometimes it is possible to produce certain pieces of equipment for science teaching in schools as a part of a teaching program. An example is production of a constant current source power supply, built in technology classes and used in chemnistry and biology laboratories at the same school in Uberlingen, Germany.

Some universities have workshops where they produce some teaching and research equipment in small quantities, for example at Fudan University in Shanghai, China. Many teachers and scientists in both developing and developed countries make low-cost equipment for their own use.

Some countries have established central units for production of teaching aids, including equipment for science education. They are often functioning as a part of the responsible Ministry (usually for education) or are non-profit organizations, and are producing equipment for the whole education system. The units usually produce a limited range of equipment, in most cases for the primary or lower secondary level.

Examples are found in Ethiopia, Uganda and Kenya. Central units may work well, but there is a danger of monopolization and, as a result, higher costs then necessary. In some countries with centrally planned economies, establishment of central production capacity can be a political issue.

Central development and assembly of equipment and kits An institution inside the country may be in charge of developing prototypes of equipment and science kits. Sometimes it includes also manufacturing of some items, while the others are bought on the domestic or international market. There are examples of institutions buying items in quantity and assembling complete science kits for distribution to schools.

In the case of Zimbabwe, for example, the Curriculum Development Unit assembles science kits for the ZIM-SCI program in lower secondary schools. Items are procured by tender from domestic and foreign suppliers. Buying certain materials in stock and repackaging them in small lots may be very economical. Typical examples are electronic components and chemicals, where the difference in price for small and large quantities may be several hundred percent.

In almost every state in India, as well as on a central level, there exists a unit for development of science equipment for lower levels of education. There are also groups developing equipment for higher levels, most notably the Edutronics Group at the University of Delhi.

In most of the countries several of the above strategies are found. A general and efficient system for the design, production and distribution of school science equipment may include local development, fabrication of prototypes, evaluation and tryout, industrial design, production in local small-scale manufacturing centers, acquisition of items on the local mnarket and import of some items, all related to the curiculum requirements.

The development of low-cost experiments fits in the general concept of low cost and locally developed curricula and equipment. There are two possibilities for adaptation of science experiments for the school use: replacement of complex methods with simpler ones or simplification of the methods. Similar approaches are used to decrease the cost of school experimentation, for example in chemistry: replacement of expensive chemicals with cheaper ones or with locally available materials.

International Cooperation

Cooperation in design and production, as well as in exchange of information on science education equipment, exists on different levels. Many developed countries have governmental and non-governmental agencies and foundations for cooperation with developing countries, for example:

Deutsche Gesellschaft fur Technische Zusammenarbeit - GTZ (Germany) together with some other German agencies is supporting development of science education equipment in India and Indonesia with funds and experts. For example, GTZ supported workshops on the production of simple teaching aids in

Afghanistan and some Latin American countries. It has also launched a project for maintenance and repair of scientific equipment at African universities.

Regional networks and cooperation projects are often included in the activities of intemational organizations, notably lUNESCO.

For exmple the Conference of African Ministers of Education, Nairobi, 1968, was convened by UNESCO and the Organization of African Unity (OAU) and attended by delegates from thirty-five countries. It recommended a problem-solving, hands-on approach in science education instead \of traditional methods based on blackboard lessons. Other conferences followed in years 1974 (Dakar) and 1976 (Lagos). In years 1978-1981 UNESCO gave support to nine regional seminars concerned with maintaining the momentum of development of school courses in science and technology.

Several international organizations are particularly active in development and provision of science education equipment: UNICEF has made kits available for primary science; some developing countries use them, for example Papua New Guinea and Solomon Islands. UNESCO is the international organization with the most experience in low-cost and locally produced equipment. Activities of some of the Regional Centers are described above. In addition, UTNESCO has launched a project on low-cost locally produced equipment together with the IUPAC - Committee on Teaching of Chemistry.

In August 1993, Chinese Chemical Society is hosting a Low-cost Equipment Workshop in Beijing, while the International Workshop on Teaching of Environmental Chemnistry will be held in December 1993 in Delhi, India, to prepare a teaching/learning package for environmental science using the items developed under the Low-cost Project. The next World Conference on Science Education will include a panel on low-cost equipment. One of its organizers, Professor Ram Lamda of the Inter American University, Puerto Rico, is an active member of the IJNESCO-IUPAC project. Exchange of information is achieved through INISTE, based in UNESCO, Paris and functioning as a clearinghouse for information.

In short, experiences from many developing countries demonstrate that the quality of science education is often unsatisfactory, especially with respect to use of equipment. In many cases, large investments in imported equipment have been made, draining limited foreign currency, without an apparent positive effect. International donor and lending organizations - the World Bank included - are often faced with expensive equipment purchases which have no demonstrated effect on the teaching.

Production of equipment in the country has advantages, such as easier service and replenishment of spare parts. If the equipment is produced locally, foreign currency is saved. At the same time, the production creates employment. It may also contribute to the development of small-scale enterprises. If the equipment is also low cost, it is more likely to be used in the classrooms, without fear of the consequences if it is accidentally broken. It has a higher local content and is generally more flexible with respect to design of new experiments. Finally, many examples show that it is possible to use the same teams for curriculum development, equipment design and teacher training, which increases the relevance of the equipment and effectiveness of its use.

Design of low-cost equipment takes place in many countries. International networks may provide information on activities in developing countries. The Ministry of Education may know which institutions are involved in curriculum development for science education. Often strong resistance against low-cost equipment is encountered since it is assumed that it leads to second-rate science teaching. However, this is not necessarily so; simpler equipment may have distinct educational advantages, particularly if it employs local materials, which are familiar to the students.

In supplying the equipment, local conditions have to be taken into consideration. Due to climatic conditions in many tropical countries (high temperature and humidity), some materials corrode very fast. The equipment should be durable and rugged. Water, electricity and gas supplies are often nonexistent. The equipment should be designed to be independent of them as far as possible. The equipment should not be too dependent on perishable items, since the supply is not always reliable.

Distribution of the equipment has to be carefully planned and coordinated with other activities for the introduction of equipment. When a new program starts in a school, the equipment should be in place with time for teachers to prepare themselves. However, equipment often arrives haphazardly to the schools. Local authorities should do their best to reduce bureaucratic delaying procedures to a minimum. There should be some flexibility in distribution to different schools. Although it is easier to prepare the same sets of the equipment for every school, an effort should be made to differentiate the supply according to the number of students, existing equipment and other local conditions.

In countries where the teachers are responsible for selecting and acquiring equipment and consumable materials, they should develop the needed managerial skills. They should know where to acquire teaching materials, and should be able to improvise to a certain extent. Improvisation makes it possible to use resources available in the local community. This may increase students' motivation, the relevance of the science teaching, and the amount of practical work performed by students. Students should become able to apply scientific concepts in their own environment.

Science Education Policy

Science education policy can be developed in two different ways. Policy formation approach most familiar to planners and policy makers is from the top down and starts with the identification national goals which can be converted into policy for different sub sectors. Most developing country national plans since the 1960s have contained commitments to invest in science and technology in the belief that this will enhance economic development. Recently it has become more common to argue that general statements of commitment are not enough, and that specific policy on science and technology is needed which is associated with particular economic development strategies. If such a policy can be articulated then the logic of this approach leads to decisions about the kinds of science and technology education and training that should be promoted.

Four overlapping national needs related to science and technology are often identified. These are to generate new technology (usually thought to be science based); to adapt technology developed elsewhere to suit local market conditions and factor endowments; to transfer technology essentially unchanged but relccated, and to devise different technologies appropriate to context which may not already exist.

A modest elaboration is justified since it is perspectives on which of these needs are dominant which are likely to shape science education policy and practice. Orthodox views of science education tend to stress the importance of discovery, invention and understandings of the natural world over application, improvement of already existing technologies, and the development of scientific knowledge related to the needs of the poor and marginalised. Role models are those of the great scientists who have shaped modern science. Much school science replicates their experiments.

The central point is that the kinds of science education and training that might prepare young people to generate new technologies, invent new products, and discover fundamental scientific truths may well not be the same as that best suited to needs to adapt the application of science and technology to new contexts.

A strategy to promote technology transfer may invite. emphasis on a secure understanding of basic concepts and their application, systematic approaches to the incremental improvement of mature technologies, and the development of diagnostic and maintenance skills, rather than on those of curiosity driven creative exploration.

If the development of alternative technologies really were to be adopted as a priority, then traditional science education and training would have to be substantially re-orientated. This might include a stress on the social context of application, the utilisation of old as well as new technologies adapted to suit needs, and more emphasis on sustainable lifestyles sympathetic to the environment. In principle, if it is possible to define a development strategy related to science and technology needs, then this can be used as a basis to identify where the emphasis in science education should lie.

This way of looking at science education policy does try to derive its rationale from national development needs. It leads to the identification of curriculum aims. Choices then have to be made on tracking (how many students should study how much science in which types of institution); science and technology knowledge, skills and values in the curriculum (valued outcomes); learning and teaching methods; and assessment and certification.

There are many criticisms of top down approaches. These include assertions that such policy is unresponsive to the needs of the mass of people and reflects the priorities of governmental and technocratic elites; that problems of participation and achievement have their roots in perceived lack of relevance to individual needs and contexts; and that marginalised groups are often over looked in the process of defining and implementing policy. Centralised planning, which generates push models for change, has not been consistently successful, though in some cases it appears to have had some impact.

Effective demand has often proved a strong countervailing force as individuals express preferences and make judgements about the attractiveness, quality and relevance of science education programmes. An alternative view of policy generation starts from individual and social needs rather than a governmental view of priorities for development. It stresses the pull of effective demand. Instead of asking the question what kind of science education policy would be consistent with national development policy designed to lead to economic growth, it explores the needs citizens express and relates these to education and training in science.

The general profiling of these needs is not difficult. Their more precise delineation varies according to circumstance, economic development level, and cultural disposition and many other factors specific to context. This bottom up view of policy development is reactive rather more than it is pro-active. It is grounded more in social demand than in priorities derived from economic development needs. It should result in the specification of educational aims and outcomes that are valued by those who participate or want to participate in science education. If stakeholders needs are recognised in the policy development process it ought to strengthen effective demand for science education of kinds relevant to meeting those perceived needs.

It is easy to exaggerate how easy it might be to adopt bottom up strategies. There are many potential pitfalls. Individual and group interests can conflict with no obvious resolution. So can those of different interest groups. An accumulation of felt needs may lack coherence and integrity if it has not been mediated in ways that create feasible educational aims and outcomes. And though the approach can in principle lead to a consensus about tracking, curriculum, learning and teaching methods and assessment and certification, it might not.

Science education policy as emergent from the bottom up does respond to some of the critiques of top down policy that many felt needs are ignored, and that participation suffers if relevance is not perceived. It cannot alone guarantee that what emerges is an efficient way to meet national needs for human resource development in science and technology that tend to require long lead times and consistent investment in institutions, curricula and teachers.

There is no simple resolution of the basic differences between the top down and bottom up approaches. It is tempting to argue that a compromise is possible. There should be a way of recognising that both have merit. National needs do have a status that is different to that of the felt needs of individuals. It is the job of democratic governments to reach accommodations in the collective interest and to identify priorities which are believed to be in the best interests of the majority, whilst protecting the position of minorities. However this is achieved, policy will only be converted into learning and teaching realities if what is proposed does enjoy some level of consensus and is seen to have benefits to individuals as well as society more generally.

One way forward is to adopt a consultative methods coupled with policy analysis of national priorities. It is possible for governments to listen to stakeholders, whilst also allowing analysis of development needs to shape policy in ways which recognise, but are not necessarily led by, the demands generated by felt needs of individuals and groups. This is more likely to be feasible in those countries where civil society is well developed, professional organisations related to science and technology established, and infrastructure is sufficient to support planned implementation of whatever may be decided. Where policy is little more than the arbitrary exercise of power, professional advice weak or ineffectual, and consultative structures fragile or nonexistent it is of course not an option.

Some issues - constraints arising from low enrolments, restricted finance, and the characteristics of demand may seem essentially top down in character. They can be viewed bottom up providing it is remembered that whatever emerges from felt needs in terms of priorities has to be addressed in ways which recognise what exists and has to be expressed in terms of feasible choices.

Similarly decisions on specialisation, the organisation of the science curriculum, learning materials, practical activity, problems of assessment and selection, and patterns of science teacher education can also be viewed either as top down planning problems or as ones which should respond to the aspirations of the various groups of stakeholders.

There are a number of factors that shape the policy context for science education in developing countries. Four are considered. The first identifies questions related to participation, the second notes the importance of financial constraints, the third explores the dimensions of supply and demand for science education, and the fourth draws attention to different needs for different groups.

The opportunity to learn science is determined by overall participation rates, and by the organisation of the curriculum and school system that makes it possible to follow science course of a general or specialised kind. Key indicators of participation in science education are overall enrolment rates at secondary, differences in enrolment between groups (rich/poor, males /females, urban/rural etc.) and the proportions specialising in science at different levels.

Middle income developing countries have the great majority of children enrolled in the secondary grades. In contrast some of the poorest countries have gross enrolment rates of between 5% and 10%. Levels of gross enrolment at secondary in most developing countries suggest that less than half the school age population experience secondary science to any depth. The gross enrolment rate places a maximum on the numbers who have the opportunity to study science at secondary level.

In many cases the organisation of the curriculum and the fact that science is not always a compulsory subject means that significantly smaller proportions take science than those enrolled. If female participation in science is relatively low in these cases it is more likely to be the result of school level policy on curriculum, specialisation and option choice, than because of overall enrolment differences.

Science at secondary level is provided in different ways, most obviously through a general or integrated common course for all students, or through specialised subject disciplines (e.g. physics, chemistry and biology). Participation rates at upper secondary are typically between 50% and 30% of those at lower secondary, as a result of attrition and policy on streaming and option choices.

These participation rates have to be interpreted in the light of the amount of time allocated to science in the curriculum. Most systems offer a range of pathways and time allocations that are impossible to summarise simply. Some allocate more than 600 hours to science and mathematics over the school year at this level.

Financial Constraints

The financial constraints on investment in science education determine the range of options that exist to provide learning materials, physical infrastructure and equipment, and consumable materials. Science education budgets are rarely identified separately. Detailed studies indicate that science education does often receive greater amounts of non-salary recurrent finance than other subject areas.

In most systems salary costs are similar for science and other subjects. In some cases science teachers are better rewarded than others, as incentives are thought to be needed to retain their services. The resources allocated to secondary schools provide some indication of the constraints that exist in different countries. The richest countries allocate more than $5000 per child per year; the poorest less than $50. Moreover most of these allocations are to teachers' salaries.

This is disproportionately so in the poorest developing countries. If even 10% of per child expenditure is retained for non-salary expenditure and of this 20% is allocated to science education then the amounts available per year in the poorest countries can be as low as $1 per child. The policy question this raises is obvious. What can be provided has to be tailored to sustainable levels of resourcing. These are very low in poor developing countries. They can be enhanced if selection and specialisation are favoured which allow the concentration of investment in a limited number of schools.

Data on participation, selection ratios, promotion rates, the output of science qualified students at different levels, and employment can provide the basis for judgements of whether there are bottlenecks in the flow of science students that need to be addressed. The basic questions revolve around an assessment of whether participation in science education is supply or demand constrained at different levels, and whether there is a case to act to increase supply or demand related to national development strategies on human resource development. On the demand side there may be a higher or lower demand from students for places in education and training at secondary and tertiary level.

Labour market signals will also indicate whether the current output of those qualified in science matches demand from employers in the public and private sectors. On the supply side enough places may be available to meet demand in education and training institutions, or there may be shortages that constrain participation.

Evidently there are circumstances in which demand for science education places may be high, but supply should not necessarily be increased. For example, this would include situations where labour market signals suggest that greater output will not be absorbed productively, or where quality is so low as to suggest that improving attainment is a prior consideration to expanding access. Where supply is high but demand low, it does not necessarily follow that supply should be reduced. The judgement depends in part on the reasons why demand is low and whether future human resource needs suggest it will rise.

Demand may also be low because of the perceived irrelevance of the science education curriculum to employment. It is also possible that demand may be low because of rigidities amongst students in terms of the kinds of employment they will accept (e.g. single subject science graduates who anticipate careers in research organisations). It then may be that changes in the science curriculum which place more stress on the applied, and greater awareness of the range of career options open to graduates, should be considered. If a top down view of policy and planning is taken, then in principle it is the current and future demands of the labour market that should shape investment in science education.

If vacancies for science trained graduates and secondary school leavers are common, expatriates are often employed in science and technology based jobs, and employers anticipate needs growing in the future, a greater output is called for from the education and training system. Conversely, if there is much evidence of unemployment amongst science graduates and science school leavers, it may be that there is over supply.

Matching supply and demand will always be an imperfect art, not least because of the difficulties of predicting labour force demand more than a short period into the future. It is also true that investment in education and training often works on a different time scale to that of changes in labour force demand. Decisions today designed to increase participation and output through investment in increased institutional capacity are only likely to have an impact on the labour market three to five years hence, by which time patterns may have changed in unanticipated ways.

In poor countries with scarce resources the trade-offs involved need careful consideration. Rapidly expanding access may diminish quality to the extent that few if any students succeed in qualifying for the next level of science education. Affirmative action, quota systems and preferential investment in science education carry with them costs which may have an impact on average levels of achievement, and on the availability of investment for general quality improvement.

Judgements about supply and demand are complicated by the need to recognise that science education caters for several different groups and several different sets of valued outcomes. This is the fourth set of contextual issues. It is important to decide what these are in undertaking policy analysis. Most simply five groups of stakeholders exist. These are those who will become qualified scientists and engineers, those destined to work in sub-professional roles which require or benefit from a grounding in science, the remaining general school population, members of marginalised groups with special needs of one kind or another, and those in the informal sector.

Historically the needs of the first group have dominated much discussion of science education policy. A concern for graduate level supply and demand for qualified scientists and engineers (QSEs) is understandable and appropriate. Outputs of university graduates are relatively easy to determine, graduate labour markets are fairly clearly defined, and the employment of QSEs tends to be more politically visible than that of science qualified school leavers. It can be noted that some countries have concentrated resources in high level, expensive and ambitious research facilities and learning and teaching science at tertiary level.

The pursuit of world class scientific capacity has resulted in some cases in skewed budgetary allocations towards higher education that may be difficult to justify by results. Second, the education of QSEs may have been biased towards the needs of research despite the fact that most graduates are more likely to be employed in areas which apply science rather than explore its leading edges. Third, tertiary science curricula tend to be based on recent developments in the most scientifically advanced countries and international networks of scientific organisations, and external examining and professional associations encourage convergence in forms of science education, training and certification at tertiary level. This may or may not have utility for local labour markets and carries implications for the quality and orientation of science education at school level.

At the sub-professional level the supply of adequate numbers of trained technicians, research assistants, skilled production process workers, and tradesmen with science and technology skills is a widespread problem. In many developing countries the supply is chronically deficient and the quality of performance lacking.

There are several planning issues. First, a view is needed about the appropriate ratios of professional to sub-professionals educated in science. There is no golden ratio but the experience of industrially developed countries suggests that between 3 to 6 to 1 or more is common and that lower levels result in under-utilisation of graduates, and qualification escalation unrelated to competence. Second, traditional patterns of technical and vocational education tends towards segmentation and specialisation of skill and are predicated on a model of employment opportunity that reflects such specialisation. But job opportunities in many countries are characterised by their multi rather than mono skilled nature.

In the formal sector many of the most successful industries have moved away from specialised single task job structuring to utilisation of labour in ways that require flexible working practices. Third, there is an unresolved debate about the best methods to support the acquisition of middle level technical skill and competence. The main issue is the extent to which the basis for this can and should be laid in school level science education. This is discussed further below.

The needs of the general school population to acquire basic scientific literacy and numeracy have already been identified. It is generally accepted that a basic education cycle should have this as one of its goals.

There are three key planning issues. If science for all is regarded as a core element of the curriculum then it will cease to be an option to the end of the basic cycle, will be allocated appropriate amounts of curriculum time, and taught by teachers with sufficient understanding of science to achieve desired outcomes.

Second, science education intended to provide a secure basis for the citizen to engage with science and technology may differ from that intended to prepare students for the next level of science education. Third, what resources are required to assure scientific literacy and numeracy of sufficient quality to have an impact on levels of scientific awareness in the general population and capabilities to apply scientific knowledge and thinking skills to everyday problems. Groups marginalised from participation in science differ. Remedies for their inclusion need to be based on an understanding of the reasons for exclusion. Key issues appear to include first, identification of which groups are considered excluded.

Impoverishment is an obvious starting point. It may be superordinate to other attributes associated with low participation in science. Second, an adequate diagnosis of the reasons for exclusion is essential. Third, if participation, retention and achievement is to be improved which strategies can be demonstrated to be most effective? There are a range of possibilities which include quota systems, special incentives to study science, and preferential access to specialised science based schools.

Finally, those working in the informal sector may often benefit from basic scientific literacy and numeracy but may fail to have acquired it from the formal school system. Their needs should not be ignored. If these are recognised then it is necessary to consider a number of factors. First, to what extent are such individuals literate and likely to benefit from self-instructional material and feasible support programmes. A range of issues that preoccupy policy makers for science education in developing countries. It is necessarily selective. These are the debate on specialisation and special science schools, the structure and organisation of the science curriculum, the provision of learning materials, the role of practical activity, problems of assessment and selection, and patterns of science teacher education.

Specialisation and Special Science Schools

Policy on specialisation in science is critical. Its results determine at what level access to science education becomes selective and curricula are differentiated to meet different needs, and it shapes the flow of students through the system and into the labour market.

There are two main reasons for specialisation. First, it is likely to be the most cost-effective way of deploying scarce resources. If there is no realistic prospect of adequately reaching all schools it may be better to provide well-found learning and teaching facilities for a selected minority. Second, some level of specialisation may be the best way of responding to the range of abilities and interests that students manifest. It allows those with most ability to study in depth, permits student preferences for science and other subjects to be expressed, and does not preclude all students from studying some science.

It is an open question as to how early pupils should be given the option of specialising in science. Those who argue in favour of early specialisation note that those who do well in science early also tend to be high achievers in science later. The supposition is that success at a young age provides motivation to continue to achieve, and that mathematical and scientific skills and attitudes benefit from early development. It should be noted that few studies address the question of what happens to those who are selected out by early specialisation who may have potential that they are unable to realise. Neither do many openly debate how accurately it is possible to identify those who should specialise, especially in those developing countries where expertise in assessment is scarce.

There are arguments against early specialisation in science. There is a compelling case that priority should be given to science for all at the primary and lower secondary levels. In most developing countries these provide the last chance to acquire the rudiments of scientific literacy.

Quality basic education must include science-based knowledge and skills. This may be at least as important for some aspects of development (equity, rural income generation) as special provision for the most talented.

Quality basic science education is also important because science learning and its outcomes at the subsequent levels depend on the foundations established over the first eight or nine years. Both for those entering the labour market and for those continuing to study an adequate grounding in science is a prerequisite. It may also be true that early specialisation reinforces differences between groups.

Thus, in many countries where secondary science is optional, girls disproportionately tend to choose against science, or concentrate only on the life sciences. One consequence is continued under-representation of girls in science-based courses at higher education level and in the physical sciences. It may be both inequitable and inefficient to allow girls to opt out of science as a result of early specialisation. Specialisation takes many different forms.

In some countries secondary students specialise through enrolment in a science stream; in others students can choose between two or more science streams offering different science and other subjects in different ways.

The degree of specialisation is a function of both the number of subjects studied and the amount of time allocated to them, which gives an indication of depth. Where two or three sciences are studied for more than about 25% of curriculum time specialisation is likely to be high. The same time allocation spread across a wider range of science based subjects offers less depth, but still a high general level of specialisation in science. Where time allocations are much smaller - say 15% or less - specialisation in science is likely to be weak. Where science is a popular choice, time in school may be complemented by much time out of formal school in private tuition in science related subjects.

Useful indicators for planners of the degree of specialisation in science are:

(i) the time (in absolute and relative terms) that those specialising in science spend on science and mathematics,

(ii) the degree to which the curriculum for those specialising in science differs from the curriculum for "non science students" (depth and difficulty),

(iii) the number of science subjects/options taken,

(iv) the weighting of science in the examinations giving access to higher education.

One clear policy option related to specialisation is to create special schools with preferential access to resources and especially well qualified staff. Several countries have opted for this approach at different times, albeit in different ways. The case that can be developed in favour of teaching science in special institutions at secondary level is based on the following arguments:

— First, good science teaching is expensive and the necessary resources are scarce (competent teachers, well found laboratories, up to date libraries). It is therefore justified to concentrate on providing quality science education to a small minority of the best students in special institutions.

— Second, an adequate supply of competent scientists and technologists is needed to fill places in further and higher education. This may be better assured through tracking the best science students into special institutions with boarding facilities etc., rather than through a dilution of effort across the whole school system.

— Third, special institutions with special admissions policies may be needed to teach science in order to increase the participation of historically marginalised groups in science and technology based education and employment.

These arguments advanced in favour of special institutions to teach secondary science have to be balanced against difficulties that commonly arise in establishing a separate track through secondary education for science students. These are likely to include:

— the reliability and validity of methods used to select students suitable for special science schools

— the risks of academicising secondary science in elite institutions to the extent that it loses relevance to national development needs

— the possibility that without separate examination arrangements approaches to learning and teaching science will simply mirror those employed in ordinary schools and lack enriching experiences

— the difficulty of assessing what level of additional costs is justified

The first implies the need for technically sophisticated selection methods that can be shown to be valid and reliable. The fewer those selected and the greater the costs of their education, the more important it will be to establish confidence in the selection process. The second invites a reminder that no growing economy employs more pure than applied scientists.

The need for science qualified school leavers is likely to be skewed in favour of those with a sound basic science education and some applied science skills. There is a risk that the prestige associated with pure science, and the preferences of teachers (a minority of whom have usually been trained as applied scientists), may reinforce each other to emphasise the theoretical at the expense of the practical, the abstract at the expense of application. It is therefore likely to be important to accord at least equal status to technology and applied science in special institutions.

The third difficulty is that learning and teaching in special science schools may not be qualitatively different in orientation and emphasis if it follows common national curricula and prepares students for the common national examinations. It may be that with the best students, creative teachers, and extensive resources, time will be found for the more exploratory, challenging and intellectually demanding activities that can stretch understanding. If special schools are to emphasise learning goals that are different and more extensive than those associated with the teaching of science in ordinary schools assessment practices may need to be refined, or additional more challenging assessment provided.

Finally, it is easy to accept that special science schools need to be more expensive than normal schools, but difficult to decide what an appropriate ratio might be. Staffing ratios may need to be more generous. If the normal pupil teacher ratio is 25:1 should it be allowed to fall to 15:1 or 10:1 or even less? Equipment costs can escalate to high levels comparable with tertiary institutions if every request with a possible justification is met. There will be a point of diminishing returns where higher costs have little effect on science achievement. Expenditure may need to be controlled by those without a stake in expanding school budgets if appropriate levels are to be set.

The evidence on the effectiveness of special science schools is mixed, as might be expected from the variety of forms they take and the systems within which they operate. Various studies suggest that such schools can contribute to a number of outcomes which include:

— An increased supply of science-qualified leavers over and above what might otherwise be the case

— Greater participation in science education by previously under represented groups

— High levels of achievement in science

— Innovative learning and teaching styles for science not found in mainstream schools

However, costs can be high and the potential disadvantages noted above have to be recognised. Choice for or against special science schools and other forms of specialisation is partly a science education policy question, but is inevitably linked to broader questions of selection and specialisation within different school systems.

Curriculum Issues

Science curriculum development in many developing countries has a long history. Systematic attempts at curriculum reform in most date back the 1960s and early 1970s when many national curriculum development centres were established. Several recent trends can be identified. These include:

— Greater attention to science-for-all programmes, alongside continued emphasis on curricula designed for those who will continue to study science and the development of primary science curricula.

— More integrated/combined/coordinated/modular approaches, especially at lower secondary level, which draw content from the traditional science disciplines and stress scientific skills and cognitive processes above content.

— Attempts to apply the results of educational research, especially on cognition, to curriculum design and special interventions

— Greater concern for applications of science through technology and more emphasis on skills needed to solve real life problems. Introduction of science and society, environmental and health issues into science curricula

— Outcomes-based approaches to curricula and assessment and evaluation.

Real world problems that relate to development often do not have their understanding in one science discipline. At lower secondary level the commonalties in aims and objectives between the sciences are far greater than the differences, especially where these relate to cognitive skills rather than content. These considerations have accelerated the movement towards integrating lower secondary courses in which science is taught as a whole without divisions into physics, chemistry and biology.

This is now very widespread with only a minority of countries continuing to adhere to separate subject teaching at the lower secondary level.

Integrated courses have several varieties. The integration may be based upon concepts, or topics or may be little more than the mixing of traditional themes drawn from different science disciplines. The most obvious benefit of integrating is to allow a focus on science reasoning skills, which are promoted across a range of learning content.

Several integrated curricula are well established and apparently successful. However, the implementation of integrated courses can be problematic. The main obstacles seem to include insufficient preparation of teachers and reluctance to work outside traditional disciplinary boundaries; lack of appropriate teaching and learning materials; and low status compared to single subject sciences. In many countries teacher training courses remain un-integrated and separate subject training of science teachers persists.

In some cases integrated courses at school level are not taught by one teacher, but subdivided between several subject specialists which would seem to undermine their basic philosophy. At upper secondary level integration is relatively uncommon, though it remains the case that the separate sciences have many common learning objectives for practical work and cognitive skills.

General science courses that group subject matter, rather than integrate it, are often provided to those who do not specialise. These can suffer from a status inferior to separate subject courses. It may be difficult to attract and retain adequately qualified science teachers to teach these curricula. This is problematic if levels of achievement are low and it is the last science that many entering the labour market experience.

The approach to technology in the curriculum raises important policy questions. Some form of technology education is part of secondary curricula in all regions of the world. A common concern is for the development of practical knowledge and capabilities, as opposed to the academic skills associated with conventional science. Traditional technology courses aimed at developing craft skills have been criticised for two major reasons.

First, rapid technological change has led to more job mobility and less need for job-specific skills. Flexible specialisation has become more attractive than mono-skill certification. Second, more concern is being expressed for awareness of and control over the technological innovations that shape peoples' lives. Attempts have been made to introduce a critical approach to the study of technology and its applications and to design and implement science, technology and society courses that place technology in its social, political, environmental and moral context.

Central issues to be addressed by planners and policy-makers are:

(i) whether it is essential to provide technology courses as part of the compulsory curriculum at lower (or upper) secondary levels or whether they should be organised at a post-compulsory stage parallel to academic programmes.

(ii) to what extent science curricula which are "technologised" can accommodate the main aims of technology education at any particular level cost effectively.

Treating technology as a separate subject increases the burden on curriculum time if all students are to follow some technology related courses. Space has to be found in what are often already overcrowded timetables. If technology teaching requires special facilities in addition to those needed for the teaching of science, these have to be provided. If these are conventionally conceived their costs may be high.

Most countries do not have trained cadres of technology teachers outside those involved in traditional subject areas where the emphasis has often been on craft skills related to single occupations (carpentry, metalwork, typing etc.). It may be difficult to attract staff into higher level technology teaching where flexible skill application and development and design capabilities are stressed along with associated cognitive achievements.

The aims of technology education may not diverge radically from those of science curricula with an emphasis on application, a focus on real world problems, and an orientation towards logical reasoning skills. If this is true then technologising the science curriculum may well be a much more cost effective alternative to introducing technology as a separate subject, especially at lower secondary level. It has the advantage that a basic grounding in science is usually a prerequisite for purposeful application of technological skill based on analysis rather than intuition.

It simplifies the logistics of providing some technological insights for students. And it offers the prospect of providing technological awareness to those who subsequently specialise in academic science. It may also succeed in offering technological learning experiences to more girls for longer than will be the case where technology is taught as a separate subject. At higher levels the balance of the arguments may be different and the importance of specialisation in areas of technology may weigh in favour of provision separated from mainstream science curricula.

Whichever pattern of curriculum organisation is chosen (integrated, single science subjects, core curriculum and electives, technologised science education) consideration must be given to resource demands. Single integrated courses should be cheaper to deliver at equivalent quality since they offer opportunities to simplify textbook production, teacher training, staffing, timetabling, and laboratory provision, and examining and enjoy economies of scale. By implication it is usually preferable to incorporate material from other areas of science into one or two courses than to attempt to teach them separately. The more options there are, the more the costs and logistic complications of provision will escalate. The planners questions are to ask:

— What is the special value of particular options that justifies the additional costs?

— What are the science learning objectives that distinguish science and technology subjects so clearly that separate curricula are needed?

— How best can different learning outcomes for science be achieved for different groups of students at different levels without multiplying needs for specialist facilities and teachers?

Cross country analysis of curricula suggest that:

— the benefits from integrating science into a single subject at lower secondary are considerable and the disadvantages marginal

— science options at upper secondary should not be allowed to proliferate unless convincing cases based on unique and valued learning outcomes can be made

— content should be reduced where possible in favour of more emphasis on systematic attempts to develop higher order cognitive capabilities than recall and content should be selected taking account of material most likely to be relevant to the majority of students studying particular programmes

— enhancing the applied and technological aspects of science curricula may be more cost effective than developing separate course, except at higher levels

Learning and Teaching Materials

There are well established connections between the availability of learning materials and achievement in schools in developing countries. A matrix can be developed that charts the main issues that relate to provision and which form the basis for policy decisions. This has four dimensions. First, judgements have to be made about the quality and relevance of existing material. If these are both low then systematic curriculum development is probably needed. If quality and relevance are judged adequate an emphasis on supporting the effective use of learning material may be more attractive. It is important to make considered judgements that do not assume that curriculum materials are necessarily the reason for unsatisfactory learning and teaching.

The developing world contains many examples of curriculum development projects that have had ambitions to change how science is taught which have not succeeded. This suggests that other factors - patterns of assessment, working practices in schools, cultural dispositions towards particular learning and teaching styles - may be at least as important as the quality and relevance of learning and teaching materials in determining how science is taught. The message from experience seems to be to only embark on resource intensive curriculum development only after establishing that it is indeed the quality and relevance of materials that is a central problem.

Second, where quality and relevance is adequate questions of distribution and availability have to be addressed. Systems vary in their ability to provide text material to students (and teachers guides). The full range of approaches exists between wholly private and wholly public systems for production and distribution. All can work effectively. If they do not, then intervention is needed once it is established where the bottlenecks lie. The choice between more and less public or private production and distribution systems is linked closely to the political preferences of different governments. Third, the range of materials available needs consideration. So also do patterns of use. If the range is narrow scope exists for enrichment, assuming resources are not too scarce.

Many possibilities exist including developing connections to internet-based sources of learning material and information. Patterns of use of materials can be very illuminating. There are cases where officially produced curriculum materials in science are considered less useful than those available from other sources. Where commercial textbook markets have developed, the pattern of sales may provide a strong indication of what kinds of materials are valued by teachers and students. These may or may not be consistent with the official curriculum.

In particular they may be highly assessment-orientated and designed to focus on the narrow range of outcomes tested by conventional external examinations.

In many countries examination guides containing key facts outsell science textbooks. If this is so then there must be concern that valued curriculum outcomes may not be being encouraged by the assessment system. It may be that these examination-orientated materials define the science curriculum in action more than do materials produced by curriculum development centres.

Fourth, the costs of learning materials may be problematic. Costs need to be at levels that ensure access. What the costs are and how they are made up is a market specific question. This is a complex area since learning materials production has become a global business. Many factors may need considering in reaching decisions that balance costs, availability, quality and relevance.

Local production in country may or may not be cheaper, adaptation of existing material may be cost effective given the commonalities that exit between science curricula, frequent changes to curricula impose high costs for new learning material, and the durability of learning material is an important factor in replacement costs. Cost recovery schemes and textbook loan systems can reduce public costs if successfully implemented.

The costs of teaching science are relatively high when compared to other subjects primarily because of the investment that takes place in providing and maintaining practical facilities and the implications these carry for the employment of ancillary staff. In some systems it is also because of the smaller groups size associated with practical subjects.

Despite the many initiatives that have occurred to simplify practical activity in many countries, the teaching of science in a conventional laboratory-based environment remains the normal expectation. This is notwithstanding widespread inability to finance the costs for all except a small minority of students. Where laboratory costs are many multiples of the cost of ordinary classrooms, running costs cannot be sustained, and where laboratories are often used as ordinary classrooms by science teachers, the purpose of high cost provision must be questioned.

The main reasons given to justify science practical work in science contain at least four assumptions. These are that practical work is essential to achieve outcomes related to inquiry and (guided) discovery; develop experimental skill; link conceptual learning to concrete experiences and motivate students; and enhance cognitive achievement in science. All these assumptions can be contested. The first assumes outcomes arising from practical work that cannot be achieved through alternative (and less costly) teaching methods.

There is much evidence that the provision of practical facilities is no guarantee that science achievement will be high or that practical work will actually be undertaken with an appropriate frequency or quality. The second anticipates that practical work will be undertaken in ways that allow students the opportunity to develop experimental skills, e.g. those of design of fair tests, interpretation of results, improvement of technique.

This may be true but the evidence is that science practical work can become characterised by ritualised replication of standard experiments undertaken more in a "minds off" rather than "minds on" manner. Third, it may be that concrete experiences are helpful to internalise science concepts. But they are clearly not the only way. Carefully organised demonstrations may be at least as effective and much less costly.

Moreover the motivational benefits associated with practical activity may be unevenly distributed amongst students. It cannot be assumed that those without a high motivation to study science will see practical activity as something that is attractive. The opposite is equally plausible. Fourth, strong links between science achievement and the provision and use of practical facilities are difficult to establish. This may be in part because conventional measures of science achievement usually do not emphasise outcomes that can be exclusively associated with practical work and which cannot be acquired through other types of learning.

The role of practical activity in science is often confused with laboratory work. The high status image of laboratory-based science can displace a focus on the thinking strategies and manipulative skills that are the most important outcomes that practical activity can support. Active engagement with problems in the physical world is part of everyday experience and most, if not all, worthwhile thinking skills associated with secondary science can be taught without expensive equipment. Many lower cost alternatives are available and demonstrations, videos and other simulations may be at least as effective, but cheaper than individual or group practical work, in promoting conceptual development.

Planners and policy makers should consider in relation to practical work:

— wherever possible practical work should be designed with costs in mind to make appropriate activities available to relatively poorly resourced schools which have large classes

— the quality and quantity of laboratory-based work should be considered in the light of the learning gains associated with it; it may be that fewer extended but simple experiments, along with simple practical activities, which may not be experimental, are a preferable and more cost effective option than curricula that assume experiments take place virtually every teaching period.

— alternatives to laboratory-based work - thought experiments, demonstrations, simulations, video presentations - should be considered as a substitute for some individual or group class work.

The costs of laboratory provision vary across an enormous range relative to the cost of ordinary classrooms. The differences may be as great as a ratio of 10:1. Where costs are many multiples of normal classroom costs and provision is well short of the number needed for all secondary schools, lower cost alternatives should be considered.

The most obvious option is to agree the design of science rooms based on ordinary classrooms that have a selected range of basic facilities adequate to teach non-specialised science through to the end of upper secondary school. This should be possible at no more than double the cost of ordinary classrooms. In summary:

— Laboratory costs should be a relatively small multiple of classroom building costs in all but the most well resourced school systems.

— The design of laboratories should, wherever possible, seek to provide a basic range of services that can be sustained and which are appropriate to location, with adequate lighting and ventilation

— Secure storge should be incorporated into the design and safety considerations should be included

— Where space permits furnishing should allow individual and small group work. Provision should allow visible demonstration work

— Science rooms should be considered as an acceptable alternative to laboratories in resource poor systems

The cost of equipment depends on what is specified and where it is produced. National lists of the minimum necessary equipment to teach science should be constructed where these do not already exist, and should be restricted to that which is essential. In summary:

— High cost individual items should be avoided especially if infrequently used. Imported equipment should always be assessed to determine whether local alternatives of adequate quality can be produced.

— Appropriately designed science kits should be considered as an alternative or as a supplement to the existing equipment base where cost precludes comprehensively equipping all schools.

If kits are deployed, advice in their use and arrangements for replenishment should be part of any implementation package. There are a number of assessment issues that have particular significance for the planning of science education. These are the significance of assessment in science for progression through the school system, the relationships between the curriculum and patterns of assessment, the problems of assessing practical work, and the ways in which assessment information can be used to plan interventions to improve quality and performance.

First, science is a component of most primary school leaving examinations that give access to secondary school and the promotion examinations that control the transition between lower and upper secondary. Typically it is one of between four to as many as fourteen subjects that are examined. In most countries mathematics counts for more than science. The weightings given to science for access to post secondary education are closely related to the subjects of higher study. Science scores may account for half or more of the marks available. In contrast science rarely carries much weight for access to non-science higher level courses. The rubric of selection subjects and the weighting of science has implications for the numbers of students studying science and the length of time they persist.

Some countries place little emphasis on science achievement for access to upper secondary school, others make it compulsory to the end of upper secondary. The acquisition of scientific literacy of a minimal kind would seem to depend on studying science at least to the end of lower secondary and attributing importance to a basic level of achievement. Second, how secondary science is taught, which topics are emphasised, and what motivation students have to acquire scientific knowledge and skills are all likely to be strongly influenced by the nature of what is assessed.

There is an extensive literature on the general effects of assessment on teaching and learning in developing countries, which illustrates the degree to which educational practice may be determined by the choices made in measuring outcomes. There is evidence that many public examinations in science continue to be heavily dependent on items that test the recall of information. This is despite much advocacy of the need to assess higher order cognitive outcomes.

Two aspects of the curriculum/assessment relationship in science subjects stand out. First, the kinds of outcomes that science curricula often aspire to can only be assessed through a combination of written tasks under examination conditions, performance of practically based activities, and study and reporting activities that may extend over a relatively long time and involve collaborative work with others.

Many valued outcomes will not be assessed unless it is possible to introduce some elements of school-based examining. This is relatively uncommon in developing countries. It is likely to have significant costs in terms of time and requires minimum levels of competence in the design and application of assessment techniques by teachers. The second aspect is concerned with opportunities to reshape the curriculum/assessment relationship through the introduction of curricula based on criteria of competency.

In principle the invitation is to define performance outcomes that profile competency at a particular level by specifying statements of mastery within relevant domains. These then provide the criterion behaviours against which students performance can be assessed. The curricula, and certainly the assessment instruments, almost write themselves since the structure and content of items are suggested by domain statements.

What seems a simple and logical approach to redefining the relationship between assessment and curricula turns out to have many difficulties in practice. Domain statements in science are not always simple statements that can define competencies very precisely. A risk is that attempts to achieve increased precision results in a very lengthy list of competencies, so long as to lose much practical application. Competency-based approaches to curriculum development may also have difficulty in defining outcomes that are both sufficiently challenging to test the most able students of a given age, and not too difficult to completely discourage the less able.

Despite these and other difficulties, policy makers and planners have begun to favour competency-based approaches to curriculum and assessment. At the very least they focus attention on attempts to define valued outcomes in measurable ways. They also draw attention to whether or not the full range of curriculum outcomes are assessed, and provide evidence on the extent to which students achieve different levels of competence.

The form the assessment takes can be used to encourage the learning outcomes that are valued. Third, assessing practical work remains problematic because it is expensive and inconvenient to organise. As noted above, there is not much evidence that public examination results are influenced by the amount and quality of practical work undertaken, and assessment of many outcomes thought to be promoted by practical work interacts with more general cognitive competencies.

The expense of practical examining arises partly from the need to assess under controlled conditions where all candidates attempt the same tasks at approximately the same time. This requires that standard apparatus and consumables should be available. If specimens of any kind are involved this may add to the problems since large numbers may have to be procured, quality assured, and distribution problems solved.

Additional costs will be involved in the setting up time needed to arrange school laboratories for examinations, which often disrupt normal teaching for substantial periods.

A further cost arises if any element of performance, as opposed to outcome, is to be assessed, since this can only be undertaken as it happens. Elements of technique, some aspects of observational skills, and design and experimental development skills can only properly be assessed by observing and following the processes a student goes through. Even if this is done using checklists the process will be time consuming.

Fourth, where national examining systems test students on technically valid and reliable items, large amounts of performance data are generated each year. This can be used to explore a whole range of questions including what differences exist between rural and urban students; what are the kinds of gender based differences in performance; which aspects of the science curriculum are consistently found difficult by different groups of students; and what characteristics are associated with improving and deteriorating performance in science at the school level.

Some types of assessment items can discriminate in favour of rural students. Overall performance differences are related to the balance of items of this type. Differences in achievement between groups can have their origins in small parts of the science curriculum rather than in all areas. Thus in some cases much of the variance in performance between boys and girls may originate from physical science in general and electromagnetism in particular.

This carries strategic implications for curriculum development and in service support. Paradoxically it is often true that high performing schools have large class sizes as a result of excess demand, and may coexist with low performing schools with small classes. Simple associations between class size and achievement in science can be misleading. School effectiveness methods can be applied to assessment and other data to gain insights into policy interventions that might have more effect than others.

Many studies suggest that more qualified and experienced science teachers are associated with higher levels of achievement in science more often than not. Attracting and retaining sufficient numbers of science graduates into the teaching profession remains a serious problem in countries where these graduates are high in demand and are better paid in the private sector in other occupations. It is often suggested that entering the teaching profession is the result of a negative choice by students who have failed to find other employment opportunities.

This is likely to be less of a problem where the output of those with science qualifications has been large and there are more applicants than places for teacher training. A surplus of science qualification holders, whether as a result of an overproduction of graduates or of a shrinking labour market means that higher quality applicants can be selected than would otherwise be the case.

There are many issues related to science teacher education in developing countries. First, the profile of science teachers in different countries varies according to the educational levels/credentials that are required for admission to training. In some developing countries a minimum entry level is defined by secondary school leaving qualification in science, in others a degree may be required.

Some countries have admissions tests organised by colleges or universities. Others, which do not have public examinations at the end of secondary, depend on university entrance tests or some other form of assessment. Levels of achievement amongst entrants to teaching are often unimpressive. It is not unusual to find that many science teacher trainees have low grade passes in science at secondary level. Where this is so it carries implications for the nature of training since subject competence is weak.

It is also the case that in a significant number of developing countries entrants into initial training have already had some experience as teachers. Practice varies between countries but often new recruits are drawn from those working as untrained teachers or teaching assistants. In some cases these trainees will have experienced some systematic on-the-job training; in others no provision will have been made. In principle, experience in teaching provides some evidence of the suitability and competence of trainees that can be used to improve selection. In practice, this is rarely done systematically.

Second, initial teacher training programmes vary in length, content and curriculum organisation The maximum length is about four years, but can be as little as two years post secondary. Where there are sufficient graduates, postgraduate one year training post-first degree is offered.

Many countries distinguish between lower and upper secondary teachers and provide different courses for each. Where the supply permits, upper secondary teachers often have graduate status. In some cases this extends to lower secondary teachers.

The major curriculum issues in most training systems are the balance between subject matter upgrading, general education and pedagogic studies, and professional studies including teaching practice. Effective science teaching undoubtedly requires an adequate level of subject matter knowledge. It also requires some theoretical understanding of how students learn and the professional skills associated with managing learning, motivating learners and presenting material in forms that can be understood by students of different ages and capabilities. Decisions on what the balance should be have to consider the subject competence of trainees on entry, the level at which they will teach, the nature of the schools in which they will teach, and the time and other resources available for training.

General education and pedagogic studies may take between 10% and 60% of the time and professional studies between 20% and 40%.

Teaching practice in most conventional full time training programmes covers a range between about 12 and 24 weeks. It is worth noting that the effectiveness of training will be associated with the extent to which training experiences are matched to likely teaching environments. One elaboration makes the point.

Pupil/teacher ratios in secondary schools in developing countries cover the range between about 15:1 and 40:1. This implies class sizes on average of between about 30:1 and 80:1, given that class teacher ratios in secondary schools are often around 2:1 since, unlike in most primary school systems, secondary teachers are generally timetabled with significant amounts of non-teaching time. If trainees are to be prepared to teach classes in excess of say 50 students, training emphasis on small group work and individual experimentation in science may be inappropriate.

Third, the deployment of science teachers is known to be problematic. Distribution is often uneven with surpluses in favoured schools co-existing with shortages in others. It may also be the case that trained science teachers are not teaching science but other subjects or are promoted to administrative posts, thus exacerbating shortages that may exist.

Few systems in developing countries have systems that deploy new science teachers in ways that could reinforce the benefits of their training. Two main systems exist. In one teachers are posted to schools by a central authority. More often than not this results in posting to less favoured schools with weak infrastructure and teaching resources since the politics of posting usually favour established teachers who move to more desirable locations.

Market systems that allow new teachers to apply for advertised jobs tend to exacerbate shortages in unfavoured locations. Either system could work more efficiently. If posting were rational and based more on need as determined by analysis of school staff and curriculum demand for science, the match between those trained in science and those teaching science should improve. Market systems will only work if there are incentives for trained teachers to apply for jobs where they are needed most. If this is not so, and there is a shortage of supply, there will be concentration in schools in favoured locations.

It is also important to establish the average length of a science teacher's career. Attrition amongst science teachers is typically higher than for other subject specialists. Alternative opportunities are often more readily available for those with science and technology skills. In those countries worst affected by HIV/AIDS attrition is also rising amongst those who are sero-positive.

The length of science teachers careers is a critical consideration. If this has been shortening then different patterns of training with lower costs are attractive. Third, although there is much enthusiasm for school-based training in the teacher education literature internationally, this is a pathway with severe limitations in resource poor countries with a high proportion of untrained teachers in schools. It is possible to imagine effective systems based on clusters of schools in which trainees work if there are a sufficient number that can demonstrate good practice. Where this is not the case school-based training will not be attractive.

Finally, the kind of training policy that is appropriate has to depend on an assessment of teacher demand. What is possible where the numbers involved are small is very different to circumstances where large numbers need some training over a short period of time.

These are questions that can only be answered with reference to broader education policy goals related to how much science should be taught to how many students at what level.

ICT and Science Education

There are several ways in which information and communication technologies can transform the educational landscape. These include allowing access to high quality learning material available from remote sites; facilitating novel learning materials; permitting open connectivity between learners and between learners and teachers independent of location; and managing learning and monitoring progress.

In principle teachers can already download a wealth of science instructional material from websites, including that which is interactive. Computers, networked or otherwise, can run software that simulates many standard science experiments, and offers interactive expeiiences that are otherwise difficult or impossible to provide. The potential for science student to learn from each other at a distance is evident, as are the possibilities for following distance courses. It is also clear that the management of science education could benefit from databases, inventory controls and ordering systems that might, in all or part, be electronically configured.

Record keeping on student progress and the analysis of assessment data to establish learning difficulties can also be more efficient using computer based systems. In order to have an impact some antecedent conditions are likely to need meeting.

Adequate hardware, software and connectivity are all essential if ICT infrastructure is to be sufficient to allow the opportunities identified to be turned into actualities. The three are interdependent. If all elements are not present, many developments cannot take place. Hardware demands imply that interface devices are available at costs and on a scale sufficient to provide frequent access to many users. Technically qualified staff are needed to maintain stand-alone or networked systems. Adequate recurrent funding is necessary to support the cost of upgrading equipment every three to five years. These are significant demands on the resources of school systems.

As important as hardware is the need to identify or develop affordable software appropriate to users' needs, defined in terms of language, application, cultural relevance, and learning needs. It is tempting to assume that the universal aspects of science curricula mean that the chances are that software is already available at a price. This may be true for discrete aspects of the science curriculum (e.g. simulations of common experiments), but it is not true of curricula as a whole, which differ significantly in emphasis and approach between countries. It is also the case that software may require maintenance to keep it configured as intended, and that its effective use benefits from training.

Lastly, but critical to connectivity, reliable connections are needed to the internet. This is problematic where telephone lines are scarce and of low quality and bandwidth. Depending on pricing regimes for telecommunications, it may also be expensive.

But without connectivity access to the internet is unavailable, restricting users to stand alone machines or local networks. It is self-evident that science education can benefit in many ways from access to computers and the internet. These include the opportunities outlined above, many of which apply to other subjects, and some of which are more specific to science (e.g. analysis of data collected with sensors; dynamic simulations of complex natural processes; solutions of equations where human calculations are impractical; and links with science and science teacher education web sites and CD-Rom distribution of learning materials).

The potential of ICTs is considerable. Properly managed and supported, and sympathetically integrated into national curricula, they offer a rich set of new opportunities. It can be noted that there is no reason why content for learning systems should not be generated in ways that reflect different national and individual needs by those who acquire the skill and have the motivation.

However, the best guess must be that the relative size of markets at a global level is likely to ensure that most applications are produced for rich country consumption and this is likely to continue to influence software and content development related to science education. This may not be optimal, but it is almost inevitable. It will have benefits. The real difficulties for developing countries are those of costs and infrastructure to sustain reliable access to learners and teachers. Data on telephone access is illuminating. East Asian tiger economies provide telephone access of 50 lines per 100 population or better.

In much of Africa line access is below 1 per 100. International telephone calls average over 250 minutes per person in Hong Kong and Singapore, but less than a minute per year in most of the poorest countries.

Estimates of the number of graduates in science and engineering give some indication of the availability of those who can technically manage and develop ICT systems. This varies from less than 2 per 10,000 inhabitants in some countries in Sub-Saharan Africa to over 100 in some European countries. Connectivity in the mid 1990s varied enormously.

The US had over 6 million internet hosts in 1996, compared to 23,000 in Singapore, 2,400 in Indonesia, 90 in Zimbabwe and 60 in Uganda. The connection costs for internet access in the poorest countries can be greater than in the richest. Subscriptions to internet service providers are often set at international levels since many of the service providers are directly or indirectly located in rich countries. The amounts invested in formal education by governments give some indication of the magnitude of recurrent public expenditure available to support ICT related developments in education.

In the poorest countries this amounts to about $5 per child per year. In middle income countries an equivalent estimation would yield about $40 per child per year and in the richest group about $430. Not all non-salary expenditure is available to support ICT based innovations.

Most will be committed to maintenance, non-ICT learning materials and equipment etc. If perhaps 20% of non-salary allocations could be linked to new developments related to ICTs this would mean that whatever was provided at school level would have to be delivered for less than $1 per child per year in the poorest countries at primary level (and perhaps $2-$5 at secondary).

At tertiary level the poorest countries allocate on average about $1,200 per student and the richest $8600. If 20% of this is non-salary spending, and 20% of this is available to support ICT-based systems then this translates into $48 per student in the poorest countries and $350 in the richest. Whatever the threshold is to meet the antecedent conditions necessary for viable and sustainable ICT-based learning systems, it is likely to be much more than $1 per child per year 2 , but conceivably less than $48.

This analysis provides clear signals that ICTs that require frequent and individualised access to a wide user group are unlikely to be feasible in the poorest countries in the near future.

Small pockets of users can be created that are connected reliably. This may include intermediaries (e.g. teacher educators, in-service co-ordinators, curriculum developers) who can share benefits with the broader community of education professionals. If there is a public strategy it will be one that provides selective access focused by resource constraints and critical areas in which ICT-based systems can have an impact that can be sustained.

Science education is one of these, but not at the level of individual mass access. In middle income developing countries, it is feasible to imagine connectivity spreading to substantial parts of the population over the next decade. How far this penetrates formal learning systems will depend on the investment decisions that governments and individuals make.

The impact of new information and communication technologies on science education is uncertain. The opportunities are extensive. They carry with them both considerable potential benefits and some risks. Reliable access to the internet is extremely varied across developing countries.

The development of professional networks of science educators across countries offers exciting possibilities that could help improve science education quality and access. The potential is not the realisation. Careful consideration has to be given to which strategies really do offer benefits at an education system level that match needs at sustainable levels of cost.

Science education is a sub-system that has it own characteristics that can be a separate focus of attention. However it does have to be seen in a more general system context if interventions, which are to have positive effects, are to be identified. This chapter is set out to locate science education policy within a general framework related to development priorities and how they are identified.

It then outlined some key contextual factors that shape policy and planing and developed perspectives on a number of issues that recur in debates on science education. It has argued that it is important to recognise that science education exists within a cultural, institutional and developmental context that differs between countries.

Some secondary school systems are very selective; others are not. Some have separate schools identified and resourced to provide high quality science and technology education, others do not.

Science curricula are organised in many different ways with differing levels of subject integration, time allocations, expectations of practical work, and emphasis on the academic or the applied. The extent to which science teachers are trained as specialists within a conventional discipline, or prepared to teach across a range of subjects also varies. All these things constitute starting points for policy and planning.

The last point is that established patterns of providing science education exist for reasons related to previous decisions and accommodations of competing methods of organising schools and curricula.

Most developing countries have a substantial history of attempts to extend access, improve curricula and revitalise learning and teaching in science and improve achievement.

There is much to learn from this history about why some innovations have taken root and many others have delivered less than they promised. Diagnosis is a starting point for policy. Those involved need to pause long enough to reflect on what has and has not worked before reinventing broken wheels.

Curriculum development alone is not a solution to problems of unsatisfactory, learning and teaching methods and low achievement, if these have their causes elsewhere. Neither is investment in facilities and equipment where these cannot be shown to have a direct relationship to improved learning outcomes.

Educating Secondary School Science Teachers

There are many factors to consider when attempting to improve student achievement in science. These factors are: the appropriateness and currency of the curriculum; the availability and quality of textbooks; the appropriateness of the assessment system; the availability of laboratories and scientific equipment; the school environment in which learning takes place; and the quality of the science teacher. Of all these factors, the one which is perhaps most frequently overlooked is the quality of the science teacher.

The educational qualifications of secondary science teachers, their ways of presenting science to their students, and their attitudes toward science have all been shown in various studies to have a significant impact on the achievement of their students. Thus, there is a great deal of interest in ensuring that the preservice and in-service education of secondary science teachers is as effective as possible.

While there are good teacher education programs, there still remains the need to evaluate the appropriateness and currency of even the very best programs, given the new expectation that modern science will be made accessible to all students. There have also been advances in cognitive research on how students learn science that have still to shape the curriculum in many teacher training institutions.

There is a consensus building on the so-called "policy parameterse associated with the preservice education of secondary science teachers. The new entry-level preservice programs are increasingly four years in length, and at a bachelors degree-level They include instruction in science, pedagogy, and general education, with an emphasis on the science content. Programs for upper secondary science teachers contain a greater percentage of science courses than programs for lower secondary science teachers The range of time typically spent on the science component of the syllabus falls within the relatively narrow margin of 60% to 70%.

The length of the program seems to be a matter of expediency or custom rather than proven value. It is argued that a shorter program will not allow sufficient time to cover both the formal coursework considered essential for a well-prepared science teacher, and the period of classroom practice which is also considered necessary. However, a longer program adds to the costs for both program sponsors and the trainees, with no definitive research data supporting the contention that a longer program is really required. The six-year preparation to teach science at a Genman "gymnasium" is a luxur few countries can afford. It is unrealistic to expect teachers to spend more than four years in a preservice program, especially in countries where teaching is a low-status occupation. For the student teacher, the financial rewards may never be sufficient to justify the greater effort, and the deferment of earnings for one or two more- years.

The content of many science teacher preparation programs needs to be re-evaluated to eliminate intellectually superficial courses from the curriculum. Expanded definitions of science content at the secondary level and a greater understanding of how students actually learn science, has implications related to the relevance of much that is currently included in the science teacher preservice program. The science component needs to cover a broader view of science than can be gained from the in-depth study of only one science. The student teacher needs to learn more than just the fats and concepts of science.

The student teacher needs to learn that: there are connections between disciplines; some scientific ideas are more important than others; science is one way of understanding reality; there are scientific modes of inquiry and habits of mind. Student teachers also need to be exposed to pedagogical content knowledge relevant to the disciplines they will teach.

Many teacher educators, whether teaching at a university or a teacher training college, do not have the educational background necessary to teach the existing teacher training curriculum effectively. They need to be upgraded in terms of both their science and pedagogical knowledge, at least to a master's degree level in science education. Increased collaboration between the faculties of science and education is absolutely essential if teacher training programs are to improve significantly. This cooperation is more likely to take place if there is some kind of intitutional support system in place to encourage and reward instructors who work together in cross-disciplinary partnerships.

Teacher training institutions need to begin to take teacher preparation seriously enough to put more thought and imagintion into program design and flexible course scheduling. Some students might be encouraged to interrupt their formal education to teach for one or two semesters, and then return to finish their degree.

As secondary education enrolments expanded, many countries allowed large numbers of unqualified students to enter teaching without any form of training. These countries are currently seeking the most cost-effective ways to provide in-service education to as many teachers as possible to bring them up to the current entry-level standards. A variety of opportunities are available to accomplish this, including residential and distance education programs. Distance education is particularly cost-effective, but needs to include sufficient hands-on science and teacher/tutor interactions to impact on the teacher's comfort-level in the laboratory.

In-service education is also used to introduce new curricula, examinations, and textbooks to teachers. Where major reforms are being introduced into the secondary science program, the cooperation of classroom teachers should be enlisted as participants in designing, conducting, and evaluating the range of in-service programs to be offered. The "cascade" model of dissemination, using teachers to train teachers, can be an effective way both to use "mastere teachers, and to reach a large number of other teachers with in-service education. However, efforts must be made to ensure the quality of the message down the cascade, perhaps through the development of well-designed instructional manuals, and supporing film loops, videos, etc.

Where in-service education is designed to bring all teachers up to some minimally acceptable level of education, or to provide a supportive introduction to a new textbook or curriculum, it is usually mandatory. All mandatory in-service science education should include a stipend for particpating teachers if the activity takes place on the teachers' time.

Finally, there remains the need to ensure that even the best prepared and functioning teachers maintain currency in their discipline(s) and in ways of presenting their subject(s) to students. Reading science and science education journals; joining science teacher organisations; attending workshops at their own expense; participating in science olympiads with their students; and organizing science fairs, are some of the activities which contribute to the professional development of the teacher.

Given the conditions under which some of these,teachers work their relzavely low pay, and probably limited prospects for career advancement, it is a tribute to science teachers in developing countries that many already participate in these blinds of continuing education opportunities with enthusiasm, dedication, and creativity. Efforts must be made to ensure that more teachers have; these opportunities to develop as professionals.

Significance of Science Education

In many nations, science and technology education are becoming increasingly identified as the background for economic stability add growth. In the past, in developed and developing countries, only the "brighter" students have been encouraged to pursue science knowledge. Science has been viewed as knowledge accessible to only the elite few. Now, however, many countries are subscribing to the goal of "science for all."

Science is increasingly being viewed as a subject of life-long utility to all students, whether or not they enter science-related careers. In the developing world, a more science literate populace is perceived as being better equipped to contribute to economic and societal development through informed decision-making in such areas as: agricultural production, nutrition and health, land and resource management, population control and industrial growth.

The "science for all" movement is driving curricular change at varying speeds in different countries and the process of school science curricula redefnition in motion worldwide. This redefinition is being accompanied by a re-examination of the classroom role of the teacher - supported by findings from cognitive psychology on how students actually learn science - from "sage on the stage, to guide on the side."

In many countries, science teachers, particularly at the lower secondary level, are unprepared to teach the existing science courses in a teacher-centered classroom. It is not just the "science for all" movement that is driving curricular change. The old disciplinary boundanes are fading in the dynamic world of science research. Biology is becoming chemistry which is becoming biology, touching on physics which shades into chemistry. It is in the bridging sciences of biochemistry, biophysics, and materials science where much of the vitality of modern science is best displayed.

Yet, on a worldwide basis, both the university courses of study and the upper secondary science stream courses tend to remain obstinately defined as chemistry, physics, and biology as they were delineated 30 years ago. This is a 'turf' problem that is presently being solved at the university level Eventually, it will be recognized that the shift to interdisciplinary science research has implications at the precollege level If the curricula for the science stream are to be modernized, secondary science teachers will have to develop a broader knowledge of the sciences than most have at present, including a better understanding of the relationships between disciplines.

Thus, whether science is to be taught to future scientists, or to future citizens, there is a pressing need to ensure that the secondary science teacher, whose role is so crucial, has the educational background necessary to rise to both challenges. The issue is not that there are no well-prepared secondary science teachers. The issue is that the purposes of science education are changing, the content and its delivery are evolving, and the expectations for student achievement are rising. This is true for both developing and developed countries.

Ten years ago, it was still generally accepted that 'teaching was telling, learning was listening, and knowledge was facts". This view of the teaching/learning exchange is being replaced by a more "agile" pedagogy, which recognizes the students' own active role in the learning process, and views the teacher as a facilitator of this process.

Today's students will be tomorrow's citizens. They will enter a workforce that needs the talents of better educated students, capable of life-long self-directed learning and of contributing to sound decision-making for their community and their country. If more students are to be taught to function at higher levels of cognition, they will need to be taught by teachers who can themselves operate as life-long, self-directed learners.

Thus, because of relatively recent changes in our views of both science and teaching, even the very best of teacher training facilities needs to re-examine and re-evaluate the currency of its mission and its curriculum.

The Importance of the Science Teacher

The educational background of the secondary science teacher is obviously only one of the variables contributing to student achievement in science. When money is scarce, countries must make the decision where money can be most effectively spent - on teacher education, higher quality textbooks, more equipment, better working conditions for teachers, higher teacher salaries, etc.

The research data do make it clear exactly which interventions are generally most cost-effective. Given the many different and interacting variables that contribute to student success in different school systems, it is not possible with current data to state unequivocally that any of point of intervention can be identified as most cost-effective. There is a need for a more systemic approach to educational reform; many points of intervention need to be addressed simultaneously.

There is evidence that the education of secondary science teachers linked to their students' achievement in a much clearer fashion than, for example, the educational background of elementary teachers is linked to their students. It would appear logical that the knowledge of the science teacher, the ways in which the teacher delivers instruction, and the teacher's attitudes toward science have an impact on student achievement.

All of these factors are related to the teacher's own education - both as a teacher, and as a former school pupil There is evidence that the formal qualifications and experience of both lower and upper secondary science teachers is positively correlated with the achievement of their students, epecially in developing countries. This has been shown for teachers in Malaysia, India, the Philippines, and several Latin American countries. It has also been shown that, for the United States, science teachers of identified "exemplar programme had a much stronger educational background than a national sample of high school science teachers, with the "exemplary" group having completed more science courses than required for most U.S. undergraduate science degrees.

In the Netherlands, the better teachers had more post-secondary education, and belonged to a science teachers association. In both the United States and Thailand, the more effective teachers were science specialists, with more post-secondary education than the less effective teachers, and they were more likely to belong to a science teachers association. For students in the science specialist streams in the final year of secondary schooling, the SISS reported that the attitudes and values of the students toward science contributed positively toward science achievement in most countries.

When the role of the science teacher is so important, how should developing countries prepare secondary science teachers, both through pre- and in-service education, to ensure the production of well-informed and enthusiastic teachers, comfortable with both the subject matter and its active delivery in the classroom?

Secondary school teachers may be educated through a variety of programs. In most developing countries, qualified and certified secondary science teachers are generally prepared either through:

(1) a three or four-year program leading to an undergraduate degree in science followed by a year of postgraduate teacher preparation for professional cerfification; or

(2) a four-year program that combines science and education courses, leading to an undergraduate degree in science education (a BSEd or BEd), with the greater percentage of the courses in science; or

(3) a three or four-year program that combines science and education courses, leading to an education degree, with the greater percentage of the courses in education; or

(4) a one- or two-year program leading to a teaching diploma or certificate that may include little more science content beyond that delivered to the student teachers while they were themselves in secondary school

This categorization of teacher preparation programs is made on the basis of the relationship between the science and education course content of teacher preparation programms rather than on specifc instituional arrangements. Degree programs may be offered by: special teacher traing colleges; the universities, through the faculty of science, an education stream within the faculty of science, the faculty of education, or a cooperative relationship between the two faculties.

Most countries offer several of these options, with the expectation that teachers at the upper secondary level will take a more science-intensive program, while teachers at the lower secondary level will take a greater percentage of education courses.

The first option (1), the science degree plus a year of postgraduate pedagogical training, is designed to ensure that teachers are familiar with their subject matter, especially those teaching at the upper secondary level Secondary teachers with a science degree plus postgraduate training in education are particularly found in many countries with a British or French colonial past. These countries include: Ghana, Kenya, Malawi, Mali, Nigeria, Senegal Uganda, Algeria, Morocco, Tunisia, Jamaica, India, Malaysia, Pakistan, and Singapore. While this option initially divorces the science content from the pedagogy, a well-designed postgraduate program can integrate the two through methods courses in the professional year. One perceived advantage of this type of program is that the initial preparation of a science teacher is the same as the undergraduate education of a future scientist, with all the academic rigor which this implies.

One disadvantage of this first option is that it is usually only possible to major in one specific science discipline, with a much lesser effort going into study of a science minor. There is rarely an opportunity to take a double or interdisciplinary science major without extending the length of the undergraduate program further. There certainly is no time to broaden the content to include other sciences, even those bridging the major and minor. This Idnd of program may be too narrow for even those teaching specialist science courses at the upper secondary level producing overspecialized teachers who are either under utilized or are assigned to teach out-of-field.

For the lower secondary school teachers who may enter teaching through this route, this degree of one-science specalisation is not ideal, particularly when they have to teach integrated science. Hence, teachers at the lower secondary level are more likely to be prepared through options 2 and 3. The second option (2) is a newer option for teachers at both the upper and lower secondary levels.

The final degree is in science education rather than in science, so this type of program is perceived in some countries as of lower status than the first. The student teachers are typically enrolled in either the education stream of the faculty of science, or consecutively enrolled in the science and education faculties. In many developing countries, the four-year, science education degree is becoming the preferred route for entry into the profession. These countries include Korea, Thailand, Brazil, and Chile.

Courses of study may be organized in a number of ways, e.g., as three years of science Instruction followed by one-year of pedagogy; as two years of science instruction followed by two years of science and pedagogy, or, the science and the pedagogy may be integrated throughout the four years. However, combining science and pedagogy in one program does not ensure that the necessary connections are made between specific science knowledge and ways of conveying this knowledge to the student.

Too often the education component of the course is taught by the faculty of education, and the science component is taught by the science faculty.

The need for the joint presentation of subject-specific pedagogy is rarely recognized. Even if recognized, there may be institutional barriers preventing this from ever happening. In practice, the schism between the science faculty and the education faculty is a problem whatever the preparation route of the secondary science teacher - and a problem in developed as well as developing nations.

The third option also leads to an undergraduate degree in education for teachers at the lower secondary level However, this option, with its greater emphasis on the pedagogical courses rather than the science, is unlikely to provide the teacher with sufficient science knowledge to teach effectively at even the lower secondary level In making this statement it is not implied that just by adding more science content the teachers will become good teachers - although they will become better teachers. Knowledge of the subject matter is but one of the competencies needed for effective science teaching. Many countries now have policies in place to ensure that all secondary science teachers, especially those at the upper secondary level, enter the profession with a bachelor's degree of some kind. In other countries, there has been a need to produce as large a number of "trained" science teachers as quickly and as economically as possible, in order to handle the rapid expansion of secondary schooling.

The confusion on how "best" to train a science teacher at any level appears to arise firm the following:

(1) The absence of a clear definition of what is meant by an "effective" science teacher and how to measure teacher "effectiveness" in practice once it has been defined.

(2) The lack of unambiguous data relating the effectiveness of a science teacher (or any teacher) to any particular model of teacher preparation.

(3) A belief that certain kinds of competencies, e.g, teaching skills, can best be acquired through experience rather than formal instruction.

Hence, teachers can best learn teaching skills by actually teaching rather than through formal course work As a consequence of this confusion, it is common, in many institutions in many countries, to segregate subject matter knowledge from pedagogy in both preservice and in-service education. This makes it difficult to give teachers instruction in pedagogical content knowledge. This confusion also results in attempts to mass-produce teachers as quickly and cheaply as possible which, apart from necessity, also arises from the misconception that it is easy to teach effectively, and to teach teachers to teach effectively.

This confusion also results in attempts to mass-produce teachers as quickly and cheaply as possible which, apart from necessity, also arises from the misconception that it is easy to teach effectively, and to teach teachers to teach effectively. Despite this confusion, there is agreement on better ways to educate secondary science teachers, based as much on common sense and individual case studies as on a firmly established research base acceptable to all. The following sections describe an "ideal" education that may be difficult to realize in practice but which defines a high standard against which to evaluate any specific teacher training program.

There is a growing consensus that science teachers must have a strong science background. This may seem obvious. However, given the lack of science content in some science teacher training programs and the belief that a good textbook or a "teacher-proof" kit is a cost-effective way to circumvent the poor science background of many teachers, it is not a position accepted by all. There are also several schools of thought regarding the agricultural science knowledge for a secondary science teacher. It is argued that:

i) the science teacher needs to know less science than a science major,

ii) the teacher needs the same knowledge as a science major,

iii) the teacher needs more (and different) science knowledge than a science major.

There is a fairly widespread concern that science instruction within the faculties of science is often very poorly presented due to: the large volume of information to be digested in a comparatively short time; the emphasis on fact and concept recall; the absence of a broad context from which to evaluate the relative importance of specific science principles; and the lack of attention paid to conveying the logic of the discipline being taught.

This is a problem common to both developed and developing countries - the sheer tedium and concept overload of much of undergraduate science instruction. This type of science instruction leads to the production of students who can solve algorithms but not apply their knowledge in problem-solving situations - nor convey the essence of their knowledge to naive learners.

This kind of science instruction does not give the novice teacher the preparation he or she needs for the classroom. (It is also not the best way to prepare future research scientists) A teacher must know the subject matter to be taught at a more sophisticated level the a the students. Ideally, whatever the reasons for teaching school science, this means that, in terms of science content teachers should know:

(1) the facts and concepts to be taught, and why these facts lead to a formulation of accepted models and theories;

(2) how these facts and concepts relate to other important ideas in a given science, as well as to the 'big" ideas in other sciences;

(3) which facts and concepts are the most important in science;

(4) haw knowledge becomes "science" knowledge, and how" accepted" science may be modified based on new data;

(5) the laboratory skills necessary to accumulate such data; and,

(6) that science is a human construct, developing over time to explain both the universe and the near environment in which we live.

Thus, the teacher's understanding of the subject matter must go beyond knowledge and comprehension into the domain of analytical thought, including the abilities to antique and apply subject matter knowledge. A commonly accepted wisdom is that a teacher's subject matter knowledge should be at least three years ahead of his/her students. However, if that knowledge is defined solely in terms of quality of knowledge recall and not quality of understanding, in other words if the teacher has not achieved some level of critical thinking in the discipline, then the teacher is not well prepared to teach that subject.

Paradoxically, it is possible that, as a teacher-learner becomes more of an expert learner, he/she may have greater difficulty explaining certain concepts to students. As a discipline becomes very familiar, its knowledge base and structure become so internalized by the learner, that recall is more or less automatic. The now expert learner begins to forget how the knowledge was constructed in the first place; which misconceptions clouded initial comprehension; and, how meaning was eventually wrestled from the abstract. If the learner becomes a researcher, it may not matter that the structure of this network of knowledge is held in the unconscious mind. However, the teachers knowledge of science needs to be "explict and self-conscious, rather than tacit".

It is perhaps because this process of knowledge storage in the unconscious mind tends to take place that those who are extremely familiar with their discipline (e.g., research scientists) are not, by virtue of their knowledge, automatically excellent teachers - although, of course, some are. Some may have moved too far away from the process of science knowledge construction to be able to assist the novice learner in understanding concepts that may be not only counterintiative but, somehow, alien to the culture in which they are being expressed.

The National Centre for Research on Teacher Learning at Michigan State University has been studying what teachers actually learn from differently structured teacher education programs. Their Teacher Education and Learning to Teach (TELT) study is following teacher-learners from their entry into a teacher education program through their first year of actually teaching. The TELT student is following teachers of writing and mathematics, but clearly lends supporting data to the position presented above in terms of science majors.

In terms of science knowledge background, it is particularly important that future science teachers are taught to be self-conscious, life-long learners in the sciences because:

(1) science continues to develop after the teacher graduates, in particular, science disciplines have increasingly fluid boundaries;

(2) a growth in teacher knowledge as teachers interact with students is an important characteristics of the most effective teachers- a commitment to continuing intellectual growth on the part of the teacher is a commitment to the continual improvement of the teacher's classroom performance; and,

(3) a commitment to continuing education is one characteristic of a professional identity - teaching will become more clearly recognized as a profession when more teachers are encouraged to behave as professionals.

While most science teachers have in-depth knowledge of only one science, a chemistry teacher at a German "gymnasium" may have studied three science subjects in-depth. Learning two (or more) science disciplines in-depth may add meaning to all of science, if both subjects are taught to emphasize the "connectedness' of the knowledge. Presuming well-taught science, should there be any difference in the science content for teachers at the upper and lower secondary levels? Teachers at the upper secondary level should be taught in-depth in at least two sciences for practical - as well as pedagogical - reasons. A coordinated two-discipline focus in training should produce a better teacher capable of more effective instruction in two sciences.

The preparation of a science teacher comfortable with teaching at least two sciences and their border areas is easier to recommend hand to accomplish. The structure of higher education in many countries in such that, especially if the training includes an undergraduate science degree, it may not be possible within the three or four years of undergraduate instruction to cover two sciences to the depth needed to teach both at the upper secondary level At the lower secondary level, science teachers are much more likely to have to teach integrated or general science courses.

These teachers need a broader exposure to the facts and main concepts of many sciences than teachers at the upper secondary level, but less in-depth factual knowledge of any one discipline. However, they do need to bring the same uailix of understanding to their broad knowledge of science and scientific inquiry as the teachers at the upper secondary level.

The well-educated science teacher is one who has developed an understanding of how different students learn science; who can help individual learners learn; and who can measure when that learning has taken place. This understanding is usually conveyed through formal "education" courses, as well as through a period of supervised teaching. The professional education of the teacher is subject to much criticism, some of it merited, in terms of the lack of intellectual content of many education courses. It is argued that the best place to team how to teach is actually in the classroom.

In designing the most effective science teacher training program, particularly if it must be short and the academic backgrounds of the student teachers are poor, it may be necessary to re-evaluate the continued existence of some traditionally compulsory courses, and the specific content of others, to eliminate both the superficial and the "not really necessary" from the curriculum.

The task of the science teacher is to identify which ideas and misconceptions are likely to be associated with particular science concepts for students of a particular level of development and culture; and to use this knowledge to help each student begin to construct satisfying scientific models of natural phenomena.

The "constructivist' model of learning is proving to be very useful in helping students understand science better. Science methods courses should both teach student teachers how to use this model and be taught by teacher educators who recognize that the student teachers are themselves harbouring naive misconceptions of science concepts.

For science teacher preparation in the developing world, general courses which are mandatory may include mathematics, economics, political science, history, languages, religion and ethics, health and physical education, etc. It is accepted that all teachers should have a liberal education much broader than the subjects they will eventually teach. However, the argument that all these courses are an essential component of science teacher training is suspect, given that, in many countries, the time devoted to these general courses in programs for lower secondary school science teachers is much higher than in programs for upper secondary school teachers.

There are two possible explanations for this discrepancy:

i) a country may not be able to afford science specialists at the lower secondary level - especially in rural areas the teacher may be expected to teach across the curriculum, or

ii) the candidates at the lower secondary level are not considered smart enough to take additional science instruction - thus, the general courses are really only serving as a "flier."

The British style of education typifies the early specialization model, at least for the elite, while the American system can accommodate a postponement of specialisation until graduate studies.

The selection of teaching as a career will depend on the actual and perceived rewards of teaching-including pay, working conditions, opportunities for further education, career ladder, status of the teacher in the community - as well as on other employment opportunities available. While conditions are relatively good in some developing countries, teacher pay, which is usually tied to civil service pay structures, is so low in others that teachers need to take two or even three jobs to pay essential bills.

Given these conditions, it is not surprising that in many countries the better science students tend to become science majors, and eventually take graduate research studies, or employment in the private sector. This leaves the future science teachers to be selected, by some combination of competitive examination and interview, from the lower achieving students. Thus, some science teacher preparation programs may be designed to accommodate the expected lower intellectual profile of the applicants.

However, it is not logical to offer future science teachers with a weak background in science fewer science courses. These student teachers should be talking as many remedial science courses as possible, together with courses in pedagogical content knowledge to help clarify their own misconceptions as well as those of their future students.

The Trainers of Teachers

In many countries, the teacher trainers do not receive any instruction in how to teach themselves. Often they are former secondary school teachers promoted out of the classroom; even then there is no guarantee that they have the explicit knowledge necessary to teach others how to teach. They may also have a weak background in modern teaching methods or in science content. Another possibility is that the teacher educators have a relatively strong background in science but have never taught at the secondary level.

Science teacher educators need to be upgraded to at least a master's degree level in science education. The course of study should include both additional science content, a science education research project, and topics with which the teacher educators may be less familiar such as: subject-specific pedagogy, continuous assessment techniques, cooperative learning, student-centered learning, concept mapping, and teaching STS. A worldwide problem alluded to previously is the lack of cooperation and respect between science and education faculty in universities. Increased collaboration between the faculties of science and education is absolutely essential if teacher training programs are to improve significantly. This cooperation is more likely to take place if there is some kind of institutional support system in place to encourage and reward instructors who work together in cross-disciplinary partnerships.

A mandate from the university administration establishing that all faculty are responsible for teacher education is a beginning. This might involve the formation of faculty teams to collaborate on an analysis of the current curriculum, and on joint recommendations for curriculum redesign. The faculty teams would then be responsible for implementing the reforms. It is also important that there be collaborations between science faculty at a university, and education faculty at a separately administered teacher training institution.

7

Conclusion

Science education in the United Kingdom is compulsory from age 5 to 16. Post-16 pupils now have to study a minimum of three subjects and are encouraged to study at least four before selecting three for their final year. None of these need be science. The curriculum exists from age 4 to 16 and is specified in a government document entitled the 'Science National Curriculum', which describes both the content and the processes of science to be taught through a programme of study divided into four strands:

- Scientific enquiry;
- Life and living processes;
- Materials; and
- Physical processes.

This curriculum is outlined for four Key Stages. Key Stage 1 (ages 5-7) and Key Stage 2 (ages 7-11) are both delivered in the primary school and currently occupy one hour a week of curriculum time on average according to recent research at King's College.

More time than this may be given under the compulsory hour a day for the teaching of literacy where science books may be used for the reading of nonfiction material. Key Stage 3 (ages 11-14) and Key (ages 11-14) and Key Stage 4 (ages 14-16) are taught in secondary school, where approximately 12-15% of the time is given over % of the time is given over to science at Key Stage 3 and 18-20% of the time at Key Stage 4.

The curriculum is dominated by the basic curriculum is dominated by the basic concepts of science rather than technology as technology is taught as a separate subject. The broad aims of science education are to stimulate and excite pupils' curiosity about phenomena and events in the world around them. It also satisfies this curiosity with knowledge.

Because science links direct practical experience with ideas, it can engage learners at many levels. Scientific method is about developing and evaluating explanations through experimental evidence and modelling. This is a spur to critical and creative thought. Through science, pupils understand how major scientific ideas contribute to technological change—impacting on industry, business and medicine and improving quality of quality of life. Pupils recognise the cultural significance of science and trace its worldwide development. They learn to question and discuss science-based issues that may affect their own lives, the direction of society and the future of the world.

Problems with Science Curricula

Science education rests on a set of ently practised, science education rests on a set of arcane cultural norms. These are 'values that emanate from practice and become sanctified with time. The more they recede into the background, the more taken for granted they become'.

A closer examination and the insights of contemporary scholarship expose these norms to be nowhere near the self-evident truths that we may think—what we might choose to call the eight 'deadly sins' of science education. For in contemporary society, research would indicate that trust in science is dependent on developing a knowledge not only of its basic concepts and ideas of science, but also how it relates to other events, why it is important, and how this particular view of the world came to be. Any science education, therefore, that focuses predominantly on the intellectual products of our scientific labour—the 'facts' of science-simply misses the point.

Science education should rest on a triumvirate of a knowledge and understanding of the scientific content; the scientific approach to enquiry; and science as a social enterprise—that is the social practices of the community. Evidence would suggest that in many countries, normative practice regards school science education as a selection mechanism for the few who will become the future scientists of contemporary society.

The predominant emphasis is on the content of science. However, society can ill afford the consequent alienation and disengagement with science that such courses generate. Moreover, where—as the modernist vision proffered scientific knowledge as a source of solutions, science is now perceived too as a source of risk. Public distrust or ambivalence with science threatens science in two ways.

— Throughout Western nations there has been a flight from science, with diminishing numbers pursuing its study at the point of choice.

— Public distrust of scientific expertise is in danger of placing unwarranted restrictions on future research and technological development. Fear of the worst is leading the public to demand a naive application of the precautionary principle to research-potentially limiting the advancements that science offers for solving the plethora of problems faced by contemporary society. In the United Kingdom, for instance, significant pressure groups have argued (using highly questionable ethical arguments) that all research on genetically modified food should be halted.

Why then is the current science education failing to develop an appropriate understanding of science, a more positive engagement with the fruits of scientific labour, and a critical but constructive understanding of its strengths and limitations? The argument here is that this failure is caused by a set of eight unquestioned norms of practice.

The myth of miscellaneous information

All too many science courses have attempted to make students memorize a series of dry facts that no practising scientist knows, such as the boiling point of water, the density of various substances, the atomic weight of different chemical elements, conversion factors from one system of units to another, the distance in light years from the Earth to various stars (and so on). However, an increasing body of work now shows that knowledge is only one component of the many competencies required of adults in their professional life and, unless it is constantly used, is rapidly forgotten.

The foundational myth

This is the myth that because scientific knowledge itself is difficult and hard won, learning and understanding science requires a similar process where the student's knowledge and understanding are assembled brick by brick or fact by fact. As a consequence only those that reach the end ever get to comprehend the wonder and beauty of the edifice that has been constructed. In effect, although the pupils can see the microscopic detail, the sense of the whole, its relevance and its value-the things that matter to the pupil—are lost.

The myth of coverage

The science we offer must be both broad and balanced. The result is an attempt to offer a smattering of all sciences and to cram more and more into an oft-diminishing pot. As the bounds of scientific knowledge expand from evolutionary biology to modern cosmology, more and more knowledge vies for a place in the curriculum. Moreover, within the disciplines themselves there is an ever-increasing fractionation. For instance, few now emerge with a degree in biology. The days of zoology and botany are long gone, replaced by the likes of molecular genetics, immunology and other specialisms. However, just as those teaching literature would never dream of attempting to cover the whole body of extant literature, choosing rather a range of examples to illustrate the different ways in which good literature can be produced, has the time not come to recognise that it is our responsibility to select a few of the major 'explanatory stories' that the sciences offer?

The myth of a detached science

Science education persists with presenting an idealised view of science as objective, detached and value-free. This is wrong on three counts.

— The public and particularly young people do not distinguish between science and technology.

— Science is a socially situated product and the language and metaphors it draws on are rooted in the culture and lives of the scientists who produce new knowledge.

— Those that engage in science are not the dispassionate, sceptical and disinterested community that Merton portrays. Science is a social practice, engaged in by individuals who share a by individuals who share a' matrix of disciplinary commitments, values and research exemplars'. Within the contemporary context, where scientists are employed by industrial companies with vested interests, it is hard to advance a case that science is simply the 'pursuit of truth' untainted by professional aspirations or ideological commitments. These days scientists are judged as much by the company they keep as the data they may gather.

— The separation of science from technology eliminates all consideration of societal implications. If science education fails to make argues, if science education fails to make the small step from science to its technological applications, how can it take the much larger step to the implications for the society in which it is embedded? Thus an approach to science education based on the consideration of Science and Technology in Society (STS) issues and materials, a student-orientated approach whose roots spread rapidly in the 1980s, is one for which there is considerable evidence of a positive affective outcome. Yet it is positive affective outcome. Yet it is an approach that has effectively withered on the vine in the hostile environment of curricula, such as the English and Welsh national curriculum, which show an obsession with science and science alone.

The myth of critical thinking

This is an assumption that the study of science teaches students reflective, critical thinking or logical analysis which may then be applied by them to other subjects of study. As examination of the conduct of the lives of scientists outside the laboratory or the study of science which shows that scientists are no more or less rational than other mortals-calls this argument into question. It is based on the fallacious assumption that mere contact with science will imbue a sense of critical rationality by some unseen process of osmosis. It is also an assumption questioned by the Wason four-card problem and the Wason 2, 4, 6 problem both of which require a standard scientific strategy of falsification to determine the correct answer and which very few, including scientists, use. In this problem, the investigator presents to the subject the following sequence of numbers: 2, 4, 6. He or she then tells the subject that there is a rule written on the other side of the card (all the numbers must be positive integers). He/she then asks the subject to work out the rule by producing further sets of three numbers. For each set of numbers that the subject produces, the investigator will tell the subject whether the numbers that they have selected do, or do not, agree with the rule. The subject is then asked to repeat this process until he or she thinks they know what the rule is, whereupon they can suggest their hypothesis to the investigator who will tell them whether they are correct. Secondly, the notion that science develops transferable skills is also an assumption questioned by a body of research which suggests that people's use of knowledge and reasoning is situated within a context and that detached knowledge is of little use to individuals until it has been reworked into a form understood by the user.

The myth of the scientific method

This is the myth that there exists a singular scientific method. The record of those who have made the important discoveries of the past shows not only that scientists rarely attempt any such logical procedure, but that the methods vary considerably between the sciences. The methods deployed by the palaeontologist working out in the field are about as similar to those used by the theoretical physicist as chalk and cheese. The mathematical tools that are available for data analysis immediately puts the study of method beyond what is learnable in a lifetime'. The procedural knowledge of science is as vast as its body of content. Yet the science that increasingly confronts the individual in the media, with its focus on environmental or biological issues, is predominantly based on correlational evidence and uses methodological devices such as clinical trials with blind and double-blind controls. Yet where and when is there any treatment of the strengths and limitations of such evidence? Is it not time to give up any notion that there is such a singular entity and turn instead to presenting a range of ideas about science and its working?

The myth of utility

This is the myth that scientific knowledge has personal utility—that it is essential to the mastery of technology; to remedy its defects; and to live at ease in the culture of technology that surrounds us. As machines become more 'intelligent', they require less care and thought for their effective use. Defunct technical artefacts are simply consigned to the garbage heap as the cost of repair is prohibitive. And those that are worthy of repair, such as the car, the washing machine or the photocopier now have a level of technological complexity which, whilst simplifying their use, renders them opaque to all but the expert. Even its economic utility is questionable as current employment trends, at least in the United Kingdom and the United States, suggest that-although we will need to sustain the present supply of scientists—there is no need to significantly improve the number going into science, which remains a small minority of the school cohort of around 10-15%.

The homogeneous myth

In many countries, science education labours under the myth that its clientele are an entity who, whilst who, whilst they might differ in aptitude and ability, nevertheless are best served by one homogeneous curriculum. Such curricula are normally defined by sets of national standards that, although they may ostensibly be voluntary, enshrine a normative expectation difficult to transcend. With their devotion to pure science, a foundationalist approach, and a 'high-stakes' assessment system, the result is a pedagogy based on transmission. Such curricula have their ideological roots firmly planted in a set of values that favour knowledge over praxis, education is, education over training, and content over process. By the onset of adolescence, the imperative of relevance increasingly challenges the delayed gratification that such a curriculum offers leading to a lack of motivation and interest. Such a curriculum also sits ill at ease with the increasing demand for a curriculum that would develop the public understanding of science.

Other research shows that understanding and inter-
Other research shows that understanding and interpreting science in the media requires a view that recognizes that science is a social practice and scientific knowledge the product of a community. For instance, new knowledge does not become public knowledge in science until it has been checked through the various institutions of science and that papers are reviewed by peers before being published in journals. Reestablishing or maintaining trust in science requires that the regulatory mechanisms that ensure the validity of scientific judgement and expertise are open to all, and understood by as many as possible. What then are the methods, practices and components of a new vision of science education that might meet these concerns?

The broad framework of such a vision has been The broad framework of such a vision has been developed in the report Beyond 2000: science education for the future.

We argued for ten recommendations that we saw would address many of the aforementioned criticisms. These were:

— science education for 'scientific literacy';

— an element of choice should be allowed at age 14;

— the curriculum needs aims;

— scientific knowledge can best be presented as a set of knowledge can best be presented as a set of 'explanatory stories';

— technology can no longer be separated from science;

— the science curriculum must give more emphasis to key 'ideas about science';

— science should be taught using a wide variety of teaching methods and approaches;

— assessment needs to measure pupils' ability to understand and interpret scientific information;

— change in the short term should be limited; and

— a formal procedure needs to be established for the testing of innovative approaches.

No such curriculum has been developed for those below age 16. A one-year course entitled 'The Public Understanding of Science' will be offered to 17-year-old students for the first time. In addition, discussions are beginning with an examination board about developing a ping a similar course pre-16. However, reforming the science curriculum to meet the challenges of contemporary society faces a number of obstacles that must be addressed and met. These are the limitations of the qualifications and abilities of the science teaching force; the problems with developing appropriate modes of assessment; the resistance of well-established stakeholders; and the culture of science teaching. There are three problems are their:

Curriculum reform

Any new curriculum that gave more emphasis to developing an understanding of the nature and processes of science would require teachers themselves to have some understanding of these dimension of science. Yet science teachers are the products of an education which has paid scant regard to history, or any examination of its social practices. And for good reason—the dominant ideology within science is one of dogmatism and authority, where the tentative nature of the roots of scientific knowledge is excised to present science as a body of unequivocal, unquestioned and uncontested knowledge which has been the successful, linear progression of the work of isolated great men, devoid of any cultural context. The outcome of such an education is a body of science teachers who have naive views of the nature of science-seeing it as an empirical process where scientific theories are inductively proven.

Similarly, how science teachers see their work as one that is dominated by content rather than process, as opposed to the contemporary treatment of history where the history teachers seek to develop an understanding of what it is to do history. The significance of empirical work to science, and in the teacher's practice, is such that they are endowed with distinctive status by the provision of specialized laboratories. Laboratories in their turn become rhetorical artefacts where the scientific world-view can be used to illustrate the predictability of nature and inspire confidence in its portrayal of nature. So this is my first problem-is it reasonable to ask science teachers to teach science with an emphasis of which they have only a limited understanding themselves? The history of educational innovation within the science curriculum shows that change, when supported with new textbooks and extensive training, has only had limited success.

Teachers then had more professional independence to select what materials and courses they felt were appropriate for their students. However, attempts to introduce change under the umbrella of the National Curriculum—particularly when those changes were later shown to be based on fallacious models of science—have met with substantive resistance and modification such that the implemented curriculum is at best a pale shadow of its intended version.

The 1991 version of the English and Welsh science curriculum in Welsh science curriculum introduced a model of practical-based investigatory work that was unfamiliar and resented by teachers who failed to share or understand its intentions. The result was a long period of adaptation whilst teachers reworked the curriculum to put into practice work that was a distorted representation of the intentions of the national curriculum document. Many teachers were alienated or disaffected by the process. The lesson of these problems is one that was clear from previous research on educational change but ignored.

— Teachers must be dissatisfied with the existing curriculum if the arguments for change are to be heard.

— If change is to occur, teachers must be supported in developing new practices, new bodies of knowledge and new pedagogic methods. At knowledge and new pedagogic methods. At the very least, that requires the rewriting of curriculum support materials, which should seek to provide exemplary illustrations of the ideas to be taught and suggestions for how it can be taught. More substantive support would require a programme of professional development delivered by individuals who are themselves competent and effective teachers, as well as have a good grasp of any new initiative.

Assessment

The role of assessment within existing national and international frameworks. Over the past twenty years, political imperatives have led to the necessity to measure the performance of the education system. The consequence has been the rise of national systems of assessment based on testing at certain key ages in the United Kingdom these are age 7, 11 and 14. A different terminal examination is also held at age 16 and the new systems being introduced will ensure that there are examinations at age 17 and 18 as well. Internationally, we have also seen the rise of comparative assessment between countries used as a measure of the overall quality of education. As a consequence, assessment has acquired an importance beyond merely providing some kind of reliable and valid measure of a child's f reliable and valid measure of a child's knowledge and understanding. Rather the emphasis has shifted to it becoming a measure of the individual teacher's capabilities; then, when summed across the school, a measure of the quality of the education provided by the school; and then when summed across the country, a measure of the effectiveness of the quality of the education system as a whole. Thus rather than assessment serving as a tool to benefit the child, providing either a formative or summative judgement of his or her capabilities, it has become a servant of a bureaucratic mentality that seeks to monitor the performance of the system. Whilst it could be argued that these two aims are not incommensurable, the reality is different. For example, most science teachers agree that practical skills are an important part of the content of a science curriculum.

An assessment of 'science', therefore, ought to assess practical skills as well as more traditional forms of scientific knowledge and capability. However, testing practical skills is expensive, and those concerned with the efficiency of the assessments point out that the results of the practical and written tests correlate very highly, so there is no need to carry on with expensive practical testing. The same sorts of arguments have dominated the debate in the United States between multiple-choice and constructed-response tests. What then happens is the practical aspects of science are dropped from the assessment.

The consequence of this, for the domain of school science, is to send the message that practical science is not as important as its written aspects. The social consequence is that teachers, understandably anxious to get their students the best possible results in the assessment because of its influence over the students' future career prospects, place less emphasis on the practical aspects of science. Because teachers are no longer teaching practical science hand-in-hand with other aspects of science, the correlation between students' performance in practical aspects of science and the written aspects weakens, so that it is no longer possible to tell anything about a student's practical competence from the score on the science assessment.

Similar problems have beset attempts to provide performance indicators in the Health Service, in the privatized railway companies and a host of other public services. A variety of indicators is selected for their ability to represent the quality of the service, but when used as quality of the service, but when used as the sole index of quality, the manipulability of these indicators destroys the relationship between the indicator and the indicated. By directing attention more and more onto particular indicators of performance they had managed to increase the scores on the indicator, but the score on the indicated was relatively unaffected.

The lesson of history then is that in seeking to make the important measurable, only the measurable has become important. The second problem is that within school science, assessment items are commonly devised by those that have been, or still are, practising science teachers. Just as it is often said that you teach only that you can teach, so assessment is often based on the normative values of what it is considered possible to assess. Hence the assessment of students' understanding of the processes of science, or its social practices, are not considered because there is not an established body of knowledge of how to assess such items. At worst, assessment experts will simply assert that it is too difficult, time-consuming or expensive to assess such understandings and at best, that they do not know how to do so. Thus within such a context generated by the importance of measuring performance of students, teachers and schools, the clear message to teachers is that the lack of any assessment of a given topic implies that it is an extraneous item of the intended curriculum and of no significance. Two messages emerge for science curriculum and policy-makers from these experiences. First, if a topic is sufficiently important to include in the curriculum, then it is sufficiently important to assess. And if there is currently a lack of experience about how to undertake such assessment, then it is important to develop items that assess students' comprehension of the full range of knowledge and performance required by the intended curriculum.

Challenging existing stakeholder

Those with the largest stake in the existing practice are the universities who see the school system as a provider of raw, novitiate students for training as future scientists. School science education should be an intensive education in the foundational concepts and ideas of science. Any attempt to weaken this aim has historically led to strong resistance with, in some cases, universities refusing to admit students who had alternative qualifications or to define which qualifications would be acceptable to them. Such a strong message severely curtails the boundaries of change that are possible and so far has been a major obstacle. Change in the school science curriculum will only happen when either school science is decoupled from academic science in universities, or at the very least when the interdependence of the two is weakened. The argument for change is twofold, having both a moral dimension and an argument based in science's own self-interest.

- For the overwhelming majority of students, school science is an end in itself. Yet to base the curriculum solely on the needs of those who will continue with a further education in science has no justification unless one believes that the education of a Platonic elite will serve the greater good.
- There is a considerable body of evidence that a school science education which gives pre-eminence to the foundational concept of science-the 'facts' of science-leaves many pupils disinterested if not alienated from science.

In an age when we are all dependent on expertise, the public's relationship with dependent on expertise, the public's relationship with any professional body is dependent on a relationship based on trust. Undermining that relationship by offering such an education means that the practice of science, and its future funding, may not be secure. Developing a relationship of trust is thus dependent not on developing a knowledge of its content but on opening the black box that is science so that the students can understand what it is to do science, how it regulates itself and why it is to be trusted that is on altering the balance of the curriculum away from its content towards a more significant emphasis on its practice. Such an education would benefit not only the future member of the lay public, but also the future scientist. For those who have the traditional academic interest in science, more academic options should be available as well.

Such a change would inevitably mean that universities would have to respond by undertaking more of the education in the foundational concepts. Current attempts at innovation are rooted in a gradualist approach. The fourth version of the national curriculum has just been published for implementation from September 2000. This gives greater emphasis to teaching some of the 'ideas about science' discussed in Beyond 2000. The United Kingdom has benefited from the rise of the 'Science Centre movement' with innovative children's galler with innovative children's at the Science Museum, the Natural History Museum and several other museums during the past fifteen years.

Millennium funding has led to the development of many more of these science centres that are enjoyed by most children who visit. However, their use is predominantly with children of age 11 and under; their aim is to provide an affective experience rather than a cognitive one; criticisms have been voiced that they provide 'infotainment'; and evidence would suggest that they are not yet effectively used by science teachers to develop children's understanding of science. Private firms sponsor the production of many materials for use by science teachers. However, research suggests that these are only used 'occasionally' and that there is poor market research by the companies as to what is needed by the schools.

The major development in United Kingdom science teaching has been the Cognitive Acceleration in Science Acceleration in Science Education project (CASE), which aims to develop children's thinking skills in science over a two-year period from age 11 to 13. Results from this work have shown that significant gains in children's performance can be achieved, in comparison to control groups, by children in their terminal examinations at age 16 in science, English and maths. The central government is now conducting The central government is now conducting pilot trials with these and other materials in

150 schools. Some may well resist such change but the question must be asked whether the status quo is acceptable for the education of the future citizen in science in the twenty-first century? In an era where scientific issues such as genetic modification of foods, global warming and others continually surface as the political and moral dilemmas confronting society, the disengagement or disenchantment of our youth with science may increase the separation that currently exists between science and society.

Such a consequence is one that an advanced industrial society can ill afford to pay, both at the individual level where it might lead to the rejection of sound scientific advice, or at the societal level where limitations may be imposed on scientific research that could have potentially beneficial outcomes for humanity. Perhaps, more tragic, will be the simple rejection of a body of knowledge that must, on any knowledge that must, on any account, represent one of the greatest cultural achievements of modern societies.

Bibliography

Adamu, A.U. (1991). *Curricular Rhetoric Class Teaching and Examinations: A Study of the New Nigerian Science Curriculum.* Science Education International, 2, (1), 6-10.

Aikenhead, G. S. (1975). *Science: A Way of Knowing. Saskatoon: Department- of Curriculum Studies, University of Saskatchewan.*

Alberta Education (1990). *STS Science Education: Unifying the Goals of Science Education.* Edmonton: Curriculum Support Branch, Alberta Education.

American Chemical Society (1988). *Chemistry in the Community.* Dubuque, Iowa: Kendall/Hunt Publishing Company.

Baez, A.V., Knamiller, G.W., and Smyth, J.C. (ods.) (1987). *The Environment and Science and Technology Education.* Vol. 8 of Science and Technology and Future Human Needs. Oxford: Pergamon Press for International Council of Scientific Unions Press.

Brophy, M., and Dudley, B. (1990). *Emergency Science Programme,* Guyana. In B.N.

Caillods, F., and Gottelmann-Duret, G. (1991). *Science Provision in Academic Secondary Schools Organisation and Condition.* Paris: United Nations Educational, Scientific and Cultural Organization.

Chisman, D. G. (1990). *What is Integrated Science Teaching: Its Beginnings and Its Place Today.* In New Trends in Integrated Science Teaching. Vol. VI. Paris: United Nations Educational, Scientific and Cultural Organization.

Cl-ghorn, A., Merritt, M., and Abagi, J. 0. (1989). *Language Policy and Science Instruction in Kenyan Primary Schools.* Comnrarative Education Review, 33, (10), 21-39.

Dock, A.W. (1983). *A Shift in Emphasis for the Zim-Sci Curriculum from Academic to Applied Science.* MISS, 3, (2), 11-14.

Gallagher, J. J., and Dawson, G. (ads.) (1986). *Science Education and Cultural Environments in the American: Report of the Inter-American Seminar and Science Education.* Washington, DC: Organization of American States.

George, J. and Glasgow, J. (1989). *Some Cultural Implications of Teaching Towards Common Syllabi in Science: A Case Study from the Caribbean.* School Science Review, 71, (254), 115-123.

Giddings, G. and Fraser, B.3. (1988). *Assessment of Students' Learning in Science Education.* In D. Layton (ad.), Innovations in Science and Technology Education. Vol. la. Paris: United Nations Educational, Scientific and Cultural Organization.

Hacker, R. G. (1984). *A Typology of Approaches to Science Teaching In Schools.* European Journal of Science Education, 6, (2), 153-167.

Hofstein, A., and Lunetta, V.N. (1982). *The Role of the Laboratory in Science Teaching: Neglected Aspects of Research.* Review of Educational Research, IU, 201-217

Holman, J.S. (1990). *The Integration of Science Teaching through Science-Technology-Society Courses.* In New Trends in Intecrated Science Teachina. Vol. VT. Paris: United Nations Educational, Scientific and Cultural Organization.

Knamiller, and J.C. Smyth (eds.), *The Environment and Science and Technology Education.* Vol. 8 of Science and Technology Education and Future Human Needs. Oxford: Pergamon Press for International Council of Scientific Unions Press.

Pensham, P.J. (1988). *Familiar but Different: Some Dilemmas and New Directions in Science Education.* In P. Fenxham (ed.), Development and Dilemmas in Science Education. London: The Falmer Press.

Index